# THE
# OXFORD MINIDICTIONARY
## OF
# FIRST NAMES

# THE OXFORD MINIDICTIONARY OF FIRST NAMES

PATRICK HANKS and
FLAVIA HODGES

Oxford   New York

OXFORD UNIVERSITY PRESS

*Oxford University Press, Walton Street, Oxford* OX2 6DP

*Oxford New York Toronto*
*Delhi Bombay Calcutta Madras Karachi*
*Petaling Jaya Singapore Hong Kong Tokyo*
*Nairobi Dar es Salaam Cape Town*
*Melbourne Auckland*

*and associated companies in*
*Berlin Ibadan*

*Oxford is a trade mark of Oxford University Press*

*Published in the United States*
*by Oxford University Press, New York*

*British Library Cataloguing in Publication Data*
*Hanks, Patrick*
*The Oxford minidictionary of first names.*
*—(Minidictionaries)*
*1. Names, Personal—English—*
*Dictionaries*
*I. Title  II. Hodges, Flavia  III. Series*
*929.4v4v0942      CS2367*
*ISBN 0–19–866135–5*

*Library of Congress Cataloging in Publication Data*
*Hanks, Patrick.*
*The Oxford minidictionary of first names.*
*1. Names, Personal-Dictionaries.  2. English*
*language—Etymology—Names.  I. Hodges, Flavia.*
*II. Title.*
*CS2377.H36  1986  929.4v4v0321  86–12544*
*ISBN 0–19–866135–5 (pbk.).*

*Printed in Great Britain*
*by Courier International*
*East Kilbride, Scotland*

# Introduction

CHOOSING a name for a child is a decision of the greatest importance in the lives of all parents and indeed for the future life of the child. Not surprisingly, then, quite a lot of care and thought generally goes into this choice. In many cases, new members of the family are named after someone: a parent or grandparent, an admired friend or relative, or a famous person. In others, the name may be chosen under the influence of some character in literature, the cinema, or television. Still other parents choose a name because it is fashionable, or on grounds of euphony: because it 'sounds nice'.

A child's first, or given, name firmly identifies him or her as a member of a particular culture. Various consequences flow from this. In the first place, for present purposes, it explains why this book is called a *Dictionary of First Names*, rather than *of Christian Names*. The Christian tradition is only one of many cultures in the world in which children are named, although it happens to figure prominently in the English-speaking world and therefore in this book. However, even in a work of this size, there are entries for Jewish names, and occasional reference is made to Arabic names (cf. *Mona*) and Indian names (cf. *Tara*). The name *David* plays a central role in the Christian tradition, and has been perennially popular. But it cannot be claimed as exclusively or even primarily Christian: it is a characteristically Jewish name as well as a Christian name. The same is true of most names of Old Testament origin. *Moses* may seem to us today to be a characteristically Jewish name, but it was not always so. In the 17th century and again in the 19th, it was common among Puritans and Dissenters and other Christian fundamentalists, who had a fondness for Old Testament names. Many of these have now, temporarily or permanently, passed out of fashion: for example *Hezekiah*, *Ezekiel*, and *Zillah*. The last, like *Adah* and for that matter *Adam*, seems to have been chosen because it occurs early in the Book of Genesis. *Eve*, on the other hand, was shunned by fundamentalist groups, as they were only too conscious that it was Eve who introduced sin into the world.

In the increasingly agnostic 20th century, direct derivation from the Bible plays a minor and diminishing role in the choice of a name. Many parents who choose the names *Peter*, *James*, *Andrew*, *John*, *Thomas*, *Philip*, *Matthew*, or *Paul* do so because they want to choose a standard and popular boy's name, not because they want to name a child after one of Christ's apostles. The fact remains that the commonest boys' given names in English today are those derived from the New Testament. Christian tradition was less well served for girls' names: there is not an equivalent set of important early Christian women in the New Testament. The common English girls' names *Jane*, *Janet*, *Jean*, and *Joan* are all derivatives of *John*, while other common girls' names are taken from the Old Testament. These include *Susan* (*Susannah*), *Deborah*, *Abigail*, *Judith*, *Rachel*, *Rebecca*, and *Ruth* and are, of course, shared in one form or another with Jewish naming traditions.

Except for Mary and Elizabeth, few women are mentioned by name in the gospels, and those few generally seem to have some drawback to them. The story of Martha, for example, might be seen as heralding a life of unremitting drudgery. *Salome*, the name of one of the women at Christ's tomb after the Resurrection, might have been a good choice as a girl's name, except that unfortunately, according to the historian Josephus, it was also borne by the daughter of Herodias, who did a strip-tease for her stepfather Herod and demanded (and got) John the Baptist's head on a plate: not the sort of person one would want to name one's daughter after. Early medieval Christianity augmented the stock of specifically *Christian* girls' names by inventing relatives for the Virgin Mary (cf. *Anne*).

A rich source of specifically Christian names is the treasure-house of stories and legends that grew up about early saints and martyrs. Christian parents through the ages have adopted names such as *Anthony*, *Gregory*, *Barbara*, and *Agnes*, in recognition of the sterling quality of the early Christians who bore them and in hope of eternal life, undeterred by their sometimes grisly earthly fates. In some cases, for example *Adrian* and *Martin*, an old Roman cognomen is preserved by this accident of Christian tradition. In others, the historical original is lost in the mists of time: in recent years, for example, the Church has expressed scepticism about the very existence of Saint George, let alone his battle with the dragon, but this has affected neither his status as the patron saint of England nor the popularity of the name.

Recourse to the Bible and to Christian tradition for names was a habit that spread only gradually from the first centres of Christianity in the early Middle Ages. Old naming habits died hard, and even after Christianity was officially instituted as the established religion, children often continued to be given traditional names of pagan origin. The most striking instances of this in English-speaking culture are the names brought to Britain by the Norman conquerors in the 11th century. Names such as *William*, *Henry*, and *Richard* are of pagan (Germanic) origin, but owe their tremendous popularity through the centuries to the fact that they were borne by kings of England. All parents would like their offspring to be and to live like kings. *Robert*, *Hugh*, *Roger*, and *Ralph* are among the many other names that were introduced by the Normans and borne by members of the nobility from the 11th century onwards. All, or almost all, Germanic names were originally 'dithematic'—that is, they were made up of two basic elements. Thus, *Roger* was composed originally of the elements *hrod* fame + *geri* spear.

Some girls' names, such as *Rosamund* and *Alice*, are of Norman origin, but once again the stock of girls' names from this other main source is not as rich as that of boys' names. This is one of the reasons why more girls' names are derivatives of boys' names than vice versa.

Adoption of a name by the royal family virtually guarantees popular success. *Charles* is a name of continental Germanic origin, and indeed was borne by Charlemagne himself. It was a common name among the kings of France, and was therefore widely popular as a French name, but was hardly used by the Normans. For this reason, it was not introduced to Britain until the Stuart kings of Scotland, who had French connections, adopted it. Once they succeeded to the throne of England its popularity was assured, although in the 18th century, when the Stuart pretenders were in exile and led rebellions in 1715 and 1745, choice of the name *Charles* was something of a political gesture.

Old English names did not, with a few exceptions such as *Edward*, survive the Middle English period, although some, such as *Alfred* and *Mildred*, were revived in the 19th century.

The other main source for everyday English

given names is Celtic legend. Arthurian romance was extremely popular in the Middle Ages, but it has not proved a particularly rich source of modern given names. *Arthur* itself is a 19th-century revival which, along with several other Arthurian names such as *Enid*, owes more to Tennyson than to medieval tradition. *Jennifer*, which is a derivation of *Guinevere*, the name of Arthur's queen, was a Cornish curiosity until the 19th century, when its popularity grew rapidly. *Lancelot* is used, but might be considered an eccentric choice nowadays; *Tristan* and *Isolde* are also occasionally used, as is *Perceval*, the name of the pure knight who is a central figure in the legend of the Holy Grail. The latter was no doubt somewhat influenced by the surname *Percy*, which was taken, erroneously, as a diminutive form of it. *Gavin* is equivalent to the name of Sir Gawain, who accepted the challenge of the Green Knight, but the name has an independent status of its own in Celtic languages, and the Arthurian connection is not prominent.

Ironically, Irish and Scottish Gaelic, whose cultures were virtually destroyed by English domination, are languages which have contributed extensively to the stock of English given names in everyday use. The Irish names *Brian*, *Neil*, *Patrick*, *Maureen*, *Eileen*, and *Deirdre*, and the Scots *Donald*, *Duncan*, and *Kenneth* are borne by hundreds of thousands of non-Celts, many of whom are unaware of the legends that lie behind the names they bear.

Specifically Welsh names, on the other hand, are very much a signal of national identity. *Geraint*, *Llewellyn*, *Myfanwy*, and *Gwyneth* are borne only by Welsh people or by admirers of Welsh culture, and can hardly be said to have achieved general currency.

Perhaps the most common of other Celtic names is *Alan*, which is of Breton origin, the name of at least two rather obscure saints who were early Breton bishops. It is surprisingly common, considering its uncertain origin, and its popularity is once again due to the Normans: it was introduced into Britain by Breton followers of William the Conqueror.

The number of given names in everyday use in the English-speaking world is remarkably small. Probably around 250 million people are named with one of the familiar everyday English names derived from one of the sources mentioned so far. There are less than 500 such boys' names, and even fewer such girls' names; there are, therefore, many hundreds of thousands of people in the English-speaking world called John or Mary. Moreover, almost all these names except for a tiny central core of a few dozen are subject to the vagaries of fashion. Earlier in the 20th century, *Reginald* and *Albert*, *Elsie* and *Edith* were in vogue, but they have since gone out again. Meanwhile, *Amy*, *Eleanor*, *Toby*, and *Nicola* have come back in.

Human beings, and children in particular, tend to mock the unfamiliar unmercifully, cruelly, and persistently. Most parents recognize this, and a primary consideration in choosing a name seems to be to ensure that their offspring are not condemned to a life of misery from teasing on account of the name bestowed upon them. There is sometimes a conflict between the desire to bestow a distinctive and stylish name and the desire to avoid bestowing an odd or old-fashioned name. Sometimes, a name that seemed smart and different at birth turns out later to be very common indeed, since many parents seem to have had the same idea at the same time: witness the number of Deborahs and Nigels born in the late 1950s. Only parents who are culturally exceptionally self-assured choose unique names for their children. A child who is going to go through life with the name *Fifi Trixiebelle* may be at least partially fortified against mockery by the knowledge that her father is Bob Geldof—although she may yet adopt a more mundane alias in order to escape the tedium of repeated comment.

Vogues for names are very strongly influenced by literature and, more recently, films. *Tracy* was hardly used as a given name until Grace Kelly played the character of Tracy Lord in the film *High Society*, but since then it has become established as one of the most popular of girls' names. *Miranda*, *Rosalind*, and *Viola* owe their popularity to their use by Shakespeare as names for his romantic heroines. *Shirley* was a boy's name, and rare, until taken up by Charlotte Brontë for the heroine of her novel of the same name, which firmly established it in the canon of conventional girls' names. Much work remains to be done on the connection between cultural change and fashions in name choice.

The small size of the stock of standard given names, coupled with the volatility of fashion, leads people from time to time to seek other sources for names for their children. These sources may be summarized as follows: variants and pet forms, inventions, revivals, surnames, place-names, vocabulary words, and foreign borrowings. A few examples of each kind will suffice.

Bearers of the names *Caroline* and *Carolyn*, which are pronounced differently although they have the same origin, generally insist on the separate identity of their names, though often to little avail as far as other people are concerned. Sometimes pet forms, for example *Peggy* and *Nancy*, acquire a life of their own, independently of the names from which they are derived.

Pure inventions are less common than might be supposed, though forms such as *Raelene* and *Charlene* have been imported from Australia and the US; inventions generally combine an existing name element with one of a small number of productive suffixes, of which -lene is the most common. They are more common for girls than for boys.

Revivals include Old English names that were taken up in the 19th century, such as *Wilfred* and *Mildred*, as well as more recent revivals of ancient Welsh names such as *Taliesin*.

Surnames are an increasingly common source of given names; for centuries the mother's maiden surname has from time to time been chosen for a new addition to the family, especially where the mother's family tradition was strong. Some of these names, such as *Dudley*, *Douglas*, *Rodney*, and *Shirley*, have passed into general use and become standard given names, especially for boys. Many new given names are now arising from this source, such as *Dean*, *Maxwell*, *Franklin*, and *Hamilton*.

Not many given names are derived directly from place-names, though several are derived indirectly via surnames that are from place-names. *Florence* is derived from the Italian city of that name, although it owes its popularity in general use to Florence Nightingale, who was named after the city, rather than to the place itself. More common are given names derived from some natural geographical feature, especially a river. The earliest such name is probably *Jordan*, which is derived from the river that flows into the Dead Sea. Crusaders returning from the Holy Land brought with them phials of water from the river in which Christ himself was baptized by John the Baptist, and they would use this water to baptize their own children. Thus, the name of the river came to be considered eminently suitable as a baptismal name. One or two other rivers have contributed their names to the general stock of given names: *Clyde* seems to have recommended itself to West Indians as a boy's name, while *Clodagh*, the name of a river in Tipperary, is now used for Irish girls.

Vocabulary words have sometimes been assigned a function as given names, especially for girls. The Puritans in the 17th century were fond of naming their daughters after abstract qualities, such as *Patience*, *Prudence*, *Faith*, *Grace*, and *Hope*, when they were not imposing on them tongue-breaking Old Testament names. In the 19th century, when girls were supposed to be pretty if not much else, names of pretty things came to be used as girls' given names—in particular flowers (*Daisy*, *Marigold*) and gemstones (*Beryl*, *Ruby*). In the U.S., and especially among Black people, words denoting ranks of the aristocracy, such as *Earl*, *Duke*, and *King*, have found favour as given names. In some cases these have been disguised slightly, for example by Frenchification, as *Leroy*, *Delroy*, *Lareine*, and so on.

Finally, we must mention foreign borrowing as a source of augmentation of the stock of conventional given names. This time-honoured practice needs to be the subject of a much larger study than the present one, especially in today's shrinking world of instant international communication. *Sophia* probably owes as much to Ms Loren as it does to Squire Weston's daughter. The French names *Yves* and *Yvette* had a brief vogue among English-speakers, as did the German *Carl* more recently. *Boris* and, very commonly now, *Tamara* have been adopted from Russia. There are hundreds of similar adoptions from other European languages. There are even occasional borrowings from further afield; *Fatima* is sometimes found in an English as well as an Islamic context, while admirers of Indian as well as Irish culture may decide to use *Tara*.

### Acknowledgements

We would like to thank friends and colleagues who have helped us with advice and comments, and in particular Ramesh Krishnamurthy, who read the whole text and greatly improved it in many ways, and Tomás de Bhaldraithe, Ian Fraser, and Hywel Wyn Owen, who advised us on problems with Irish, Gaelic, and Welsh pronunciations and other matters. Responsibility for the published text rests, of course, with the authors.

P.W.H.

F.M.H.

*April 1986*

# Key to Pronunciations

IN this dictionary a guide to the pronunciation of each name is given in the International Phonetic Alphabet. The accent represented is the educated speech of southern England and elsewhere, sometimes referred to as 'Received Pronunciation' (RP). With a few minor exceptions, the system is that of the *English Pronouncing Dictionary* (14th edn, ed. A. C. Gimson, 1977). In a few cases, Welsh, Irish, Gaelic, and other foreign pronunciations are given; these are labelled as such. For transcriptions of foreign pronunciations, the reader is recommended to consult the Duden *Aussprachewörterbuch* (ed. Max Mangold, 1974).

The values of the symbols are as follows: b, d, f, h, k, l, m, n, p, r, s, t, v, w, and z have their normal English value; other symbols are to be interpreted according to the key below.

## ENGLISH SOUNDS

### VOWELS

| | | | |
|---|---|---|---|
| ɑː | as in *father* /ˈfɑːðə/ | ɪə | as in *dear* /dɪə/ |
| æ | as in *fact* /fækt/ | ɒ | as in *hot* /hɒt/ |
| aɪ | as in *life* /laɪf/ | əʊ | as in *hope* /həʊp/ |
| aɪə | as in *fire* /faɪə/ | ɔː | as in *order* /ˈɔːdə/ |
| aʊ | as in *loud* /laʊd/ | ɔɪ | as in *boy* /bɔɪ/ |
| aʊə | as in *power* /paʊə/ | ʊ | as in *good* /ɡʊd/ |
| ɛ | as in *red* /red/ | uː | as in *food* /fuːd/ |
| eɪ | as in *face* /feɪs/ | ʊə | as in *tour* /tʊə/ |
| ɛə | as in *fair* /fɛə/ | ə | as in *about* /əˈbaʊt/ |

| | | | |
|---|---|---|---|
| ɪ | as in *ship* /ʃɪp/ | ɜ: | as in *third* /θɜːd/ |
| iː | as in *sheep* /ʃiːp/ | ʌ | as in *cut* /kʌt/ |

STRESS: the symbol ' is placed before stressed syllables.

LENGTH: the symbol : is placed after long vowels.

CONSONANTS:

| | | | |
|---|---|---|---|
| g | as in *good* /gʊd/ | dʒ | as in *joke* /dʒəʊk/ |
| j | as in *yellow* /'jɛləʊ/ | θ | as in *thin* /θɪn/ |
| ʃ | as in *ship* /ʃɪp/ | ð | as in *there* /ðeə/ |
| tʃ | as in *china* /'tʃaɪnə/ | ŋ | as in *ring* /rɪŋ/ |
| ʒ | as in *measure* /'mɛʒə/ | | |

# FOREIGN SOUNDS

VOWELS:

a as in French *ami* /am'i/, German *Mann* /man/
e as in French *été* /e'te/, German *sehr* /zeːr/
o as in French *mot* /mo/, German *Boot* /boːt/
ɔ as in French *mort* /mɔr/
y as in French *tu* /ty/, German *fünf* /fynf/

NASALIZATION:

Nasalized vowels, as for example in French *maison*
/meˈzɔ̃/, are marked with ˜ over them.

CONSONANTS:

x as in Scots *loch* /lox/, German *ach* /ax/, an unvoiced
    velar fricative.
ɣ as in Spanish *Aragon* /ara'ɣɔn/, a voiced velar frica-
    tive.
ç as in German *ich* /ɪç/, an unvoiced palatal fricative.
β as in Spanish *Havana* /a'βana/, a voiced bilabial frica-
    tive.
ɥ as in French *lui* /lɥi/, a bilabial semivowel.
ɫ is the Welsh lateral fricative, an l in which air passes
    on one side or other of the tongue.

### PALATALIZATION:

In Irish Gaelic all consonants are either velarized or palatalized. In this book, velarized consonants are unmarked. Palatalized consonants are generally marked with a glide /j/ following them, as in *few* /fju:/, but in fact the two sounds are pronounced together. Palatalized /r/ is marked as /rz/, as it is often heard by English speakers as /z/.

### STRESS:

In some languages word stress is not as important as it is in English, where meaningful differences between words can be expressed by stress alone, as in the difference between the verb and the adjective *abstract*, and where a word wrongly stressed can become unrecognizable.

In French, for example, phrase stress is more important, being expressed by a slight lengthening of the last syllable in a phrase, rather than by the combination of pitch and loudness differences as in English. In Gaelic, stress usually falls at the beginning of a word or phrase. In these languages, a stress mark has been added to the transcriptions of names to remind English speakers of the characteristic patterns of these languages, even though there may in theory be good reasons to object to any attempt to show stress on words or names listed in isolation.

# Glossary of Terms

**Anglicization**: alteration of the form of a name to conform to the normal sound pattern and spelling of English. For example, *Moira* is an Anglicization of Irish Gaelic *Máire*. Sometimes an existing English name may be taken as an Anglicization of a name with which it is not etymologically connected, as when *Hugh* is taken as an Anglicization of the Gaelic name *Aodh*. Many names of French or German origin, such as *Martin* and *Curt*, have been thoroughly Anglicized in pronunciation, although the spelling remains unaffected.

**aphetic**: formed by removal of the first syllable of another name. For example, *Becky* is an aphetic formation of *Rebecca*. Aphetic forms occur quite often in English as pet forms, but are even more common in some other languages, such as Russian and Polish.

**baptismal name**: a Christian name given specifically during the service of baptism. The term is often used to distinguish the baptismal name from the name by which someone is ordinarily known, in cases where the former has been abandoned in favour of some adopted name which the bearer prefers.

**baronial name**: a surname, such as *Melville*, which was originally borne by a family of Norman barons in Britain after the Conquest, usually derived from the name of the place in northern France from which the family originally came or where they still had estates. Some of these baronial names, like other surnames, have yielded given names.

**bilabial**: pronounced using both lips. The sounds /p/ and /b/ are bilabial plosives; that is, they are pronounced with the sudden release of both lips. Spanish has a voiced bilabial fricative, represented in the phonetic alphabet as /β/, which to English ears sound like a cross between /v/ and /b/.

**byname**: a name acquired in addition to the given name, often derived from some physical characteristic of the bearer. Bynames were like nicknames, except that they were used more seriously, as a second or replacement personal name. *Algernon*, for example, originated as a byname for someone with a moustache (Norman French *al gernon*). *Mungo*, which is occasionally found as a given name in Scotland, was originally a byname for Saint Kentigern, although its etymology is unknown. The term *byname* is often used with reference to the period before surnames were in use.

**calque**: a name formed by translating the elements of a name in another language. For example, *Amadeus* was formed in medieval Latin as a calque on the Greek name *Theophilos*: in both cases, the elements mean 'love' and 'God', although the order has been reversed.

**Celtic**: denoting the group of languages spoken in the British Isles until they were gradually displaced, from the 6th century AD onwards, by Anglo-Saxon (Old English). There are two main groups of Celtic languages: the Brittonic group, which includes Welsh, Breton, and the extinct languages of Cornwall, Cumbria, Strathclyde, and elsewhere, and the Goidelic group, which consists of Scottish and Irish Gaelic and Manx, the extinct language of the Isle of Man.

**Christian name**: a name given to a child at birth or shortly after birth (strictly, in Christian tradition, at baptism). In Britain, this is the usual term for a given name, but it is not much used in this book, partly because some names are listed which are never or hardly ever used by Christians (e.g. *Chaim*), and partly because even the names which are used by Christians have become generally adopted and are used by many people who are not Christians.

**classical**: referring to the ancient culture of Greece and Rome, which flourished in Greece for over five centuries before Christ, and in Rome from about the 3rd century BC to the 5th century AD, when the Roman Empire was overrun by Germanic tribes, and the pagan civilization of both Greece and Rome had already been replaced by Christianity. Classical names did not generally survive the introduction of Christianity, although modern Greeks may be named *Sophocles*, *Aristocles*, and so on. In a few cases, such as *Claudius* (*Claude*), a Roman family name has survived in general use, usually by the accident of having been borne by an early Christian saint.

**cognate**: having the same origin. Latin *Maria*, French *Marie*, Irish *Máire*, and English *Mary* are all cognate names, since they all derive from the same New Testament original.

**contraction**: a shortening in which the first and last letters, and often the whole of the first and last syllables, remain the same, but sounds are left out in the middle. Thus *Minette* is a French name that arose as a contraction of *Mignonette* 'Darling'.

**derivative**: a name or form that comes from another name or from a word in the vocabulary of a language.

**diminutive**: denoting a name form that has been altered by the addition of a suffix such as -*et*(*te*), -*in*(*e*), or -*on*(*ne*), that originally suggested smallness, and thus was a way of expressing affection. Compare SHORT FORM and PET FORM.

**dissimilation**: alteration of one of the consonants in a word or name with two consonants in it that are identical or that are pronounced in very similar ways. The name *Annabel* is probably derived from *Amabel*, the *m* being changed to *n* in order to dissimilate it from the nearby *b*, both *m* and *b* being pronounced with closure of the lips.

**dithematic**: see ELEMENT.

**element**: a word or suffix from ordinary language that has been joined with other elements to make a name. Old English and Germanic names were almost all made up of two elements. Thus *Alfred* is made up of the elements *alf*, meaning 'elf', and *rad*, meaning 'advice' or 'counsel'. These were ordinary words in the vocabulary of Old English. Name elements are sometimes referred to in names studies as 'themes', and Germanic names with two themes are called 'dithematic'.

**ethnic name**: a name for a national group. Some ethnic names gave rise to surnames, and a few of these have been adopted as given names. Thus *Brett* was originally a vocabulary word meaning 'Breton'; it gave rise to a surname, which in turn has been adopted as a given name.

**etymology**: the linguistic origin of a word or name, which is a matter of scientific study. The aim of etymology in names studies is to trace all names back to their origins as words in the vocabulary of some language or other. This is often a very long road. In the case of *Dudley*, for example, it leads from given name to surname to place-name and back to a personal name. Sometimes the trail peters out before the facts can be established: *Dudley* comes via a surname from a place in the West Midlands, which was named in Old English as 'Dudda's clearing', but who Dudda was, or what his name meant, is unknown. The etymologies of names often take us into ancient languages such as Hebrew, Aramaic (the language of the Holy Land at the time of Christ), Greek, and Latin. In other cases, names have their origins in languages which have died out completely, such as ancient Germanic, so that we can only reconstruct the ancient forms by comparing modern cognates.

**first name**: the familiar name by which someone is ordinarily known to family and friends. A first name is chosen for a person, usually by the parents or guardian at birth, but occasionally by the individual himself or herself. Compare SURNAME, BAPTISMAL NAME, GIVEN NAME.

**folk etymology**: an explanation of the origin of a name which is or has been widely believed but is in fact wrong. The analysis of *Rosamund* as meaning 'pure rose' (Latin *rosa munda*) is a piece of folk etymology; the name is actually from the Germanic elements *hrod* fame and *mund* protection.

**Frenchified**: invented or altered to look like French, rather than actually existing in that language. Compare GALLICIZATION.

**fricative**: pronounced by very nearly, but not quite, closing the passage through which the airstream passes, in most cases by using the tongue or lips, so that a noise is made by the friction of the air passing through. The sounds /f/, /v/, /s/, /z/, /θ/, /ð/, /ʃ/, /ʒ/, and /h/ are the fricatives of English.

**Gaelic**: either of the two ancient Celtic languages of Scotland and Ireland, still spoken by a few hundred thousand people. Scots Gaelic, often pronounced /ˈgælɪk/, was brought to Scotland from Ireland in the 6th century AD, and gradually became differentiated. Irish Gaelic /ˈgeɪlɪk/ is often referred to simply as 'Irish'.

**Gaelicization**: alteration of the form of a name to conform to the spelling and sound pattern of Gaelic, especially Irish Gaelic.

**Gallicization**: alteration of the form of a name to conform to the spelling and sound pattern of French; the French equivalent of English *Anglicization*.

**Germanic**: the ancient language, of which virtually no records survive, which gave rise to modern Danish, Swedish, and Icelandic (North Germanic), German and Dutch (West Germanic), and English, which is basically a West Germanic language, but with a strong Romance (Latin) added element and a smattering of North Germanic, especially in Scots dialects. Germanic was spoken in Europe about 2000 years ago. Except for occasional references by Roman historians such as Tacitus, all that we know of Germanic is derived from a comparison of the modern languages derived from it. It plays an important part in names studies because many surnames, given names, and place names are derived from ancient Germanic personal names. Germanic names influenced English names in three main ways: by introduction with the Anglo-Saxon invaders who came across the North Sea in the 5th, 6th, and 7th centuries, whose language is now known as Old English; by introduction with the Vikings from Scandinavia in the 8th, 9th, and 10th centuries, and, most importantly of all, via the Normans, whose names were influenced by the French tradition which they had adopted. This French culture contained names derived from continental West Germanic, the vernacular language spoken at the court of Frankish kings such as Charlemagne. Many current English given names, such as *Rosamund*, *Alice*, *Robert*, and *Herbert*, are ultimately of continental West Germanic origin.

**given name**: a name given to a child by its parents or guardians at birth. In this book, the term 'given name' means much the same as 'first name', but it is used for names which may occur as the first, second, or even

third item in a string of names borne before the surname.

**Hispanicization**: alteration of the form of a name to
conform to the spelling and sound pattern of Spanish.

**hypercorrection**: the practice of 'correcting' the
spelling or pronunciation of a word or name to a form
that is believed to be correct but is actually wrong. The
-h- in *Anthony* was introduced by hypercorrection.

**hypocoristic**: denoting a pet form of a name or a
suffix added to create a pet form. *Sally* is a hypocoristic
alteration of *Sarah*; the most common hypocoristic suffix in English is -*ie*.

**Latinate**: altered to look like Latin, although not
actually existing in that language. For example,
*Roberta* and *Philippa* are Latinate coinages as names in
their own right. Although they have the typical Latin
feminine ending -*a*, they were not used in classical
Latin.

**Latinization**: alteration of the form of a name to
conform to the usual spelling and sound pattern of the
Latin language. For example, *Phoebe* is a Latinization
of the Greek name *Phoibē*.

**lenition**: in Irish and Scots Gaelic, one of the types of
alteration that take place in both the sound and spelling
of an initial consonant in a word, depending on where
the word occurs in a sentence and what word precedes
it. For non-Gaelic speakers, the most noticeable case of
lenition in a name is when it occurs in the vocative after
*A* (meaning 'O'). Lenition alters the sound of the initial
consonant to a different speech sound altogether, but
the spelling is altered merely by the addition of -*h*- after
the consonant, so that in the spelling at least the relationship of the lenited form of the name to its basic
form can be clearly seen. The following table shows the

alterations that take place through lenition in Irish (which are quite similar to those that occur in Scots Gaelic):

Basic initial consonant:  p t c b d g m s f

Lenited form (spelled):  ph th ch bh dh gh mh sh fh
(pronounced):  /f/ /h/ /x/ /v/ /γ/ /γ/ /ṽ/ /h/ /-/

Thus, for example, the Irish form of Patrick, *Pádraig*, is lenited in the vocative: *A Phádraig*. Scots Gaelic *Seumas* shows both lenition and inflection in the vocative: *A Sheumais* (O James), whence the Anglicization *Hamish*.

**local name**: a surname derived from a place name. Some local names, for example Morton, have been adopted as given names.

**metronymic**: a surname derived from the given name of somebody's mother, rather than his or her father. The surname *Nelson* may in some cases be a metronymic from *Nell* rather than a patronymic from *Neil*.

**Middle English**: the English language from the time of the Norman Conquest (1066) to the mid-15th century. Most English surnames were formed in the Middle English period and common modern surnames preserve Middle English given names and hypocoristic forms that have otherwise fallen out of use. For example, the common surname *Hopkins* is derived from the Middle English given name *Hob*, a short form of *Robert*, with the hypocoristic suffix *-kin*, which was added to many such names.

**mutation**: change in the form of a word. In Celtic languages, mutation denotes the alteration of the initial consonant of a word that occurs in certain positions in a sentence and in particular after certain other words. In

Welsh there are three types of mutation, known respectively as the soft mutation (in which *t*, for example, becomes *d*), the aspirate mutation (in which *t* becomes *th*), and the nasal mutation (in which *t* becomes *nh*). In Irish and Scottish Gaelic the main mutation is LENITION.

**nasal**: pronounced with some air or vibration from the vocal cords passing through the nose as well as or instead of through the mouth. /m/ and /n/ are specifically nasal consonants. In French, Portuguese, and many other languages (but not English), a distinction is made between specifically nasal forms of vowels and non-nasal forms.

**nasalization**: pronunciation of a speech sound with a nasal quality in addition to its ordinary quality. Some languages are characteristically more nasalized than others: for example, the general quality of vowels in Gaelic and Portuguese is typically more nasal than in English.

**nickname**: an additional name given to someone, often referring to some physical feature. For example, *Lofty* is often used as a nickname for a very tall person (and occasionally, ironically, for a very short person). In other cases nicknames are associated with particular surnames: people with the surname *Miller* are often nicknamed *Dusty*, no doubt because millers were always covered in flour from their occupation; people with the surname *Clark* are often nicknamed *Nobby*. See also BYNAME.

**occupational name**: a surname derived from a person's occupation or status in society, such as *Baker*, *Cooper*, or *Franklin*. A few of these occupational names have been adopted in recent years as given names.

**Old English**: the English language from the time when it was a collection of Germanic dialects, first brought to the British Isles by invaders across the North Sea in the 5th century, up to the Norman Conquest in the 11th century, after which it underwent a number of changes and is known as Middle English. Old English personal names generally did not survive beyond the Middle English period, so that *Ethelred*, *Wulfstan*, and so on are not now generally found as given names. An exception is *Edward*, which survived partly because it was bestowed in honour of King Edward the Confessor, and was borne by eight further English kings. In the 19th century there was a vogue for the revival of Old English names; examples which were widely adopted include *Alfred*, *Wilfred*, and *Mildred*.

**palatal**: pronounced with the tongue coming close to or even touching the hard palate (the arch that forms the roof of the mouth). A distinction is made in many languages between palatal and velar sounds: for example the two pronunciations of the German fricative -*ch*-, as in *ich* /iç/, which is a palatal, and *ach* /ax/, which is velar.

**palatalization**: pronunciation of a consonant in such a way that not only is it pronounced in the usual way, but also the tongue comes close to the hard palate. In Irish Gaelic all consonants have both palatalized and velarized forms. The palatalized forms often sound to English ears as if they are pronounced with a *y* /j/ sound or, in the case of palatal *r*, with a *z*. Compare VELARIZATION.

**patronymic**: denoting a name derived from the personal name of somebody's father; a very common source of surname formation. A patronymic surname may have a patronymic suffix, as in the case of *Jackson* and *Jefferson*, or it may take the father's personal name unaltered, as where *John*, *Jack*, *Patrick* etc, are used as surnames. Often the patronymic suffix is reduced to *-s*, as in *Roberts*; the significance of this *-s* is not always clear, since it coincides with the genitive case and may therefore mean 'of Robert', which could apply to a retainer or servant, as well as to a son or descendant. In the days before surnames came into general use, personal names were often composed of a given name plus a patronymic. In Icelandic, names still have this form; *Herman Pálsson* is Herman son of Pál, and his own son would be Sigurd Hermansson. In Russian, although surnames are in use, people are still generally addressed by their Christian name plus patronymic; *Nikita Sergeyevich* is Nikita son of Sergei.

**personal name**: a name bestowed on a person. The term is used very generally, but in this book and elsewhere is often applied specifically to a single name that was in use to identify an individual in the period before the current pattern of given names plus surname became the norm.

**pet form**: a form of a name used to show affection, generally created by addition of the suffix *-ie* or *-y* to a name or a short form of it, as in *Timmy* from *Timothy*. So strong is the notion that the ending *-y* indicates a pet form that some names ending in *-y*, for example *Terry* and *Gary*, are now generally assumed to be pet forms, even though in fact they are not.

**plosive**: pronounced with a sudden release of air from some point in the mouth that has been closed. The points of closure are generally the lips (*p* and *b*), the tongue and the teeth or the alveolar ridge just behind the teeth (*t* and *d*), or the tongue and the back of the mouth (*k* and *g*).

**short form**: a form of a name created by shortening it, especially by cutting off syllables at the end, as in

*Fred* from *Frederick* and *Flo* from *Florence*. Sometimes creation of a short form is accompanied by alteration of consonants, as in *Bob* from *Robert*. Short forms are widely used as friendly and colloquial terms of address, but are less intimate and affectionate than pet forms.

**surname**: the name inherited by a child from its father, in contrast to a FIRST NAME, which is a matter of conscious choice. Surnames as we know them originated among the Normans in the 12th century and were in widespread use in England by the end of the 13th. There were four main sources of surnames: PATRONYMICS, NICKNAMES, LOCAL NAMES, and OCCUPATIONAL NAMES. Sometimes a child will receive a surname as a given name, especially if it is the mother's original surname, and some of these, for example *Dudley*, *Percy*, *Douglas* and *Maxwell*, have been adopted into more general use, augmenting the stock of conventional given names.

**unattested**: denoting a form of a word or a name that is known or believed to have existed because of circumstantial evidence, such as cognates or derived forms, but not actually found in any of the surviving literature. Unattested forms in etymological studies are sometimes written with an asterisk (*) in front of them.

**unvoiced**: see VOICED.

**velar**: pronounced with the back of the tongue raised towards the 'velum' or soft palate at the back of the mouth. Languages such as Spanish and modern Greek, have a voiced velar fricative, written /γ/ in the phonetic alphabet. Compare PALATAL.

**velarization**: pronunciation of a consonant in such a way that not only is it pronounced in the usual manner, but also the back of the tongue is raised towards the soft palate. Many English consonants are ordinarily velarized, especially when they occur after a back vowel such as /uː/. For example, the /l/ in *fool* is velarized, while that in *fill* is not. However, the distinction in English is not important in the way that it can be in Gaelic. Compare PALATALIZATION.

**vocabulary word**: an ordinary word in a language, a term used in this book to distinguish such words from name forms. Occasionally given names are still derived directly from vocabulary words, as in the case of *Faith*, *Prudence*, and the flower names and gemstone names, such as *Daisy* and *Beryl*, which were introduced in the 19th century.

**voiced**: pronounced with vibration of the vocal cords. Voiced consonants in English include /b/, /d/, /g/, /v/, /ð/, /z/, and /ʒ/. Each of these consonants has an UNVOICED counterpart, namely /p/, /t/, /k/, /f/, /θ/, /s/, and /ʃ/. Other voiced consonants are /m/, /n/, /ŋ/, /r/, /l/, and /w/.

**Note**: Cross-references from one entry to another are shown by the use of small capitals.

# A

**Aaron** /ˈɛərɒn/ (*m.*) Old Testament: name of the
brother of Moses, who was appointed by God to be
Moses' spokesman, and became the first High Priest
of the Jewish nation (Exod. 4:14). It is of uncertain
origin and meaning but most probably, like MOSES, of
Egyptian rather than Hebrew origin. The traditional
derivation from Hebrew *har-on* 'Mountain of
Strength' is no more than a folk etymology. The
name has been used fairly infrequently by Christians,
rather more commonly by Jews.

**Abbey** /ˈæbi:/ (*f.*) Short form of ABIGAIL, now used as
an independent name in its own right. The spelling
**Abbie** is also used.

**Abe** /ˈeɪb/ (*m.*) Short form of ABRAHAM.

**Abel** /ˈeɪbəl/ (*m.*) Old Testament: name of the
younger son of Adam and Eve, who was murdered
out of jealousy by his brother Cain (Gen. 4:1–8). The
Hebrew form is *Hevel*, ostensibly representing the
vocabulary word *hevel* breath, vapour, and so taken
to imply vanity or worthlessness. Abel is considered
by the Christian Church to have been a pre-Christian
martyr (cf. Matt. 23:25), and is invoked as a saint in
the litany for the dying. Nevertheless, his name has
not been much used either before or after its brief
vogue among the Puritans.

**Abigail** /ˈæbɪɡeɪl/ (*f.*) Old Testament: name (meaning
'Father of Exaltation' in Hebrew) borne by one of
King David's wives, who had earlier been married to
Nabal (I Sam. 25:3), and by the mother of Absalom's
captain Amasa (II Sam. 1:25). The name was popular
in the 17th cent. under Puritan influence. It was a
common name in literature for a lady's maid, for
example in Beaumont and Fletcher's play *The Scorn-*

*ful Lady* (1616), partly no doubt because the biblical
Abigail refers to herself as 'Thy Servant'.

**Abner** /'æbnə/ (*m.*) Old Testament: name (meaning
'Father of Light' in Hebrew) of a relative of King
Saul, who was in command of Saul's army (I Sam.
14:50, 26:5). It is not common as a given name in
England, but has enjoyed a steady modest popularity
in America, where it was brought in at the time of the
earliest Puritan settlements.

**Abraham** /'eɪbrəhæm/ (*m.*) Old Testament: name of
the first of the Jewish patriarchs, who entered into a
covenant with God that his descendants should pos-
sess the land of Canaan. The Hebrew form is *Avra-
ham*, of uncertain derivation. In Gen. 1:5 it is
explained as 'Father of a Multitude (of nations)'
(Hebrew *av hamon* (*goyim*)). It has always been a
popular given name among Jews, and was occasionally also chosen by Christians, sometimes in honour
of the various early saints of the Eastern Roman
Empire who were so named. Its present (modest)
currency in the United States is largely due to the
fame of President Abraham Lincoln (1809–65).

**Abram** /'eɪbrəm/ (*m.*) Old Testament: variant of
ABRAHAM. It was originally a distinct name (meaning
'High Father' in Hebrew), which, according to Gen.
17:5, was changed by divine command to the longer
form. From the Middle Ages, however, if not before,
it was taken to be a contracted version.

**Absalom** /'æbsələm/ (*m.*) Old Testament: name
(meaning 'Father of Light' in Hebrew, or, according
to some, 'Father of Peace') of the third son of King
David, who rebelled against him and was eventually
killed when he was caught by the hair in an oak tree
as he fled, to the great grief of his father (II Sam.
15–18). The name has never been particularly com-

**Adam**

mon in the English-speaking world, but the Scandinavian form AXEL is familiar in the United States.

**Achilles** /əˈkɪliːz/ (*m.*) From Greek mythology: Achilles, son of the sea nymph Thetis and the mortal Peleus, was the leading warrior of the Greek army attacking Troy. In the *Iliad,* Homer relates how he withdrew from the siege as a result of a slight to his honour, until his lover Patroclus was killed wearing his armour, whereupon he rejoined the fray in order to avenge him. The Greek form of his name is *Akhilleus,* and is of unknown, possibly pre-Greek, origin; it may be connected with that of the river Akheloos. The name has been used only rarely in the English-speaking world, usually as a result of recent continental influence. Although there were various minor early saints so named, it has normally been chosen by parents who wished to take advantage of the licence given by the Catholic church to select names borne by classical heroes as well as those of saints.

**Ada** /ˈeɪdə/ (*f.*) Of uncertain origin, apparently not generally bestowed before the late 18th cent. To some extent, this is a pet form of ADELE and ADEL-AIDE, and so it may go back to a Germanic girl's personal name, a short form of various compound names with the first element *adal* noble. Alternatively it may have originated as a variant of ADAH. Ada was the name of a 7th-cent. abbess of Saint-Julian-des-Prés at Le Mans.

**Adah** /ˈeɪdə, ˈɑːdə/ (*f.*) Old Testament: Authorized Version spelling of the name (meaning 'Adornment' in Hebrew) of the wives of Esau (Gen. 36:2) and of Lamech (Gen. 4:19).

**Adam** /ˈædəm/ (*m.*) Old Testament: name borne by the first man (Gen. 2–3). It probably derives from Hebrew *adama* earth; it is a common feature of creation legends that the god responsible fashioned the

first human beings from earth or clay and breathed
life into them. The name was subsequently borne by
a 7th-cent. Irish abbot of Fermo in Italy. It has
enjoyed something of a resurgence in the English-
speaking world since the 1960s.

**Adela** /ə'delə/ (f.) Latinate form of ADÈLE, especially
popular in the late 19th cent.

**Adelaide** /'ædəleɪd/ (f.) Norman French: of Germanic
origin, composed of the elements *adal* noble + *heid*
kind, sort. It was borne in the 10th cent. by the wife
of the Holy Roman Emperor Otto the Great. She
became regent after his death and was revered as a
saint. The given name increased in popularity in England during the 19th cent., when it was borne by the
wife of King William IV; she was the daughter of the
holder of the German duchy of Saxe-Meiningen. The
Australian city of Adelaide was named in her
honour.

**Adèle** /ə'dɛl/ (f.) From French: of Germanic origin,
representing a short form of various compound
names with the first element *adal* noble. It was popular among the Normans as a result of the fame of a
7th-cent. saint, a daughter of the Frankish king
Dagobert II. It was also the name of William the
Conqueror's youngest daughter (*c.* 1062–1137), who
became the wife of Stephen of Blois and was likewise
revered as a saint. It was revived in England in the
late 19th cent., being the name of a character in
Johann Strauss's opera *Die Fledermaus*. Its popularity was further reinforced in the 1930s as the name of
a character in the novels of Dornford Yates.

**Adeline** /'ædəliːn, 'ædəlaɪn; *French* ad'liːn/ (f.)
French: diminutive of ADÈLE. The Latinate form
**Adelina** is also found. Both enjoyed a brief vogue in
the 19th cent.

**Adolf** /ˈædɒlf/ (*m.*) From Germanic: composed of the elements *adal* noble + *wolf* wolf. This form of the name was first introduced into Britain by the Normans, displacing the Old English cognate *Æthelwulf*, but it did not become common until it was re-introduced by the Hanoverians in the 18th cent. The association with Adolf Hitler (1889–1945) has meant that the name has hardly been used since World War II.

**Adolphus** /əˈdɒlfəs/ (*m.*) Latinized form of ADOLF (the *ph* a result of hypercorrection). This has been a recurring name in the Swedish royal family, and this form has also been used occasionally in the English-speaking world.

**Adrian** /ˈeɪdrɪən/ (*m.*) Usual English form of the Latin name *Hadriānus* 'man from Hadria'. Hadria was a town in northern Italy which has given its name to the Adriatic Sea; it is of unknown derivation, and the initial *H-* has always been very volatile. The name was borne by the Roman emperor Publius Aelius Hadrianus, during whose reign (AD 117–38) Hadrian's Wall was built across northern England. The name was later taken by several early popes, including the only English pope, Nicholas Breakspeare (Adrian IV). It has become particularly popular in the English-speaking world during the past thirty years.

**Adrienne** /ædrɪˈɛn, eɪdrɪˈɛn; *French* adriˈɛn/ (*f.*) French feminine form of ADRIAN.

**Agatha** /ˈægəθə/ (*f.*) Latinized version of the Greek name *Agathē*, from the feminine form of the adjective *agathos* good, honourable. This was the name of a Christian saint popular in the Middle Ages; she was a Sicilian martyr of the 3rd cent. who suffered the fate of having her breasts cut off. According to the traditional iconography, she is depicted holding them on a platter. In some versions they look more like loaves, leading to the custom of blessing bread on her feast day (5 February). The name was revived in the 19th cent., but has faded again since.

**Aggie** /'ægi:/ (*f.*) Pet form of AGNES and AGATHA.

**Agnes** /'ægnis/ (*f.*) Latinized version of the Greek name *Hagnē*, from the feminine form of the adjective *hagnos* pure, holy. This was the name of a young Roman virgin martyred under Diocletian; she became a very popular saint in the Middle Ages. Her name was associated with Latin *agnus* lamb, leading to the dropping of the initial *H-* and to her representation in art accompanied by a lamb. The name was strongly revived in the 19th cent., especially in Scotland.

**Agnethe** /'ægneitə; *German, Swedish* 'agne:tə/ (*f.*) German and Scandinavian form of AGNES, derived from the Latin genitive case *Agnētis*. It has occasionally been used in the English-speaking world during the 20th cent.

**Aidan** /'eidən/ (*m.*) From Irish (Gaelic **Aodhán** /'e:gɑ:n/): diminutive of AODH. This was borne by various early Irish saints, principally the 7th-cent. apostle of Northumbria, in whose honour it is normally bestowed. It has enjoyed a growth of popularity recently, not only in areas of Celtic influence.

**Aileen** /'aili:n, ai'li:n/ (*f.*) Variant spelling of EILEEN.

**Aimee** /'eimi:/ (*f.*) Frenchified variant of AMY.

**Al** /ael/ (*m.*) Short form of ALBERT, ALAN, and other boys' names beginning with this syllable.

**Alan** /'ælən/ (*m.*) Of Celtic origin and uncertain derivation (probably a diminutive of a word meaning 'rock'). It was introduced into England by Breton followers of William the Conqueror, most notably Alan, Earl of Brittany, who was rewarded for his services with vast estates in the newly conquered kingdom. In Britain the variants **Allan** and **Allen** are considerably less frequent, and generally represent transferred uses of surname forms, whereas in America all three forms of the name are approximately equally common.

**Alana** /ə'lɑ:nə/ (*f.*) Feminine form of ALAN, a comparatively rare 20th-cent. coinage.

**Alasdair** /'aləstɛ:r/ (*m.*) Scots: Gaelic version of ALEXANDER; see ALISTAIR. The form **Alastair** is also used.

**Alban** /'ælbən/ (*m.*) Romano-British: name of the first British Christian martyr, the Latin form of which is *Albānus*. This may be an ethnic name from one of the numerous places in the Roman Empire called Alba. Alternatively, it may represent a Latinized form of a British name derived from the Celtic element *alp* rock, crag. The 3rd- or 4th-cent. Romano-British saint was executed at the place now known as St Albans, from the Benedictine abbey founded there in his memory by King Offa. The name was in use in the Middle Ages, and was revived in the 19th cent. In some people's minds it may have been associated with Albion, a poetic name for Britain.

**Albert** /'albə:t/ (*m.*) Norman: of Germanic origin, composed of the elements *adal* noble + *berht* bright, famous. The Norman form displaced the Old English cognate *Æþelbeorht*. The name is popular in a variety of forms in Western Europe, and has been traditional in a number of European princely families. Its great popularity in England in the 19th cent. was due largely to Queen Victoria's consort, Prince Albert of Saxe-Coburg-Gotha.

**Aldous** /'ɔ:ldəs/ (*m.*) Of uncertain origin; probably a short form of any of various Norman names, such as

*Aldebrand, Aldemund,* and *Alderan,* containing the Germanic element *ald* old (cf. the common Italian name *Aldo*). It was relatively common in East Anglia during the Middle Ages, but is now rare, known mainly as the given name of the novelist Aldous Huxley (1894–1963).

**Alec** /ˈælɪk/ (*m.*) Short form of ALEXANDER, now less popular than ALEX.

**Alethea** /ælɪˈθiːə, əˈliːθɪə/ (*f.*) Learned coinage, not found before the 17th cent. It represents the Greek word *alētheia* truth, and seems to have arisen as a result of the Puritan enthusiasm for using terms for abstract virtues as girls' names. See also ALTHEA.

**Alex** /ˈælɪks/ (*m., f.*) Short form of ALEXANDER, ALEXANDRA, or ALEXIS; also commonly used as a given name in its own right. The spelling **Alix** is occasionally found.

**Alexa** /əˈlɛksə/ (*f.*) Short form of ALEXANDRA or variant of ALEXIS.

**Alexander** /ælɪksˈɑːndə/ (*m.*) Latin form of the Greek name *Alexandros,* which is composed of the elements *alexein* to defend + *anēr* man, warrior (genitive *andros*). The compound seems to have been coined originally as a title of the goddess Hera, consort of Zeus. It was also borne as a byname by the Trojan prince Paris. The name became extremely popular in the post-classical period, and was borne by several characters in the New Testament and early Christian saints. Its use as a common given name throughout Europe, however, derives largely from the fame of Alexander the Great, King of Macedon (356–323 BC), around whom a large body of popular legend grew up in late antiquity, much of which came to be embodied in the medieval 'Alexander romances'.

**Alexandra** /ælɪks'ɑ:ndrə/ (*f.*) Feminine form of ALEX-
ANDER. It was very little used in the English-speaking
world before the 20th cent., when it was brought in
from Scandinavia and Eastern Europe. It owes its
sudden rise in popularity in Britain at the end of the
19th cent. to Queen Alexandra, Danish wife of
Edward VII:

**Alexia** /ə'leksɪə/ (*f.*) Variant of the girl's name ALEXIS.

**Alexis** /ə'leksɪs/ (*m.*, *f.*) Greek: short form of various
compound names with the first element *alexein* to
defend. It was originally a boy's name, but in the
English-speaking world it is now more commonly
given to girls. This name and its variants are particularly common in Eastern Europe, as a result of the
fame of a 5th-cent. Edessan saint revered in the Orthodox Church.

**Alf** /ælf/ (*m.*) Short form of ALFRED. The pet form
**Alfie** also occurs, but is rarely if ever used as an independent given name.

**Alfred** /'ælfrɪd/ (*m.*) Old English: composed of the
elements *ælf* elf, supernatural being + *ræd* counsel.
It was a relatively common name before the Norman
Conquest of Britain, being borne most notably by
Alfred the Great (849–99), King of Wessex. After the
Conquest it was adopted by the Normans in a variety
of more or less radically altered forms, and provides a
rare example (see also EDWARD) of a distinctively Old
English name that has spread widely on the Continent. It was strongly revived in the 19th cent., along
with other names of pre-Conquest historical figures
(such as *Hereward*), but has faded since.

**Alger** /'ældʒə/ (*m.*) Old English: composed of the
elements *ælf* elf, supernatural being + *gār* spear; it is
possible that this form may also have absorbed other
names with the first elements *æþel* noble, *ēald* old,

and *ēalh* temple. The name was not common either
before or after the Norman Conquest, but was
revived in the 19th cent., along with other Germanic
names. It is relatively common in America, where it
seems to have been taken up as a more 'manly' short
form of ALGERNON.

**Algernon** /ˈældʒənɒn/ (*m.*) Norman French: originally a byname meaning 'Moustached' (from *grenon,
gernon* moustache, of Germanic origin). The Normans were as a rule clean-shaven, and this formed a
suitable distinguishing nickname when it was applied
to William de Percy, a companion of William the
Conqueror. In the 15th cent. it was revived, with a
sense of family tradition, as a byname or second
given name for his descendant Henry Percy
(1478–1527), and thereafter regularly used in that
family. It was subsequently adopted into other families connected by marriage with the Percys, and eventually became common property.

**Algie** /ˈældʒi/ (*m.*) Short form of ALGERNON.

**Alice** /ˈælɪs/ (*f.*) Norman French: variant of ADELAIDE,
representing an Old French spelling of a dramatically
contracted version of Germanic *Adalheidis*. It was
regarded as a distinct name when it was revived in the
19th cent. It was the name of the child heroine of
Lewis Carroll's *Alice's Adventures in Wonderland*
(1865) and *Through the Looking Glass* (1872), who
was based on his child friend Alice Liddell (b.1852),
daughter of the Dean of Christ Church College,
Oxford.

**Alicia** /əˈlɪʃə/ (*f.*) Modern Latinate variant of ALICE.

**Aline** /əˈliːn/ (*f.*) In the Middle Ages this represented a
contracted form of ADELINE. In modern use it is either
a revival of this or a respelling of AILEEN.

**Alison** /ˈælɪsən/ (*f.*) Norman French: diminutive of

ALICE, with the addition of the diminutive suffix *-on*. It was a popular name in medieval England, but died out in the 15th cent. However, it survived in Scotland, with the result that until its general revival in the 20th cent. the name had a strongly Scottish flavour.

**Alissa** /əˈlɪsə/ (*f.*) Variant of ALICIA.

**Alistair** /ˈælɪstə/ (*m.*) Of Scottish origin: from Gaelic **Alasdair**, a version of ALEXANDER. Alexander has long been a popular name in Scotland, having been borne by three early medieval kings of the country. This name has a large number of spelling variants, including **Alisdair**, **Alastair**, and **Alister**.

**Allan** /ˈælən/ (*m.*) Variant spelling of ALAN.

**Allegra** /əˈlɛgrə/ (*f.*) From the feminine form of the Italian adjective *allegro* gay, jaunty (familiar in English as a musical tempo). It seems to have been an original coinage when it was given to Byron's illegitimate daughter (1817–22), but since then it has been taken up by parents in many English-speaking countries. It is not used as a given name in Italy.

**Allen** /ˈælən/ (*m.*) Variant spelling of ALAN, in Britain generally found only as a surname, but in the United States equally common as a given name.

**Alma** /ˈælmə/ (*f.*) A relatively modern creation, of uncertain origin. It had a temporary vogue following the Battle of Alma (1854), which is named from the river in the Crimea by which it took place; similarly *Trafalgar* had occasionally been used as a girl's name earlier in the century. Nevertheless, the historical event seems only to have increased the popularity of an existing, if rare, name. Alma is also the feminine form of the Latin adjective *almus* nourishing, kind (cf. *alma mater* fostering mother, the clichéd phrase for an educational establishment). In Tennessee Wil-

liams's play *Summer and Smoke* (1948), a bearer of
the name explains that it is 'Spanish for "soul"' (Latin
*anima*), but this seems to be only coincidental.

**Aloysius** /ˌæləʊˈɪʃəs/ (*m.*) Of unknown origin, possibly
a Latinized form of a Provençal version of LOUIS. It
was relatively common in Italy in the Middle Ages,
and has subsequently enjoyed some popularity
among Catholics in honour of St Aloysius Gonzaga
(1568–91), who was born in Lombardy.

**Althea** /ˈælθiːə/ (*f.*) From Greek mythology.
Although often considered a contracted form of
ALETHEA, this is a quite distinct name (Greek
*Althaia*), of uncertain origin. It was borne in classical
legend by the mother of Meleager, who was given a
brand plucked from the fire at the instant of her son's
birth, with the promise that his life would last as long
as the brand did; some twenty years later she destroyed it in a fit of pique and he died. The name was
revived by the 17th-cent. poet Richard Lovelace, as a
poetic pseudonym for his beloved.

**Alun** /ˈælɪn/ (*m.*) Welsh: probably a cognate of ALAN.
It is borne in the *Mabinogion* by Alun of Dyved, a
character mentioned in passing several times. It was
adopted as a bardic name by John Blackwell
(1797–1840) and became popular as a result of his
fame.

**Alvar** /ˈælvɑː/ (*m.*) From a medieval English name,
representing an Old English personal name, *Ælfhere*,
composed of the elements *ælf* elf, supernatural being
+ *here* army. In modern use it is either a revival of
this (or a transferred use of the surname derived from
it) or an Anglicized form of the Spanish given name
*Alvaro*. The latter is of Germanic (Visigothic) origin
but uncertain derivation; it seems to be composed of
elements meaning 'all' + either 'truth' or 'guard'.

**Alvin** /'ælvɪn/ (*m.*) From an Old English personal name composed of the elements *ælf* elf, supernatural being + *wine* friend. The medieval name was not especially common in Britain either before or after the Norman Conquest, but the modern form has recently become fairly popular in the United States. The reasons for this are not entirely clear; association with CALVIN may be a factor, but a more plausible (though less elevated) reason may be that it was the name given to the naughty chipmunk in a popular TV cartoon series of the 1960s.

**Alwyn** /'ælwɪn/ (*m.*) Variant of ALVIN.

**Alys** /'ælɪs/ (*f.*) Variant spelling of ALICE.

**Alyssa** /ə'lɪsə/ (*f.*) Variant spelling of ALISSA.

**Amabel** /'æməbel/ (*f.*) Old French: from Latin *amābilis* lovable. This name is now very rare in the English-speaking world, but lies behind the much commoner ANNABEL and MABEL. It gained some currency from being borne by the character Amabel Rose Adams in Angela Thirkell's *Barsetshire Chronicles* (1933 onwards).

**Amadeus** /æmə'deɪəs/ (*m.*) Occasionally bestowed in honour of the Austrian composer Wolfgang Amadeus Mozart (1756–91). His middle name is a medieval Latin coinage composed of the elements *ama-* love + *Deus* God, a calque on Greek *Theophilos*. The Italian derivative, *Amedeo*, and the German calque *Gottlieb*, enjoyed consistent popularity in central Europe throughout the Christian era.

**Amanda** /ə'mændə/ (*f.*) A 17th-cent. coinage, but popular only since the 1940s. It represents the feminine form of the gerundive from the Latin verb *amāre* to love, i.e. 'she who is fit to be loved', and seems to have been modelled on MIRANDA. The masculine form *Amandus*, borne by various saints of the 4th to

7th cents., is unlikely to have been the model for the
feminine form.

**Amber** /'æmbə/ (*f.*) From the vocabulary word for the
gemstone *amber*, a word derived via Old French and
Latin from Arabic *ambar*. This was first used as a
given name at the end of the 19th cent., but has
become particularly popular in the past couple of
decades. In part it owes its popularity to Kathleen
Winsor's novel *Forever Amber* (1944).

**Ambrose** /'æmbrəʊz/ (*m.*) English (and Old French)
form of the post-classical Greek name *Ambrosios*
'Immortal'. This was borne by various early saints,
most notably a 4th-cent. bishop of Milan. The name
has never been common in England, but has enjoyed
considerably greater popularity in Catholic Ireland.

**Amelia** /ə'miːliə/ (*f.*) Probably the result of a cross
between the Latin-origin *Emilia* (see EMILY) and the
Latinized Germanic *Amalia*, a short form of various
compound names with the first element *amal* work. It
was first used by Henry Fielding for the heroine of his
novel *Amelia* (1751).

**Amos** /'eɪmɒs/ (*m.*) Old Testament: Amos was a
Hebrew prophet of the 8th cent. BC, whose sayings
are collected in the book of the Bible that bears his
name. This is of uncertain derivation, but may be
connected with the Hebrew verb *amos* to carry. It
was popular among the Puritans, and survived relatively well into the 19th cent., but is little used today.

**Amy** /'eɪmɪ/ (*f.*) Anglicized form of Old French *Amee*
'Beloved'. This originated in part as a vernacular
nickname, in part as a form of Latin *Amāta*. The latter is ostensibly the feminine form of the past participle of *amāre* to love, but in fact it may have had a
different, pre-Roman, origin; it was borne in classical
mythology by the wife of King Latinus, whose

daughter Lavinia married Aeneas and (according to the story in the *Aeneid*) became the mother of the Roman people.

**Anastasia** /ænə'steɪzɪə/ (*f.*) Feminine form of the Greek male name *Anastasios* (a derivative of *anastasis* resurrection). It has always been popular in Eastern Europe as a result of the fame of a 4th-cent. saint who was martyred at Sirmium in Dalmatia, and in the Middle Ages it was in use in England too. Its modern use in the English-speaking world seems, however, to reflect the recent fashion for names of Russian origin. One of the daughters of the last tsar of Russia bore this name. She was probably murdered along with the rest of the family by the Bolsheviks in 1918, but in 1920 a woman claiming to be the Romanov princess Anastasia came to public notice in Germany. A film was subsequently based on this story (1956).

**Andrea** /'ændrɪə, æn'dreɪə/ (*f.*; occasionally *m.*) Feminine equivalent of ANDREW, in use since the 17th cent., and identical in spelling with an Italian (masculine) version of *Andrew*. It seems to have originally represented an Anglicized form of the Greek abstract noun *andreia* manliness, virility.

**Andrew** /'ændruː/ (*m.*) English form of the Greek name *Andreas*, a short form of any of various compound names with the first element *andr-* man or, in particular, warrior. This was the name of the first disciple to be called by Jesus. After the Resurrection, St Andrew preached in Asia Minor and was probably crucified at Patras in Achaia. He was one of the most popular saints of the Middle Ages and was adopted as the patron of Scotland, Russia, and Greece. A recent increase in popularity is due to Prince Andrew (b. 1960).

**Andy** /'ændi/ (*m.*) Pet form of ANDREW.

**Aneurin** /æ'neɪrɪn/ (*m.*) Welsh, of uncertain deriva-

tion. It may be a version of the Latin name *Honorius*
(see HONORIA), derived directly from the time when
Latin was spoken in Britain, before the Anglo-Saxon
invasions. It was borne by the first known Welsh
poet, who lived AD *c.* 600. The 'Book of Aneurin' is a
13th-cent. manuscript which purports to preserve his
work, including the *Gododin*, a long work about the
defeat of the Welsh by the Saxons.

**Angela** /'ændʒələ/ (*f.*) From Church Latin: feminine
form of the much rarer boy's name *Angel* (post-classical Latin *Angelus* 'Angel', from Greek *angelos* messenger). It has been in use in Britain and America
since the 18th cent., increasing steadily in popularity.

**Angelica** /æn'dʒelɪkə/ (*f.*) From the feminine form of
the Latin adjective *angelicus* angelic, often used as an
elaboration of ANGELA.

**Angelina** /ændʒə'liːnə/ (*f.*) Latinate elaboration of
ANGELA.

**Angeline** /ændʒə'liːn/ (*f.*) French diminutive of
ANGELA.

**Angharad** /*Welsh* æŋ'hæræd/ (*f.*) Welsh: composed
of an old Celtic intensive prefix + an element meaning 'dear, beloved'. This was the name of the mother
of the 12th-cent. chronicler Giraldus Cambrensis
('Gerald the Welshman'). In the *Mabinogion*, Angharad Golden Hand at first rejects Peredur's suit, but
later falls in love with him. The name has been
strongly revived in Wales since the 1940s.

**Angie** /'ændʒi:/ (*f.*) Pet form of ANGELA.

**Angus** /'æŋɡəs/ (*m.*) Scottish (Gaelic **Aonghus**):
composed of old Celtic elements meaning 'one' and
'choice'. The Irish forms are **Aongas** and **Aonaos**
/'eːnɪːs/. This name is first recorded in Adamhnan's
'Life of St Columba', where it occurs in the form

*Oinogus(s)ius* as the name of a man for whom the saint prophesied a long life and a peaceful death. This is also almost certainly identical with the name of the 8th-cent. Pictish king variously recorded as *Onnust* and *Hungus*.

**Aniela** /ænɪˈɛlə/ (*f.*) Polish form of ANGELA, now adopted in the English-speaking world, but sometimes respelled **Anniela** (by association with ANNE) or **Aniella** (by association with the Italian diminutive suffix *-ella*).

**Anita** /əˈniːtə/ (*f.*) From Spanish: diminutive of *Ana*, the Spanish version of ANNE. It is now widely used in English-speaking countries with little awareness of its Spanish origin.

**Ann** /æn/ (*f.*) Variant spelling of ANNE. *Ann* was the more common of the two spellings in the 19th cent., but is now losing ground to the form with final *-e*.

**Anna** /ˈænə/ (*f.*) Latinate variant of ANNE. Among people with a classical education, it has from time to time been associated with Virgil's *Aeneid*, where it is borne by the sister of Dido, Queen of Carthage. This Phoenician name may ultimately be of Semitic origin, and thus cognate with the biblical *Anne*. However, there is no direct connection, as has sometimes been assumed.

**Annabel** /ˈænəbɛl/ (*f.*) Sometimes taken as an elaboration of ANNA, but more probably a dissimilated form of AMABEL. It has been common in Scotland since the 12th cent. and in the rest of the English-speaking world since the 1940s. The Latinized form **Annabella** is sometimes used, and occasionally also the Gallicized **Annabelle**.

**Anne** /æn/ (*f.*) English form (via Old French, Latin, and Greek) of the Hebrew girl's name *Chana* 'He (God) has favoured me (i.e. with a child)'. This is the

name borne in the Old Testament by the mother of
Samuel (see HANNAH), and according to non-biblical
tradition also by the mother of the Virgin Mary. It is
the widespread folk cult of the latter that has led to
the great popularity of the name throughout Europe.
The simplified form **Ann** was in the last century very
much more common, but the elaborated form with
final -*e* has grown in popularity during the 20th cent.,
partly no doubt due to *Anne of Green Gables* (1908),
a girls' story by L.M. Montgomery, and partly due to
Princess Anne (b. 1950). A large number of diminutives of this name have been borrowed from various
languages; many are now used as given names in their
own right. Among the most common are ANNETTE,
ANITA, and ANNIKA.

**Annette** /ə'nɛt/ (*f.*) French diminutive of ANNE.

**Annie** /'ænɪ:/ (*f.*) Pet form of ANNE or ANN.

**Annika** /'ænɪkə/ (*f.*) Scandinavian diminutive of
ANNE.

**Anona** /ə'nəʊnə/ (*f.*) Of uncertain origin, apparently
not recorded before the 1920s. It seems most likely
that it arose as an artificial combination of elements
from existing names, for example ANNE and FIONA. In
form it resembles Latin *annona* corn supply, but this
is unlikely to have influenced the formation of the
name.

**Anselm** /'ænsɛlm/ (*m.*) From Italian *Anselmo*, a name
of Germanic origin, composed of the elements *ans*
divinity + *helm* helmet. This name seems to have
been largely confined to Italy; the Christian saint who
served as archbishop of Canterbury in the late 11th
and early 12th cents. was born at Aosta in Piedmont.
He is honoured by Christians as a Doctor of the
Church. The given name is borne mostly by Roman
Catholics.

**Anthea** /'ænθi:ə/ (f.) Anglicized spelling of Greek *Antheia*, feminine form of the adjective *antheios* flowery. This was used in the classical period as a byname of the goddess Hera at Argos, but as a modern given name it was reinvented in the 17th cent. by English pastoral poets such as Robert Herrick.

**Anthony** /'æntəni:/ (m.) The usual English form of the old Roman family name *Antōnius*, which is of uncertain (probably Etruscan) origin. The spelling with *-th-* (not normally reflected in the pronunciation) represents a learned but erroneous attempt to associate it with Greek *anthos* flower. In the post-classical period it was a common name, borne by various early saints, most notably a 3rd-cent. Egyptian hermit monk. The spelling **Antony** is also found, and the French **Antoine** and German **Anton** are also used as less common variants in the English-speaking world.

**Antoinette** /æntwə'nɛt/ (f.) French feminine diminutive of *Antoine* (the French form of ANTHONY), which has become quite popular in the English-speaking world, unlike the masculine form.

**Antonia** /æn'təuni:ə/ (f.) Feminine form of ANTHONY, representing the pure classical form, without the intrusive *-h-* of the masculine.

**Antonina** /æntə'nainə/ (f.) Latin elaboration of ANTO-NIA, occasionally used in the English-speaking world.

**Aodh** /i:, e:/ (m.) Irish: from the name of the old Celtic god of the sun and of fire, *Aed*. It has been revived as a given name in Ireland, and is sometimes found Anglicized as HUGH. AIDAN is in origin a diminutive of this.

**Aoife** /'i:fjə/ (f.) Irish: an ancient Gaelic name which has been revived in recent times. It is probably connected with Gaelic *aoibh* beauty, and is often Anglicized as EVA.

**Aphra** /'æfrə/ (*f.*) Of uncertain origin: perhaps a hypercorrected spelling of Latin *Afra*, originally an ethnic name for a woman from Africa (in Roman times meaning the area around Carthage). This was used in the post-classical period as a nickname for someone with dark colouring and eventually became a given name, being borne, for example, by saints martyred at Brescia under the Roman emperor Hadrian and at Augsburg under Diocletian. The respelling of the name may have been prompted by Micah 1:10 'in the house of Aphrah roll thyself in dust', where *Aphrah* is often taken as a personal name, but is in fact a place name meaning 'Dust'.

**April** /'eɪprɪl/ (*f.*) From the month (Latin [*mensis*] aprīlis, probably a derivative of *aperīre* to open, as the month when buds open and flowers appear). It forms a series with the more common names MAY and JUNE, all taken from months associated with the spring, a time of new birth and growth, and may originally have been intended as an English version of the supposedly French name AVRIL.

**Arabella** /ærə'belə/ (*f.*) Of Scottish origin and uncertain etymology: it probably represents an alteration of *An(n)abella* (see ANNABEL). The form **Arabel** is now rare, but was common in the Middle Ages, when it was also sometimes found as *Orabel*, apparently the result of derivation, by folk etymology, from Latin *\*orābilis* invokable (from *orāre* to pray to), i.e. a saint who could be invoked.

**Archibald** /'ɑːtʃɪbɒld/ (*m.*) Norman French: of Germanic origin, composed of the elements *ercan* genuine + *bald* bold, brave. It has always been largely associated with Scotland, where it was taken, surprisingly enough, as an Anglicized form of *Gillespie* (Gaelic *Gille-easpuig*, 'Servant of the Bishop').

**Archie** /'ɑːtʃiː/ (*m.*) Short form of ARCHIBALD. Also spelled **Archy**.

**Arlene** /'ɑːliːn, ɑːˈliːn/ (*f.*) Modern coinage, most common in the United States. It is of unknown origin, probably a fanciful coinage based on MARLENE and/or CHARLENE.

**Arnold** /'ɑːnɒld/ (*m.*) Norman French: of Germanic origin, composed of the elements *arn* eagle + *wald* rule. An early saint of this name, whose cult contributed to its popularity, was a musician at the court of Charlemagne. He was apparently a Greek by birth and at what stage he acquired his Germanic name is not clear. The name had died out in England by the end of the Middle Ages and was revived in the 19th cent., along with a large number of other medieval Germanic names.

**Arthur** /'ɑːθə/ (*m.*) Of Celtic origin. King Arthur was a British king of the 5th or 6th cent., about whom virtually no historical facts are known. He ruled in Britain after the collapse of the Roman Empire and before the coming of the Germanic tribes, and a vast body of legends grew up around him in the literatures of medieval Western Europe. His name may be connected with the Gaelic element *art* stone, or with some lost Celtic form of the Indo-European term for the bear (reflected in Latin *ursus* and Greek *arktos*). Others believe that it is a Celticized form of a Latin name, perhaps *Arcturus* (from Greek *arktouros* bear-keeper). The spelling with *-th-*, now universally reflected in the pronunciation, is not found before the 16th cent., and seems to represent no more than an artificial embellishment. The name became particularly popular in the 19th cent., partly as a result of the fame of Arthur Wellesley (1769–1852), Duke of

# Asa

Wellington, partly because of the popularity of Tennyson's *Idylls of the King* (1842–85), and partly because of the enormous Victorian interest in things medieval in general and in Arthurian legend in particular.

**Asa** /ˈeɪsə/ (*m.*) Old Testament: name of one of the early kings of Judah, who reigned for forty years, as recorded in I Kings and II Chronicles. It was originally a byname meaning 'Doctor, Healer' in Hebrew, and is still a common Jewish name. It was first used among English-speaking Christians by the Puritans in the 17th cent., and although now far from common it has never completely dropped out of use. In the 20th cent. it is largely known as the given name of the historian Asa Briggs and of the footballer Asa Hertford.

**Ashley** /ˈæʃli/ (*m.*, *f.*) From the English surname, which comes from any of numerous places in England named in Old English with the elements *æsc* ash + *lēah* wood. Its use as a given name may have been first inspired by admiration for the humanitarian work of Anthony Ashley Cooper (1801–85), Earl of Shaftesbury.

**Astrid** /ˈæstrɪd/ (*f.*) Scandinavian: composed of the Old Norse elements *ans* god + *friðr* fair, beautiful. It has become fairly common in the English-speaking world during the 20th cent.

**Auberon** /ˈɔʊbərɒn/ (*m.*) Norman French, from Germanic. There is much doubt about the form and meaning of the elements of which it was originally composed; it may be connected with AUBREY, or may derive from the elements *adal* noble + *ber(n)* bear.

**Aubrey** /ˈɔːbri/ (*m.*) Norman French form of the Germanic name *Alberic*, composed of the elements *alb* elf + *ric* power. This was the (appropriate) name, according to Germanic mythology, of the king of the elves. The native Old English cognate, *Ælfrīc*, borne by a 10th-cent. archbishop of Canterbury, did not long survive the Conquest. *Aubrey* was a relatively common given name during the Middle Ages, but has since fallen out of favour. Its occasional occurrence since the 19th cent. seems in part to reflect a transferred use of the surname, which was derived from the given name in the Middle Ages.

**Audrey** /ˈɔːdrɪ/ (*f.*) Drastically reduced form of the Old English girl's name *Æðelþryð*, composed of the elements *æðel* noble + *þryð* strength. This was the name of a 6th-cent. saint (normally known by the Latinized form of her name, *Etheldreda*), who was a particular favourite in the Middle Ages. According to tradition she died from a tumour of the neck, which she bore stoically as a divine punishment for her youthful delight in necklaces. The name went into a decline at the end of the Middle Ages, when it came to be considered vulgar, being associated with *tawdry*, i.e. cheap lace and other goods sold at fairs held in her name (the word deriving from a misdivision of *Saint Audrey*). Shakespeare bestowed it on Touchstone's comic sweetheart in *As You Like It*. In the last century such associations have largely been forgotten, and the name has enjoyed some revival of popularity. The form **Audra** is also used, especially in the Southern U.S. in double names such as *Audra Jo* and *Audra Rose*.

**Augusta** /ɔːˈɡʌstə/ (*f.*) Latin: feminine form of *Augustus*.

**Augustine** /ɔːˈɡʌstɪn/ (*m.*) English form of the Latin name *Augustīnus* (a derivative of AUGUSTUS). The most famous bearer of this name is St Augustine of Hippo (354–430), perhaps the greatest of the Fathers of the Christian Church. He formulated the principles followed by the numerous medieval communities named after him as AUSTIN canons, friars, and nuns. Also important in England was St Augustine of Canterbury, who brought Christianity to Kent in the 6th cent.

**Augustus** /ɔːˈɡʌstəs/ (*m.*) Latin: from the adjective *augustus* great, magnificent (from *augēre* to increase). This word was adopted as a title by the Roman emperors, starting with Octavian (Caius Julius Caesar Octavianus), the adopted son of Julius Caesar, who assumed it in 27 BC and is now generally known as the Emperor Augustus. This name, together with AUGUSTA, was revived in the 18th cent., but it has now again declined in popularity.

**Aurelia** /əˈriːliə/ (*f.*) Feminine form of Latin *Aurelius*, an old Roman family name derived from *aureus* golden. Its most famous bearer was the 2nd-cent. emperor Marcus Aurelius Antoninus, who is also noted as a philosophical writer. It was later borne by various saints, including a 5th-cent. archbishop of Carthage who was a friend of St Augustine. It has not, however, enjoyed much popularity in the Middle Ages or since; the modern use of the feminine form since the 17th cent. seems to be the result of its relatively transparent etymology ('golden').

**Aurora** /əˈrɔːrə/ (*f.*) From Latin *aurōra* dawn, also used in the classical period as the name of the personified goddess of the dawn. It was not used as a given name in the post-classical or medieval period, but is a reinvention of the Renaissance, and has generally been bestowed as a learned equivalent of DAWN by parents conscious of its etymology.

**Austin** /ˈɒstɪn/ (*m.*) Medieval contracted form of the Latin name *Augustīnus*; see AUGUSTINE. The present-day use of the name in this form is probably the result of its survival as a surname, for the full forms are rare in the English-speaking world. The variant **Austen** is also sometimes used as a given name.

**Ava** /ˈɑːvə, ˈeɪvə/ (*f.*) Of uncertain origin: probably Germanic, from a short form of various girls' compound names containing the element *av* (cf. AVIS). St Ava or Avia was a 9th-cent. abbess of Dinart in Hainault and a member of the Frankish royal family. On the other hand, evidence for its use between the early Middle Ages and the mid-20th cent. is lacking, and it may be an arbitrary modern invention.

**Avice** /ˈeɪvɪs/ (*f.*) Variant spelling of AVIS.

**Avis** /ˈeɪvɪs/ (*f.*) Norman French form of the Germanic name *Aveza*, derived from a short form of various girls' compound names containing the first element *av* (of uncertain meaning). The name probably owes its modest popularity in the later Middle Ages and subsequent centuries to its correspondence in form to the Latin feminine noun *avis* bird.

**Avril** /ˈævrɪl/ (*f.*) Although generally taken as the French form of the name of the fourth month (see APRIL), this probably represents an Old English name composed of the elements *eofor* boar + *hild* battle. The variant **Averil** preserves a slightly fuller form.

**Axel** /ˈæksəl/ (*m.*) Scandinavian form of ABSALOM, sometimes used in the U.S.

**Aylwin** /ˈeɪlwɪn/ (*m.*) Variant of ALWYN.

# B

**Babs** /bæbz/ (*f.*) Pet form of BARBARA.

**Baptiste** /bæp'tiːst/ (*m.*) French: meaning 'Baptist' (Late Latin *baptista*, Greek *baptistēs*, from *baphein* to dip), the epithet of the most popular of the numerous saints called JOHN. It is rarely used in the English-speaking world.

**Barbara** /'bɑːbrə/ (*f.*) From Latin, meaning 'Foreign Woman' (a feminine form of *barbarus* foreign, from Greek, referring originally to the unintelligible chatter of foreigners, which sounded to the Greek ear like no more than *bar-bar*). St Barbara has always been one of the most popular saints in the calendar, although there is some doubt whether she ever existed. According to legend she was imprisoned in a tower and later murdered by her father, who was then struck down by a bolt of lightning; accordingly she is the patron of architects, stonemasons, and artillerymen. The name is now occasionally spelled **Barbra**, in the case of Barbra Streisand (b. 1942).

**Barnabas** /'bɑːnəbəs/ (*m.*) From New Testament Greek: Barnabas was a companion of St Paul, whose name was Aramaic, meaning 'Son of Consolation'.

**Barnaby** /'bɑːnəbiː/ (*m.*) Usual English form of BARNABAS.

**Barney** /'bɑːniː/ (*m.*) Pet form of BARNABY, now sometimes used, especially in the U.S., as an independent name. It is notably borne by Barney Rubble, the friend and neighbour of the prehistoric cartoon character Fred Flintstone. The name is also sometimes spelled **Barny**.

**Barry** /'bæriː/ (*m.*) From the surname: occasionally used as a given name since the mid 19th cent., and very frequently since the mid 20th cent., especially in

Australia. The surname has various origins, but is most common in Ireland, where it represents in part a Norman baronial name from various places called *Barri* 'Rampart', in part an Anglicized form of various Gaelic names, such as *Ó Bearaigh* 'Descendant of Bearach', a personal name meaning 'Spear'. The modern Irish Gaelic form of the name, **Barra** /ˈbarə/, is sometimes used in Ireland.

**Bartholomew** /bɑːˈθɒləmjuː/ (*m.*) New Testament: the name of an apostle mentioned in all the synoptic gospels (Matthew, Mark, and Luke) and in the Acts. It is an Aramaic formation meaning 'Son of Talmai', and has been assumed by many scholars to be a byname of the apostle Nathaniel. *Talmai* is a Hebrew name, said to mean 'Abounding in Furrows', which appears in the Old Testament (Num. 13:22).

**Basil** /ˈbæzəl/ (*m.*) From the Greek name *Basileios* 'Royal' (from *basileus* king). It was borne by several early saints martyred in the East, and above all by Basil the Great, an important early theologian.

**Bathsheba** /bɑːθˈʃiːbə/ (*f.*) Old Testament: meaning 'Daughter of the Oath' in Hebrew. This was the name of the woman who became the wife of King David, after he had disposed of her previous husband Uriah, and the mother of King Solomon (II Sam. 11–12). It was popular with the Puritans, and is occasionally revived today by parents in search of an unusual name.

**Bazza** /ˈbæzə/ (*m.*) Australian colloquial pet form of BARRY.

**Beatrice** /ˈbɪətrɪs/ (*f.*) Italian or French form of BEATRIX. It is most famous as the name of Dante's beloved (probably Beatrice Portinari).

**Beatrix** /ˈbɪətrɪks/ (*f.*) Church Latin: the name of a saint executed in Rome, together with Faustinus and

Simplicius, in the early 4th cent. The original form of
the name seems to have been *Viātrix*, a feminine version of *Viātōr* 'Voyager (through life)', which was
common among early Christians. This was then
altered by association with Latin *Beātus* 'Blessed'
(*Via-* and *Bea-* being pronounced very similarly in
Late Latin).

**Becky** /'bɛkiː/ (*f.*) Aphetic pet form of REBECCA, commonly used as an independent given name, especially
in the 18th and 19th cents.

**Belinda** /bə'lɪndə/ (*f.*) Of uncertain origin: it seems to
be exclusively English, having no established cognates in ordinary use in other European languages. It
was used by Sir John Vanbrugh for a character in his
comedy *The Provok'd Wife* (1697), was taken up by
Alexander Pope in *The Rape of the Lock* (1712), and
has enjoyed a steady popularity ever since. It is not
certain where Vanbrugh got the name from. The
notion that it is Germanic (with a second element *lind*
lime tree) does not seem to be well-founded. In Italian literature it is the name ascribed to the wife of
Orlando, vassal of Charlemagne, but this use is not
supported in Germanic sources. The name may be an
Italian coinage from *bella* beautiful (see BELLA) +
*-inda* as in LUCINDA.

**Bella** /'bɛlə/ (*f.*) Aphetic short form of ISABELLA, the
Italian version of ISABEL, but associated with the
adjective *bella*, feminine of Italian *bello* handsome,
beautiful (Late Latin *bellus*).

**Belle** /bɛl/ (*f.*) Variant of BELLA, reflecting the French
feminine adjective *belle* beautiful.

**Ben** /bɛn/ (*m.*) Short form of BENJAMIN, or less commonly of BENEDICT or BENNETT.

**Benedict** /'bɛnədɪkt/ (*m.*) From Church Latin *Bene-
dictus* 'Blessed'. This was the name of the saint (*c.*

480–*c.* 550) who composed the Benedictine rule of
Christian monastic life that is still followed in essence
by all Western orders. The name is used mainly by
Roman Catholics.

**Benjamin** /'bɛndʒəmɪn/ (*m.*) Old Testament: Benjamin was one of the founders of the twelve tribes of
Israel, the youngest of the twelve sons of Jacob. His
mother Rachel died in giving birth to him, and in her
last moments she named him *Benoni*, meaning 'Son
of my Sorrow'. His father, however, did not wish him
to bear such an ill-omened name, and renamed him
*Benjamin* 'Son of the Right Hand' (Gen. 35:16–18;
42:4). In the Middle Ages the name was often given
to sons whose mothers had died in childbirth. Today
it has no such unfortunate associations, but is still
mainly a Jewish name.

**Bennett** /'bɛnɪt/ (*m.*) The normal medieval form of
BENEDICT, now sometimes used as an antiquarian
revival or, more probably, taken from the surname
*Bennett*, which is derived from the medieval name.
There are also variants **Benett**, **Bennet**, and
**Benet**.

**Berenice** /bɛrə'naɪsiː/ (*f.*) From Greek *Berenike*, a
name that seems to have originated in the royal house
of Macedon. It is almost certainly a Macedonian dia-
lectal form of the Greek name *Pherenīkē* 'Victory
Bringer'. The name was introduced to the Egyptian
royal house by the widow of one of Alexander the
Great's officers, who married Ptolemy I. It was also
borne by an early Christian woman mentioned in
Acts 25, for which reason it was felt to be acceptable
by the Puritans in the 17th cent. It has now fallen out
of fashion again.

**Bernard** /'bɜːnəd; *American* bərˈnɑːrd/ (*m.*) Germanic: composed of the elements *ber(n)* bear + *hard*
hardy, brave, strong. A native Old English form,

*Beornheard*, existed, but was replaced at the time of the Norman Conquest by the continental form.

**Bernardette** /bɜːnə'dɛt/ (*f.*) French feminine diminutive of BERNARD. Its use in Britain and Ireland is now almost exclusively confined to Catholics, who take it in memory of St Bernardette Soubirous of Lourdes (1844–79), the French peasant girl who had visions of the Virgin Mary and uncovered a spring where miraculous cures are still sought. The spelling **Bernadette** is also used in English.

**Bernice** /'bɜːnɪs/ (*f.*) Contracted form of BERENICE, becoming increasingly common in the English-speaking world.

**Bert** /bɜːt/ (*m.*) Short form of any of the various names containing this syllable as a first or second element, for example ALBERT and BERTRAM.

**Bertha** /'bɜːθə/ (*f.*) Latinized version of a Germanic name, a short form of various compound girls' names containing the element *berht* famous (cognate with Modern English *bright*). It probably existed in England before the Conquest, and was certainly reinforced by Norman use, but as a modern given name it is a 19th-cent. reintroduction from Germany.

**Bertram** /'bɜːtrəm/ (*m.*) Norman French: of Germanic origin, composed of the elements *berht* famous + *hramn* raven. Ravens were traditional symbols of wisdom in Germanic mythology; Odin was regularly accompanied by ravens called Hugin and Munin.

**Bertrand** /'bɜːtrənd/ (*m.*) Variant of BERTRAM which originated in the Middle Ages. In modern times it has been made famous by the philosopher Bertrand Russell (1872–1970).

**Beryl** /'berəl/ (*f.*) One of several girls' names taken from gemstones that came into fashion at the end of the 19th cent. Beryl is a pale green stone (of which emerald is a variety). Other colours are also found. The word is from Greek, and is ultimately of Indian origin.

**Bess** /bɛs/ (*f.*) Diminutive of ELIZABETH, commonly used in the days of Elizabeth I, 'Good Queen Bess'.

**Bessie** /'bɛsi:/ (*f.*) Pet form of BESS, with the addition of the hypocoristic suffix -*ie*. It is occasionally used as an independent given name, and the spelling **Bessy** is also occasionally found.

**Beth** /bɛθ/ (*f.*) Modern short form of ELIZABETH, probably not used before the 19th cent., when it became popular in the U.S. and elsewhere after publication of Louisa M. Alcott's novel *Little Women* (1868), in which Beth March is one of the central characters. The form **Bet** is also found.

**Bethan** /'bɛθən/ (*f.*) Probably a shortened form of BETHANY, in spite of its Celtic appearance.

**Bethany** /'bɛθəni:/ (*f.*) New Testament: originally a place name, that of the village just outside Jerusalem where Jesus stayed during Holy Week, before going on to Jerusalem and crucifixion (Matt. 21:17, Mark 11:1, Luke 19:29, John 12:1). Its Hebrew name means 'House of Dates'. The given name is largely favoured by Catholics, given in honour of Mary of Bethany, sister of Martha and Lazarus. She is sometimes identified with Mary Magdalene (see MADELEINE), although the grounds for this identification are very poor.

**Betsy** /'bɛtsi:/ (*f.*) Pet form of ELIZABETH; a cross between BESSIE and BETTY.

**Bettina** /bɛ'ti:nə/ (*f.*) As an English name this seems to be a Latinate elaboration of BETTY. It is in use in Italy as a feminine diminutive of *Benedetto*, the Italian version of BENEDICT, and has also long been popular in Germany.

**Betty** /'bɛti:/ (f.) Pet form of ELIZABETH, dating from the 18th cent.

**Beulah** /'bju:lə/ (f.) Old Testament: a name applied to the land of Israel by the prophet Isaiah (Isa. 62:4). It means 'Married' in Hebrew, but 'the land of Beulah' has sometimes been taken as a reference to Heaven. It was taken up as a girl's given name at the time of the Reformation.

**Beverley** /'bɛvəli:/ (f.; also m.) From the English surname, which comes from a place in Yorkshire named in Old English with the elements *beofor* beaver + *lēac* stream. The spelling **Beverly** is apparently used exclusively for girls, and is the usual form of the girl's name in the U.S.

**Bianca** /bɪ'ænkə/ (f.) Italian: from *bianca* white (i.e. 'pure', but cf. BLANCHE). The name was used by Shakespeare for characters in two of his plays that are supposed to take place in an Italian context: the mild-mannered sister of Katharina, the 'shrew' in *The Taming of the Shrew*, and a courtesan in *Othello*.

**Biddy** /'bɪdi:/ (f.) Pet form of BRIDE or its variant BRIDGET. It was formerly quite common, but is now seldom used outside Ireland.

**Bill** /bɪl/ (m.) Pet form of WILLIAM, not used before the 19th cent. The reason for the change in the initial consonant is not clear.

**Billie** /'bɪli:/ (f., m.) Variant of BILLY, now mainly used for girls, and sometimes bestowed at baptism as a feminine equivalent of WILLIAM.

**Billy** /'bɪli:/ (m.) Diminutive of BILL.

**Blaise** /bleɪz/ (m.) French: the name (Latin *Blasius*, probably from *blaesus* lisping) of a saint popular throughout Europe in the Middle Ages but almost forgotten today. He was a bishop of Sebaste in Armenia, and was martyred in the early years of the 4th cent.; these bare facts were elaborated in a great number of legends that reached Europe from the East at the time of the Crusades. The name is rare in the English-speaking world; its modern popularity in France is partly due to the 17th-cent. French philosopher and mathematician Blaise Pascal.

**Blake** /bleɪk/ (*m.*) From the English surname, which has two quite distinct etymologies. It is both from Old English *blæc* black and from Old English *blāc* pale; it was originally a nickname given to someone with hair or complexion that was either remarkably dark or remarkably light.

**Blanche** /blɑːntʃ/ (*f.*) Originally a nickname for a blonde, from *blanche*, feminine of Old French *blanc* white (of Germanic origin), but also associated with the notion of whiteness as indicating purity. A pale complexion and light hair has long been an ideal of beauty in Europe (cf. Modern English *fair*, which meant first 'beautiful' and then, from the 16th cent., 'light in colouring').

**Blodwen** /ˈblodwen/ (*f.*) Welsh: composed of the elements *blodau* flowers + *gwen* white, feminine of *gwyn* white, fair, holy.

**Bob** /bɒb/ (*m.*) Short form of ROBERT, a later development than the common medieval forms *Hob*, *Dob*, and *Nob*, all of which, unlike *Bob*, have given rise to English surnames.

**Bobbie** /ˈbɒbɪ/ (*f.*) Feminine variant of BOBBY, sometimes also used as a pet form of ROBERTA.

**Bobby** /ˈbɒbɪ/ (*m.*; also *f.*) Diminutive of BOB or variant of BOBBIE.

**Bonita** /bəˈniːtə/ (*f.*) Apparently coined in America in the 1940s, probably from the feminine form of Spanish *bonito* pretty, although this is not actually used as a given name in Spanish-speaking countries. *Bonita* looks like the feminine form of a medieval Latin boy's given name, *Bonītus* (from *bonus* good), which was borne by an Italian saint of the 6th cent. and a Provençal saint of the 7th. However, the feminine form is not found in medieval records, nor indeed in any records until the 20th cent.

**Bonnie** /ˈbɒni/ (*f.*) Affectionate nickname from the Scots word *bonnie* pretty; now also used as a pet form of BONITA. Its popularity may be attributed to the character of Scarlett O'Hara's infant daughter Bonnie (her name was really Eugenie Victoria, but she had 'eyes as blue as the bonnie blue flag') in the film *Gone with the Wind* (1939), based on Margaret Mitchell's novel of the same name. Bonnie Parker was the accomplice of the American bank robber Clyde Barrow; their life together was the subject of the film *Bonnie and Clyde* (1967).

**Boris** /ˈbɒrɪs; *Russian* baˈriːs/ (*m.*) Russian: introduced to the English-speaking world in the 20th cent., but never as popular as many of the girls' names from the same source. The name is apparently not of Slavonic etymology, and is probably from the Tartar nickname *Bogoris* 'Small'. St Boris is one of the most important saints of the Eastern church and the patron of Moscow. It is as a result of his influence that *Boris* is one of the very few non-classical names that the Orthodox Church allows to be taken as baptismal names (although the saint himself bore the baptismal name *Romanus*).

**Brad** /bræd/ (*m.*) Short form of BRADFORD and BRADLEY, used mainly in the U.S.

**Bradford** /ˈbrædfəd/ (*m.*) From the English surname, derived from any of the numerous places in England named in Old English with the elements *brād* broad + *ford* ford.

**Bradley** /'brædli:/ (*m.*) From the English surname,
derived from any of the numerous places in England
named in Old English with the elements *brād* broad
+ *lēah* wood, clearing.

**Brenda** /'brɛndə/ (*f.*) Until the 20th cent. this was an
exclusively Scottish name. Its origin is not certain,
but it seems to be of Scandinavian rather than Celtic
origin (in spite of its similarity to BRENDAN), and may
be a short form of various compound names containing the element *brand* (flaming) sword.

**Brendan** /'brɛndən/ (*m.*) Irish: the name of two 6th-
cent. Irish saints, Brendan the Voyager and Brendan
of Birr. The Gaelic form of their name is **Breandán**
/'brɛndɑ:n/. According to legend the former was the
first European to set foot on North America. Irish
monks in the early Middle Ages had a habit of push-
ing out westwards into the Atlantic in their coracles,
with a little food and water and their trust in God to
sustain them. St Brendan was one such. The name
may be connected with BRIAN, but according to
another theory it is a nickname meaning 'Stinking
Hair', from Gaelic *breda* + *ron*.

**Brent** /brɛnt/ (*m.*) From the English surname, which is
derived from various places in Devon and Somerset
which are on or near prominent hills, and seem therefore to have been named with a Celtic or Old English
term for a hill.

**Brett** /brɛt/ (*m.*; occasionally *f.*) From the English surname, which originated in the Middle Ages as an ethnic name for one of the Bretons who arrived in
England in the wake of the Norman Conquest; it is
most common in East Anglia, where Breton settlement was particularly concentrated.

**Brian** /'braɪən, *Irish* 'brʒɪən/ (*m.*) Celtic: apparently
from an element meaning 'hill', 'eminence'. In the

Middle Ages the name was relatively common in East
Anglia, to which it was introduced by Breton settlers,
and in north-west England, to which it was introduced by Scandinavians from Ireland, where it has
been perennially popular, largely on account of the
fame of Brian Boru (Gaelic *Brian Boroimhe*), a 10th-
cent. High King of Ireland.

**Bride** /braɪd/ (*f.*) Irish: variant of BRIDGET, from the
modern Gaelic form **Bríd** /brzɪːdj/, Old Irish *Brighid*, genitive *Brighde*. This name has recently become
fairly popular in the English-speaking world, perhaps
helped by association with the Modern English vocabulary word *bride*.

**Bridget** /ˈbrɪdʒɪt/ (*f.*) Anglicized form of Irish *Brighid*
or *Bríd* (see BRIDE). This was the name of an ancient
Celtic goddess, which may have meant originally
'The High One'. Many of the legends surrounding St
Bridget of Kildare (*c.* 450–*c.* 525) seem to be Christianized versions of pagan legends concerning the
goddess.

**Bridie** /ˈbraɪdiː/ (*f.*) Diminutive of BRIDE, largely confined to Ireland.

**Brigid** /ˈbrɪdʒɪd/ (*f.*) Variant of BRIDGET.

**Brigit** /ˈbrɪdʒɪt/ (*f.*) Variant of BRIDGET, owing something to continental influence (cf. BRIGITTE).

**Brigitte** /*French* briˈʒit, *German* briˈgitə/ (*f.*) French
and German form of BRIDGET, made famous
especially by the French film star Brigitte Bardot (b.
1934).

**Bronwen** /ˈbrɒnwen/ (*f.*) Welsh: composed of the
elements *bron* breast + *gwen* white, feminine of
*gwyn* white, fair, holy.

**Bronya** /ˈbrɒnjə/ (*f.*) From Russian: introduced into
the English-speaking world in the 20th cent. It is a

short form of various Slavonic compound names containing the element *bron* armour, protection.

**Bruce** /bruːs/ (*m.*) From the Scottish surname: now used as a given name throughout the English-speaking world (but particularly associated with Australia). The surname was originally a Norman baronial name, but a precise identification of the place from which it was derived has not been made (there are a large number of possible candidates). The Bruces were an influential family in Scottish affairs in the early Middle Ages; its most famous member was Robert 'the Bruce' (1274–1329), who is said to have drawn inspiration after his defeat at Methven from the perseverance of a spider in repeatedly climbing up again after being knocked down.

**Bruno** /'bruːnəʊ/ (*m.*) A recent introduction to the English-speaking world from Germany (i.e. later than the revival of many Germanic names in the 19th cent., which was stimulated by Queen Victoria's German connections). Its popularity may have been partly influenced by Lewis Carroll's *Sylvie and Bruno* (1889), but more probably it was first used by settlers of German ancestry in the U.S. It is a Germanic name meaning 'Brown', which was in use in many of the ruling families of Germany during the Middle Ages, being borne by a 10th-cent. saint, son of the Emperor Henry the Fowler, and by the Saxon duke who gave his name to Brunswick (German *Braunschweig*, i.e. 'Bruno's settlement').

**Bryan** /'braɪən/ (*m.*) Variant spelling of BRIAN, influenced by the usual form of the associated surname.

**Bryn** /brɪn/ (*m.*) Welsh: a 20th-cent. coinage from the Welsh topographical term *bryn* hill, no doubt influenced by the well-established Irish given name BRIAN.

**Bryony** /'braɪəni:/ (*f.*) From the name of the plant (Greek *bryonia*). This is one of the more recently coined (20th cent.) of the class of flower names.

**Bud** /bʌd/ (*m.*) American: originally a short form of the nickname or vocabulary word *buddy* friend, which is an alteration, perhaps a nursery term, from *brother*. It is now occasionally used as a given name in its own right, especially in America.

**Burt** /bɜːt/ (*m.*) In the case of the American film actor Burt Lancaster (b. 1913), this is a short form of BUR-TON, but it has also been used as a variant spelling of BERT. The pianist and composer Burt Bacharach (b. 1928) was the son of a Bert Bacharach, and his first name is presumably simply a variation of his father's.

**Burton** /'bɜːtən/ (*m.*) From the English surname, which is derived from any of the dozens of places in England so called, in most cases from Old English *burh* fortress, fortified place + *tūn* enclosure, settlement.

**Byron** /'baɪrən/ (*m.*) Surname used as a given name, apparently originally in honour of the poet Lord Byron (George Gordon, 6th Baron Byron, 1784–1824). The surname derives from the Old English phrase *æt ðæm bȳrum* 'at the byres or cattlesheds', and was given to someone who lived there because it was his job to look after the cattle.

# C

**Caesar** /'siːzə/ (m.) From Latin: an old Roman family name, of uncertain meaning. It has been connected with Latin *caesaries* head of hair, but this is probably no more than folk etymology; the name may be of Etruscan origin. Its most notable bearer was Gaius Julius Caesar (?102–44 BC) and it also formed part of the full name of his relative Augustus (Gaius Julius Caesar Octavianus Augustus). Subsequently it was used as an imperial title and eventually became a vocabulary word for an emperor (leading to German *Kaiser* and Russian *tsar*). The occasional modern use as a given name in the English-speaking world seems to reflect this; cf. DUKE, EARL, KING, and PRINCE.

**Caitlin** /*Irish* 'kætjiːlɪːnj/ (f.) Irish Gaelic form of KATHERINE, from the Old French dissimilated form *Catheline*. The name is becoming popular in this form in parts of the English-speaking world outside Ireland.

**Caleb** /'keɪleb/ (m.) Old Testament: borne by an early Israelite, one of the only two original migrants who set out with Moses from Egypt and lived long enough to enter the Promised Land (Num. 26:65). The name, which means 'Dog' in Hebrew, was popular with the Puritans and was introduced by them to America, where it is still occasionally used.

**Callum** /'kæləm/ (m.) From Scots **Calum** or Irish **Colm**, Gaelic forms of the Late Latin name *Columba* 'Dove'. This was popular among early Christians because the dove was a symbol of gentleness, purity, peace, and the Holy Spirit. Columba was the name of one of the most important of all Celtic saints, who lived in the 6th cent. He was born in Donegal and was responsible for converting Scotland and Northern England to Christianity.

**Calvin** /'kælvɪn/ (m.) From the French surname, used

as a given name among Nonconformists in honour of the French Protestant theologian John (Jean) Calvin (1509–64). The surname meant originally 'little bald one', from a diminutive of *calve*, a Norman or Picard form of French *chauve* bald. (The theologian was born in Noyon, Picardy.)

**Cameron** /'kæmrən/ (*m.*) From the Scottish surname, used as a given name usually only by people with Scottish connections. The Camerons were one of the great Highland clans, deriving their name from an ancestor with a 'crooked nose' (Gaelic *cam shron*). There were also Camerons in the Lowlands, apparently the result of an assimilation to the famous clan name of a Norman baronial name derived from Cambernon in Normandy.

**Camilla** /kə'mɪlə/ (*f.*) Feminine form of the old Roman family name *Camillus*, of obscure and presumably non-Roman origin. According to tradition, recorded by the Roman poet Virgil, Camilla was the name of a warrior maiden, who was queen of the Volscians, and fought in the army of Aeneas (*Aeneid* 7:803–17).

**Campbell** /'kæmbəl/ (*m.*) From the Scottish surname, used as a given name usually only by people who have some connection with Scotland or more specifically with the Clan Campbell. The Campbells were one of the great Highland clans, deriving their name from an ancestor with a 'crooked mouth' (Gaelic *cam beul*).

**Candice** /'kændɪs/ (*f.*) Apparently a respelling of the ancient Ethiopian name *Candace*, the hereditary name of a long line of Queens of Ethiopia. One of them is mentioned in the Bible, when the apostle Philip baptizes 'a man of Ethiopia, an eunuch of great authority under Candace queen of the Ethiopians, who had charge of all her treasure' (Acts 8:27). The

spelling may well have been influenced by that of
CLARICE or by a folk etymology deriving the name
from Late Latin *canditia* 'whiteness'.

**Candida** /'kændɪdə/ (*f.*) From Late Latin, meaning
'White'. The colour was associated in Christian imagery with purity and salvation (cf. Rev. 3:4 'thou hast
a few names even in Sardis which have not defiled
their garments; and they shall walk with me in white:
for they are worthy'). This was the name of several
early saints, including a woman supposedly cured by
St Peter himself.

**Candy** /'kændi/ (*f.*) Originally an affectionate nickname from the American vocabulary word·*candy*
sweets; now occasionally used as a given name in its
own right in America, but rare in England. The word
*candy* is from French *sucre candi* 'candied sugar', i.e.
sugar boiled to make a crystalline sweet. The French
word is from Arabic *qandi*, which is in turn of Indian
origin. *Candy* could in theory also be a short form of
CANDICE and of CANDIDA, but there is no evidence for
this.

**Caoimhín** /'kɪːvjɪːn/ (*m.*) Irish Gaelic form of KEVIN, 
a simplified form of the older spelling **Caoimhghin**.

**Cara** /'kɑːrə/ (*f.*) Modern coinage, not in use before
the 20th cent., from the Italian term of endearment
*cara* 'beloved'. This is not, however, used as a given
name in Italy, where such innovations are held in
check by the insistence of the Catholic Church that
baptismal names should have been borne by saints.

**Caradoc** /kə'rædok/ (*m.*) From Welsh: respelling of
the ancient Celtic name *Caradog*, which is apparently
derived from an element meaning 'love', of which a
form was borne by the British chieftain *Caratacus* or
*Caractacus*. He revolted against Roman rule in the
1st cent. AD, and although the rebellion was swiftly

put down he is recorded by the Roman historian
Tacitus as having impressed the emperor Claudius by
his proud bearing in captivity, and has become an
honourable figure in British national legend.

**Carl** /kɑːl/ (*m.*) Variant spelling of **Karl**, the German
version of CHARLES, now increasingly used in English-
speaking countries, especially since CAROL and CARYL
have been adopted as girls' names.

**Carla** /'kɑːlə/ (*f.*) Latinate feminine form of CARL.

**Carlotta** /kɑː'lɒtə/ (*f.*) Italian form of CHARLOTTE,
occasionally used in the English-speaking world.

**Carlton** /'kɑːltən/ (*m.*) From the English surname,
which is of the same origin as CHARLTON, being
derived from any of various places (in Beds.,
Cambs., Co. Durham, Leics., Lincs., Northants,
Notts., Suffolk, and Yorks.) named with the Old
English elements *ceorl* man, labourer + *tūn* settlement, i.e. 'settlement of the common people'. The
initial consonant has been affected by Scandinavian
influence.

**Carmel** /'kɑːməl/ (*f.*) Of early Christian origin, referring to 'Our Lady of Carmel', a title of the Virgin
Mary. Carmel is the name (probably meaning 'God's
vineyard' in Hebrew) of a hill in the Holy Land that
was populated from very early Christian times by her-
mits, who were later organized into the Carmelite
order of monks. The name is favoured mainly by
Roman Catholics.

**Carmen** /'kɑːmɛn/ (*f.*) Spanish form of CARMEL, which
is now occasionally used as a given name in the English-speaking world, in spite of or perhaps because of
its association with the unfortunate but tragically
romantic heroine of Bizet's opera *Carmen* (1875),
based on a short story by Prosper Mérimée. The

name is identical in form with the Latin word *carmen* song, and may sometimes be chosen because of this.

**Caro** /'kærəʊ/ (f.) Recently coined short form of CARO-LINE and CAROLYN.

**Carol** /'kærəl/ (f., originally m.) Anglicized form of *Carolus* (see CHARLES), or of its feminine derivative *Carola*. It has never been common as a boy's name in England, and has become even less so since its growth in popularity as a girl's name. This seems to be of relatively recent origin (not found much before the end of the 19th cent.) and may have originated as a short form of CAROLINE. For its use as a boy's name in Ireland, see CARROLL.

**Carole** /'kærəl; *French* ka'rɔl/ (f.) French form of CAROL, formerly quite commonly used in order to make it clear that a girl's name was in question. Now that *Carol* is used almost exclusively for girls, *Carole* has become rarer.

**Caroline** /'kærəlaɪn/ (f.) From a French or German form of Latin or Italian *Carolina*, a feminine diminutive of *Carolus* (see CHARLES).

**Carolyn** /'kærəlɪn/ (f.) Variant of CAROLINE, coined under the influence of the suffix *-lyn* (see LYNN).

**Carrie** /'kæri:/ (f.) Short form of CAROLINE or occasionally of other girls' names beginning with the syllable *Car-*. It was first used in the 19th cent. and is now popular in its own right, *Caro* having to a large extent taken over the role of the short form.

**Carroll** /'kærəl/ (m.) An Irish boy's name, found in Gaelic as **Cearúll** /'kjæru:l/, derived from an Irish surname which in turn is from the old Gaelic personal name *Cearbhall*. This is of uncertain origin, possibly a nickname for a violent warrior, connected with *cearbh* hacking. The given name was taken as an Irish form of CHARLES, adopted especially among Roman Catholic supporters of the Stuarts in the 18th and 19th cents., in some cases specifically in honour of Prince Charles Stuart, 'Bonnie Prince Charlie', leader of the 1745 rebellion in Scotland and England.

**Cary** /'keəri/ (*m.*) From the English surname, which comes from the River Cary in Somerset (the name of which is of Celtic origin). *Cary* became popular as a given name around the middle of the 20th cent., due to the fame of the film actor Cary Grant (b. 1904), who made his first theatrical appearances under his baptismal name of Archie Leach.

**Caryl** /'kærəl/ (*m.*, sometimes *f.*) Of uncertain origin, probably of Irish origin, a variant of CARROLL. As a girl's name, it is a variant of CAROL, possibly influenced by BERYL.

**Casey** /'keɪsi/ (*m.*, now occasionally also *f.*) From the Irish surname: used as a given name as a result of the fame of the American engine driver and folk hero 'Casey' Jones (1864–1900), who saved the lives of passengers on the 'Cannonball Express' at the expense of his own. He was baptized Jonathan Luther Jones, and nicknamed from his birthplace in Cayce, Kentucky. The Gaelic form of the surname is *Ó Cathasaigh* 'Descendant of *Cathasach*', a byname meaning 'Vigilant, Wakeful'. As a girl's name it is probably a variant of CASSIE.

**Caspar** /'kæspə/ (*m.*) German and Central European form of JASPER. According to legend, this was the name of one of the three magi who brought gifts to the infant Christ. The magi are not named in the Bible, but early Christian tradition assigned them the names *Caspar*, *Balthasar*, and *Melchior*.

**Cass** /kæs/ (*f.*) Medieval and modern short form of CASSANDRA.

seems to be a relatively late and artificial creation,
modelled on the classical Muses, and her name was
formed from transparently appropriate elements.
This is said to have been the name of the mother of
the semi-mythical 6th-cent. Welsh hero Taliesin, but
it is not clear whether this represents an early use of
the given name or whether it is being stated that the
poet was the son of the goddess.

**Chad** /tʃæd/ (*m.*) Modern English spelling of Old English *Ceadda*, name of a 7th-cent. saint who was for a
time Archbishop of York. This is of uncertain derivation. The name is comparatively rare, even among
Roman Catholics, by whom it is chiefly favoured.

**Chaim** /haɪm/ (*m.*) Jewish: variant spelling of HYAM.

**Chantal** /French ʃã'tal/ (*f.*) French: bestowed in
honour of St Jeanne Françoise Frémiot (1572–1641).
In 1592 she married the Baron de Chantal (a place in
Saône-et-Loire, so called from a dialect form of Old
Provençal *cantal* stone, boulder) and adopted his
family name. After his death she became an associate
of St Francis of Sales and founded a new order of
nuns. The name is sometimes also spelled **Chantale**.

**Charis** /'kærɪs/ (*f.*) From Greek *kharis* grace. This was
a key word in early Christian thought, but was not
used as a name in the early centuries after Christ or in
the Middle Ages. As a given name it seems to be an
invention of the 17th cent., chosen either to express
the original idea of charity, or else as a reference to
the three Graces (Greek *kharites*) of classical mythology (Aglaia, Euphrosyne, and Thalia, of which the
first and third have also been occasionally used as
given names).

**Charity** /'tʃærɪti/ (*f.*) From the English vocabulary
word, denoting originally the Christian's love for his
fellow man (Latin *caritas*, from *carus* dear). In spite

of St Paul's words 'and now abideth faith, hope, charity, these three; but the greatest of these is charity' (I Cor, 13:13), *Charity* is now rarely used as a given name in comparison with the shorter FAITH and HOPE.

**Charlene** /ʃɑːˈliːn, ˈʃɑːliːn/ (*f.*) Recent coinage, originating either as a respelling of French *Charline* (a feminine diminutive of CHARLES), or else as an independent formation from *Charles* and the suffix *-ene*, *-een*.

**Charles** /tʃɑːlz/ (*m.*) From French: originally from a Germanic word meaning 'man', cognate with Old English *ceorl* man. The name originally owed its popularity in Europe to the Frankish leader Charlemagne (?742–814), who in 800 established himself as Holy Roman Emperor. His name (Latin *Carolus Magnus*) means 'Charles the Great'. *Charles* or KARL (the German form) was a common name among Frankish leaders, including Charlemagne's grandfather Charles Martel (688–741). The name was also borne by a succession of Holy Roman Emperors and ten kings of France. It was hardly used among the Normans, and was introduced to Britain by Mary Queen of Scots (1542–87), who had been brought up in France. She chose the names *Charles James* for her son (1566–1625) who later became King James VI of Scotland and, from 1603, James I of England. His son and grandson both reigned as King Charles, and the name thus became established among English and Stuart Scottish supporters of the monarchy. In the 19th cent. the popularity of the name was further increased by romanticization of the story of 'Bonnie Prince Charlie', Stuart pretender to the throne and leader of the 1745 rebellion. This popularity continued in the 20th cent. with the birth in 1948 of Prince Charles.

**Charlie** /tʃɑːliː/ (*m.*, sometimes *f.*) Pet form of CHARLES and, occasionally, of CHARLOTTE.

**Charlotte** /ˈʃɑːlət/ (f.) French: feminine diminutive of
CHARLES, used in England since the 17th cent., but
most popular in the 18th and 19th cents., in part due
to the influence of firstly Queen Charlotte
(1744–1818), wife of George III, and secondly the
novelist Charlotte Brontë (1816–55).

**Charlton** /ˈtʃɑːltən/ (m.) From the English surname:
used as a given name largely as a result of the fame
of the film actor Charlton Heston (b. 1924; *Charlton* was his mother's maiden name). The surname
originally denoted someone who came from one of
the numerous places in England named in Old English as the 'settlement of the common people', Old
English *ceorlatūn*. The first element of the place
name is ultimately connected with the source of
CHARLES.

**Charmaine** /ʃɑːˈmeɪn/ (f.) Possibly a variant of CHAR-
MIAN, but more probably an invented name based on
the vocabulary word *charm* + *-aine* as in LORRAINE. It
enjoyed some popularity in the 1960s due to The
Bachelors' hit song of this name.

**Charmian** /ˈʃɑːmɪən/ (f.) From the Late Greek name
*Kharmion* (a diminutive of *kharma* delight). The
name was used by Shakespeare in *Antony and Cleopatra* for one of the attendants of the Egyptian
queen; he took it from Sir Thomas North's translation of Plutarch's *Parallel Lives*.

**Chauncey** /ˈtʃɔːnsiː/ (m.) American coinage from a
well-known New England surname. It seems to have
been originally chosen as a given name in honour of
the Harvard College president Charles Chauncey
(1592–1672), the New England clergyman Charles
Chauncy (1705–87), or the naval officer Isaac Chauncey (1772–1840). All these men were almost certainly
descended from a single family; the surname is found

in England in the Middle Ages, and probably has a Norman baronial origin, but now seems to be extinct in Britain.

**Cherry** /ˈtʃɛri/ (*f.*) Now generally regarded as an Anglicized spelling of the French word *chérie* darling (cf. CARA). However, Dickens used it as a pet form of CHARITY: in *Martin Chuzzlewit* (1844) Mr Pecksniff's daughters Charity and MERCY are known as Cherry and Merry. Nowadays the name is sometimes also taken as referring to the fruit.

**Cheryl** /ˈtʃɛrəl/ (*f.*) Not found before the 1920s, and not common until the 1940s. It seems to be an artificial creation, perhaps the result of a blend between CHERRY and BERYL.

**Chester** /ˈtʃɛstə/ (*m.*) From the English surname, which originally denoted someone from the town of Chester, a Roman settlement of some size and importance; it gets its name from an Old English form of Latin *castra* 'legionary camp'.

**Chloe** /ˈkləʊi:/ (*f.*) From a Late Greek given name (*Khloe*), originally used in the classical period as an epithet of the fertility goddess Demeter. It seems to be connected with CHLORIS. It occurs only fleetingly in the New Testament (I Cor. 1:11), but its use as a given name in the English-speaking world almost certainly derives from this, having been adopted by 17th-cent. Puritans. It has survived much better than the majority of the minor biblical names taken up in the 17th cent.

**Chloris** /ˈklɒrɪs/ (*f.*) From Greek mythology: *Khlōris* was a minor goddess of vegetation; her name derives from Greek *khlōros* green. It was used by the Roman poet Horace for one of his loves (cf. LALAGE), and was taken up by Augustan poets of the 17th and 18th cents.

**Chris** /krɪs/ (*m.*, *f.*) short form of CHRISTOPHER, CHRISTINE, or any other name beginning with this syllable.

**Chrissie** /'krɪsi:/ (*f.*) Pet form of CHRISTINE.

**Christabel** /'krɪstəbɛl/ (*f.*) A 19th-cent. coinage: from the first syllable of CHRISTINE combined with the productive suffix *-bel* (see BELLE). The coinage was apparently made by Samuel Taylor Coleridge (1772–1834) in a poem called *Christabel* (1816). The name was also borne by the suffragette Christabel Pankhurst (1880–1958). The forms **Christabelle** and **Christabella** have also been occasionally used.

**Christian** /'krɪstjən/ (*m.*, occasionally also *f.*) From Latin *Christiānus* 'Follower of Christ', in use as a given name in the Middle Ages, and sporadically ever since. The name *Christ* itself (Greek *Khristos*) is a translation of the Hebrew term *Messiah* 'Anointed'.

**Christie** /'krɪsti:/ (*f.*, *m.*) Usually a pet form of CHRISTINE. In Scotland and Ireland it is often a boy's name, a pet form of CHRISTIAN and CHRISTOPHER.

**Christina** /krɪs'ti:nə/ (*f.*) Simplified form of Latin *Christiāna*, feminine of *Christiānus* (see CHRISTIAN), or a Latinized form of Middle English *Christin* 'Christian' (Old English *christen*, from Latin).

**Christine** /krɪs'ti:n/ (*f.*) From French: a form of CHRISTINA, not much used in Britain until the end of the 19th cent. Until fairly recently it was principally associated with Scotland, but now it is extremely popular in all parts of the English-speaking world.

**Christmas** /'krɪstməs/ (*m.*) Occasionally given to a boy born on Christmas Day (so called from *Christ* (see CHRISTIAN) + *mass* festival, feast). See also NOEL and NATALIE.

# Christopher

**Christopher** /ˈkrɪstəfə/ (*m.*) From Greek *Khristo-pheros*, a name composed of the elements *Khristos* Christ + *pherein* to bear. This was popular among early Christians, conscious of the fact that they were metaphorically bearing Christ in their hearts. A later, over-literal interpretation of the name gave rise to the legend of a saint who actually bore the Christ-child over a stream; he is the patron of travellers.

**Christy** /ˈkrɪsti:/ (*f.*, *m.*) Variant spelling of CHRISTIE.

**Chuck** /ˈtʃʌk/ (*m.*) Informal American pet form of CHARLES.

**Ciarán** /*Irish* ˈkjiərɑːn/ (*m.*) Irish: Gaelic form of KIERAN, a byname meaning 'little black one'. This was the name of two important Irish saints, of the 5th and 6th cents.

**Cicely** /ˈsɪsəli:/ (*f.*) Variant spelling of CECILY. This was a common form of the name in the Middle Ages.

**Cillian** /*Irish* ˈkjiljiən/ (*m.*) Irish Gaelic: apparently from a diminutive of *ceall* cell, church. It was borne by various early Irish saints, including the 7th-cent. author of a life of St Bridget and missionaries to Artois and Franconia.

**Cindy** /ˈsɪndi:/ (*f.*) Pet form of CYNTHIA or, less often, of LUCINDA, now very commonly used as a given name in its own right, especially in America. It has occasionally also been taken as a short form of the fanciful *Cinderella*, which in fact is not related to it, being the name of a character in a fairy-tale (French *Cendrillon*), a derivative of *cendre* cinders.

**Claire** /klɛə/ (*f.*) French form of CLARA, introduced to Britain by the Normans but subsequently abandoned. It has occasionally been revived in the past hundred years for the sake of variety.

**Clancy** /ˈklænsi:/ (*m.*) From the Irish surname, now

occasionally used as a given name, especially in America. The Gaelic form of the surname is *Mac Fhlannchaidh* 'Son of Flannchadh', which in turn is a personal name composed of the elements *flann* red, ruddy + *cadh* warrior.

**Clara** /'klɑːrə, klɛərə/ (*f.*) Post-classical Latin name, from the feminine of *clārus* famous. The modern name is a re-Latinization of the regular English form CLARE.

**Clare** /klɛə/ (*f.*) The normal English spelling of CLARA during the Middle Ages and since. The name has always been particularly popular in Italy (in the form *Chiara*) and has been borne by several Italian saints, notably Clare of Assisi (*c.* 1193–1253), an associate of Francis of Assisi and founder of the order of nuns known as the Poor Clares.

**Clarence** /'klærəns/ (*m.*) English coinage: in use from the end of the 19th cent., but now rare. It was first used in honour of the popular elder son of Edward VII, who was created Duke of Clarence in 1890, but died in 1892 before he could ascend the throne. His title (*Dux Clarentiae* in Latin) originated with a son of Edward III who in the 14th cent. was married to the heiress of Clare in Suffolk (which is so called from a Celtic river name and has no connection with the given name CLARE). It has been held by various British royal princes at different periods in history.

**Clarice** /'klærɪs/ (*f.*) Medieval English and French form of the Latin name *Claritia*. This seems to have meant 'Fame' (an abstract derivative of *clārus* famous), but it may simply have been an arbitrary elaboration of CLARA. It was borne by a character who features in some versions of the medieval romances of Roland and the other paladins of Charlemagne.

**Clarinda** /klə'rɪndə/ (*f.*) Elaboration of CLARA with

the suffix *-inda* (cf. BELINDA and LUCINDA). *Clarinda* first appears in Spenser's *Faerie Queene* (1596). The formation seems to have been influenced by the name *Clorinda*, which occurs in Torquato Tasso's *Gerusalemme Liberata* (1580), and is probably a similarly arbitrary elaboration of CHLORIS. Robert Burns (1759–96) wrote four poems *To Clarinda*.

**Clarissa** /kləˈrɪsə/ (*f.*) Latinate form of CLARICE; occasionally found in medieval documents. It was revived by Samuel Richardson as the name of the central character in his novel *Clarissa* (1748).

**Clark** /klɑːk/ (*m.*) From the English surname (originally denoting a *clerk* or secretary, in the Middle Ages a man in minor holy orders, who earned his living by his ability to read and write). It is now quite commonly used as a given name, especially in the U.S. The word *clerk* derives from Latin *clēricus*, but this more common form of the surname and given name reflects a widespread medieval shift in pronunciation from *-er-* to *-ar-* (preserved in the British but not the American pronunciation of the vocabulary word).

**Claud** /klɔːd/ (*m.*) Anglicized spelling of CLAUDE.

**Claude** /klɔːd/ (*m.*) French: from the Latin name *Claudius* (itself occasionally used as a modern given name), which was an old Roman family name derived from the nickname *Claudus* 'Lame'. It was borne by various early saints, but its popularity in France is largely due to the fame of the 7th-cent. St Claude of Besançon. In France, *Claude* also occurs as a girl's name.

**Claudette** /klɔːˈdet/ (*f.*) French feminine diminutive of CLAUDE.

**Claudia** /ˈklɔːdɪə/ (*f.*) From the Latin girl's name, a feminine form of *Claudius* (see CLAUDE). The name receives a fleeting mention in one of St Paul's letters to Timothy (II 4:21 'Eubulus greeteth thee, and Pudens, and Linus, and Claudia, and all the brethren'), from which it was taken up in the 16th cent. (cf. CHLOE).

**Claudine** /klɔ:'di:n/ (f.) French feminine diminutive of CLAUDE, made popular at the beginning of the 20th cent. as the name of the heroine of a series of novels by the French writer Colette (1873–1954).

**Claus** /klaus/ (m.) German short form of *Niklaus* or *Niclaus*, contracted versions of NICHOLAS. In America this name tends to be associated with the figure of *Santa Claus* (originally *Sankt Niklaus*), which inhibits serious use of it. In German the name is now usually spelled **Klaus**.

**Clemence** /'klɛmǝns/ (f.) Medieval French and English form of Latin *Clementius* (a masculine derivative of *Clemens*; see CLEMENT) or of *Clementia* (feminine version of *Clementius* or an abstract noun meaning 'mercy'). It has never been particularly common, but is still occasionally used as a girl's name.

**Clemency** /'klɛmǝnsi/ (f.) English: rare variant of CLEMENCE or a direct use of the abstract noun, on the model of CHARITY, FAITH, MERCY, etc.

**Clement** /'klɛmǝnt/ (m.) Medieval English form of the Late Latin name *Clemens* 'Merciful'. This was borne by several early saints, notably the fourth pope and the early Christian theologian Clement of Alexandria (Titus Flavius Clemens, AD ?150–?215).

**Clementine** /'klɛmǝntain, -ti:n/ (f.) French feminine diminutive of CLEMENT; first used in the 19th cent., and for a time very popular. It is now largely associated with the popular song with this title. The Latinate form **Clementina** is also found.

**Cleo** /'kli:ǝu/ (f.) Short form of CLEOPATRA.

**Cleopatra** /kliːəˈpɑːtrə, kliːəˈpætrə/ (*f.*) Greek name
(*Kleopatra*, composed of the elements *kleos* glory +
*patēr* father) borne by a large number of women in
the Ptolemaic royal family of Egypt. The most
famous (?69–30 BC) was the lover of Mark Antony,
and has always figured largely in both literature and
the popular imagination as a model of a passionate
woman of unsurpassed beauty, who 'gave all for love'
and in the process destroyed the man she loved. She
had previously been the mistress of Julius Caesar.
The name is occasionally chosen, especially in Black
families.

**Cliff** /klɪf/ (*m.*) Short form of CLIFFORD, now used as an
independent given name and more common than the
original, especially since the rise to fame in the 1950s
of the pop singer Cliff Richard. It has sometimes also
been associated with CLIVE.

**Clifford** /ˈklɪfəd/ (*m.*) From the English surname,
which is derived from any of several places (Gloucs.,
Herefords., Yorks.) named in Old English with the
elements *clif* cliff, slope + *ford* ford.

**Clint** /klɪnt/ (*m.*) Short form of the surname *Clinton*,
made famous by the actor Clint Eastwood (b. 1930).
It was apparently first used as a given name in America in honour of the Clinton family, whose members
included the statesman George Clinton (1739–1812),
governor of New York, and his nephew De Witt Clinton (1769–1828), who was responsible for overseeing
the construction of the Erie Canal. It was also borne
by Sir Henry Clinton (1735–95), British commander-
in-chief in America during the Revolution.

**Clio** /ˈklaɪəʊ, ˈkliːəʊ/ (*f.*) From classical mythology:
Clio (Greek *Kleio*) was the name both of one of the
nymphs and of one of the Muses. It is probably ultimately connected with the word *kleos* glory; cf. CLEO-

PATRA. The name is now sometimes used as a variant of CLEO.

**Clitus** /'klaɪtəs/ (*m.*) From Greek history: *Kleitos* was the name of one of Alexander the Great's generals. His name seems to be ultimately connected with *Kleio* (see CLIO). It has occasionally been used as a given name in America in recent years.

**Clive** /klaɪv/ (*m.*) From the English surname, which is originally from any of the various places (Ches., Shrops.) so called from Old English *clif* cliff, slope. As a given name it seems to have been originally chosen in honour of 'Clive of India' (Robert Clive, created Baron Clive of Plassey in 1760).

**Clodagh** /'kləʊdə/ (*f.*) Irish: in Gaelic now spelt **Clóda**. Its use as a given name seems to be of recent origin. It is probably from *Clóideach*, the name of a river in Tipperary, but there may also have been some association with the Latin name *Clōdia* (borne by the mistress of the Roman poet Catullus), a variant of CLAUDIA.

**Clyde** /klaɪd/ (*m.*) Apparently derived from the name of the river in south-west Scotland that runs through Glasgow. This did not give rise to a surname in Britain and so the given name must have been taken directly from the river. The name is comparatively popular among West Indian and American Blacks; Dunkling points out that geographical names such as *Aberdeen* and *Glasgow* were bestowed on slaves in the Southern U.S. A large number of plantation owners were of Scottish origin. *Clyde*, unlike other such names, seems to have survived, and even gained some currency among Southern Whites. The bank robber Clyde Barrow became something of a cult figure, especially after the film *Bonnie and Clyde* (1967).

**Coinneach** /'kʌnʌx/ (*m.*) Scots Gaelic form of KEN-
NETH.

**Colette** /kə'lɛt/ (*f.*) French feminine diminutive of the
medieval name *Col(le)*; cf. COLIN and NICOLETTE. This
diminutive was given particular currency from the
1920s onwards by the fame of the French novelist
Colette (1873–1954), although it was actually her surname.

**Colin** /'kɒlɪn/ (*m.*) English and French medieval diminutive of the old name *Col(le)*, a short form of
NICHOLAS. It has been enduringly popular and is now
normally regarded as an independent name rather
than as a pet form of *Nicholas*. Its popularity in Scotland and Ireland was increased by association with
surnames derived from the Gaelic words *cailean*
(Scottish) and *coiléan* (Irish), meaning 'Pup, Cub'.

**Colleen** /kɒ'li:n/ (*f.*) From the Anglo-Irish vocabulary
word *colleen* girl, wench (Gaelic *cailín*). The name
arose during the period of enthusiasm for Irish names
in the 1940s and became especially popular in America and Australia, although it is not in fact used as a
given name in Ireland. It is sometimes used as a feminine of COLIN.

**Colm** /*Irish* 'kɔləm/ (*m.*) Irish form of CALLUM.

**Columbine** /'kɒləmbaɪn/ (*f.*) A comparatively
unusual name nowadays, from Italian *Colombina*, a
diminutive of *Colomba* 'Dove'. In the tradition of the
*commedia dell'arte* this is the name of Harlequin's
sweetheart. The modern English name, however,
was probably coined independently as one of the
class of names taken in the 19th cent. from flowers.
The columbine gets its name from the fact that its
petals are supposed to resemble five doves clustered
together.

**Conan** /ˈkəʊnən/ (*m.*) From an Old Irish personal name, a diminutive form of CONN.

**Conn** /kɒn/ (*m.*) From an Old Irish personal name meaning 'High'. It is now also used as a short form of CONNOR and of various non-Irish names beginning with the syllable *Con-*.

**Connie** /ˈkɒniː/ (*f.*) Pet form of CONSTANCE.

**Connor** /ˈkɒnə/ (*m.*) From an Old Irish personal name (Gaelic **Conchobar** /ˈkvʊhuːr/), composed of the elements *con(n)* high + *cobar* desire. Modern use as a given name in part reflects the surname *Ó Conchobhair* 'Descendant of Conchobar', Anglicized as *Connor(s)*. Conchobar was an Irish king who lived shortly after the time of Christ.

**Conrad** /ˈkɒnræd/ (*m.*) Anglicized spelling of German *Konrad*, a Germanic personal name composed of the elements *kuoni* bold + *rad* counsel. It was used occasionally in Britain in the Middle Ages in honour of a 10th-cent. bishop of Constance in Switzerland, but modern use in the English-speaking world represents a re-importation dating mainly from the 19th cent.

**Constance** /ˈkɒnstəns/ (*f.*) Medieval English and French form of the Late Latin name *Constantia*, which is either a feminine form of *Constantius*, a derivative of *Constans* (see CONSTANT), or an abstract noun meaning 'Constancy'.

**Constant** /ˈkɒnstənt/ (*m.*) Medieval English and French form of the Late Latin name *Constans* 'Steadfast', but not common in the Middle Ages. It was taken up by the Puritans because of its transparent meaning, as an expression of their determination to 'resist steadfast in the faith' (I Peter 5:9).

**Constantine** /ˈkɒnstəntaɪn/ (*m.*) Medieval English and French form of the Latin name *Constantīnus* (a derivative of *Constans*; see CONSTANT). This was the name of Constantine the Great (?288–337), the first Christian emperor of Rome.

**Cora** /'kɔːrə/ (*f.*) Apparently coined by James Fenimore Cooper for one of the characters in *The Last of the Mohicans* (1826). It could represent a Latinized form of Greek *Korē* 'Maiden'. In classical mythology this was a euphemistic name of the goddess of the underworld, Persephone, and would not have been a well-omened name to take.

**Coral** /'kɒrəl/ (*f.*) Late 19th-cent. English coinage: one of the group of girls' names taken from the vocabulary of jewellery. Coral is a beautiful pink calcareous material found in warm seas; it actually consists of the skeletons of millions of tiny sea creatures. The word is from Late Latin *corallium* and is probably ultimately of Semitic origin.

**Cordelia** /kɔː'diːlɪə/ (*f.*) The name used by Shakespeare for King Lear's one virtuous daughter. It is not clear where he got it from; it does not seem likely to have a genuine Celtic origin. It may be a fanciful elaboration of Latin *cor* heart, and certainly this association has been made by many of those who have subsequently chosen it.

**Corinna** /kə'rɪnə/ (*f.*) Greek name (*Korinna*, probably from *Korē*; cf. CORA), borne by a Boeotian poetess of uncertain date, whose works survive in fragmentary form. The name was also used by the Roman poet Ovid for the woman addressed in his love poetry. The French form **Corinne** is also used in the English-speaking world.

**Cormack** /'kɔːmæk/ (*m.*) Irish and Scottish, from a Gaelic personal name, **Cormac** /'kɔrəmək/, which is of great antiquity, meaning 'son of the raven', from *corb* raven + *mac* son.

**Cornelia** /kɔːˈniːliə/ (*f.*) From Latin: feminine form of the old Roman family name CORNELIUS. It was borne most notably in the 2nd cent. BC by the mother of the revolutionary reformers Tiberius and Gaius Sempronius, and is still occasionally bestowed in her honour.

**Cornelius** /kɔːˈnɪːliəs/ (*m.*) From an old Roman family name, which is of uncertain origin, possibly a derivative of Latin *cornu* horn.

**Cosima** /ˈkɒzɪmə/ (*f.*) From Italian: feminine form of COSMO, occasionally used in the English-speaking world. The most famous bearer is probably Cosima Wagner (1837–1930), daughter of Franz Liszt and wife of Richard Wagner.

**Cosmo** /ˈkɒzməʊ/ (*m.*) Italian form (also found as **Cosimo**) of the Greek name *Kosmas* (a short form of various names containing the element *kosmos* order, beauty). This was borne by a Christian saint martyred, together with his brother Damian, at Aegea in Cilicia in the early 4th cent. It was first brought to Britain in the 18th cent. by the Scottish Dukes of Gordon, who had connections with the ducal house of Tuscany. The name was traditional in that family, having been borne most famously by Cosimo de' Medici (1389–1464), its founder and one of the chief patrons of the Italian Renaissance.

**Courtney** /ˈkɔːtniː/ (*m., f.*) From the English surname, originally a Norman baronial name from any of various places in Northern France called *Courtenay* ('domain of Curtius'). However, from an early period it was taken as a nickname from Old French *court nez* 'short nose'. It is also used as a girl's name, especially in America.

**Craig** /kreɪɡ/ (*m.*) From the Scottish surname, derived from any of several places in Scotland named with the Gaelic element *creag* rock. It is now widely fashionable throughout the English-speaking world and is chosen as a given name by people who have no connection with Scotland.

**Cressida** /'krɛsɪdə/ (*f.*) From a medieval legend, told by Chaucer and Shakespeare among others, set in ancient Troy. Cressida is a Trojan princess, daughter of Calchas, a priest who has defected to the Greeks. When she is restored to her father, she jilts her Trojan lover Troilus in favour of the Greek Diomedes. The story is not found in classical sources. Chaucer used the name in the form *Criseyde*, getting it from Boccaccio's *Criseida*. This in turn is ultimately based on Greek *Khryseis* (a derivative of *khrysos* gold), the name of a Trojan girl who is mentioned briefly as a prisoner of the Greeks at the beginning of Homer's *Iliad*. Chaucer's version of the name was Latinized by Shakespeare as *Cressida*. In spite of the unhappy associations of the story, the name has enjoyed some popularity in the 20th cent.

**Crispian** /'krɪspɪən/ (*m.*) Medieval variant of CRISPIN; now very rarely used as a given name.

**Crispin** /'krɪspɪn/ (*m.*) English form of the Latin name *Crispīnus*, a derivative of the old Roman family name *Crispus* 'Curly(-headed)'. St Crispin was martyred with his brother Crispinian in *c.* 285, and the pair were popular saints in the Middle Ages.

**Crystal** /'krɪstəl/ (*f.*) English 19th-cent. coinage: one of a group of names taken from or suggestive of gemstones. The word *crystal*, denoting high-quality cut glass, is derived from Greek *krystallos* ice. (As a boy's name, *Crystal* originated as a Scottish pet form of CHRISTOPHER, but it is hardly if ever used today.)

**Curt** /kɜːt/ (*m.*) Probably an Anglicized spelling of German *Kurt* (a contracted form of *Konrad*; see CONRAD), but now also used as a short form of CURTIS.

Association with the vocabulary word *curt* 'brusque' does not seem to have harmed its popularity.

**Curtis** /'kɜ:tis/ (*m.*) From the English surname, which was originally given as a nickname to someone who was 'courteous' (Old French *curteis*). At an early date, however, it came to be associated with Middle English *curt* short + *hose* leggings; cf. COURTNEY.

**Cuthbert** /'kʌθbət/ (*m.*) Old English: composed (somewhat tautologously) of the elements *cūð* known + *beorht* bright, famous. It was borne by two pre-Conquest English saints: a 7th-cent. bishop of Lindisfarne and an 8th-cent. archbishop of Canterbury who corresponded with St Boniface.

**Cynthia** /'sɪnθɪə/ (*f.*) From the Greek name *Kynthia*, an epithet applied to the goddess Artemis, who was supposed to have been born on Mount Kynthos on the island of Delos. The mountain name is of pre-Greek origin. *Cynthia* was later used by the Roman poet Propertius as the name of the woman to whom he addressed his love poetry. The English given name was not used in the Middle Ages, but dates from the classical revival of the 17th and 18th cents.

**Cyril** /'sɪrɪl/ (*m.*) English form of the (post-Classical) Greek name *Kyrillos*, a derivative of *kyrios* lord. It was borne by a large number of early saints, most notably the theologians Cyril of Alexandria and Cyril of Jerusalem. It was also the name of one of the Greek evangelists who brought Christianity to the Slavonic regions of Eastern Europe; in order to provide written translations of the gospels for their converts, they devised the alphabet still known as Cyrillic.

**Cyrus** /'saɪrəs/ (*m.*) From the Greek form (*Kyros*) of the name of several kings of Persia, most notably Cyrus the Great (d. 529 BC). The origin of the name is not known, but in the early Christian period it was associated with Greek *kyrios* lord, and borne by various saints, including an Egyptian martyr and bishops of Carthage and Pavia. Present-day use of the given name seems to be more or less confined to America, and is probably an example of the revival of names from ancient history.

# D

**Daisy** /ˈdeɪzi/ (*f.*) English: from the name of the flower, Old English *dægesēge*, the 'day's eye', so called because it uncovers the yellow disc of its centre in the morning and closes its petals over it again at the end of the day. The name seems to have been used early on as a punning pet form of MARGARET, by association with French *Marguerite*, which is both a version of that name and the word for the flower.

**Dale** /deɪl/ (*m.*) From the English surname, originally a topographical name for someone who lived in a *dale* or valley. It is now commonly used as a given name, especially in the U.S., along with other monosyllabic surnames of topographical origin (cf., e.g., DELL and HALE).

**Daley** /ˈdeɪli/ (*m.*) From the Irish surname, the Gaelic form of which is *Ó Dalaigh* 'Descendant of Dalach', a personal name derived from *dal* assembly, gathering. The spelling **Daly** is also found. It is possible that this name is now taken as a diminutive of DALE.

**Damaris** /dəˈmɑːrɪs/ (*f.*) New Testament: the name of a woman mentioned as being converted to Christianity by St Paul (Acts 17:34). Its origin is not clear, but it is probably Greek, perhaps a late form of *Damalis* 'Calf'. It was taken up in the 17th cent., along with the names of other characters fleetingly mentioned in the New Testament, and has been occasionally used ever since.

**Damian** /ˈdeɪmɪən/ (*m.*) From Greek *Damianos*, the name of the brother of Cosmas (see COSMO), who was martyred together with him at Aegea in Cilicia in the early 4th cent. The origin of the name is not certain, but it is probably connected with DAMON. It is sometimes spelled **Damien**.

**Damon** /'deɪmən/ (*m.*) From a classical Greek name, derived from *damān* to tame or subdue (often a euphemism for 'kill'). This was made famous in antiquity by the story of Damon and Pythias. Pythias was condemned to death in the early 4th cent. BC by Dionysius, ruler of Syracuse. His friend Damon offered to stand surety for him, and took his place in the condemned cell while Pythias put his affairs in order. When Pythias duly returned to be executed, rather than absconding and leaving his friend to his fate, Dionysius was so impressed by the trust and friendship of the two young men that he pardoned both of them. The name was not used in the early centuries of the Christian era or during the Middle Ages. Its modern use seems to date from the 1930s and is probably due to the fame of the American short-story writer Damon Runyon (1884–1946). It is sometimes taken as a variant of DAMIAN.

**Dan** /dæn/ (*m.*) Short form of DANIEL.

**Daniel** /'dænjəl/ (*m.*) Old Testament: name (meaning 'God is my Judge' in Hebrew) borne by the prophet whose story is told in the book of Daniel. He was an Israelite slave of the Assyrian king Nebuchadnezzar, who obtained great favour through his skill in interpreting dreams and the 'writing on the wall' at the feast held by Nebuchadnezzar's son Belshazzar. His enemies managed to get him cast into a lions' den, but he was saved by God. This was a favourite tale in the Middle Ages, often represented in miracle plays. The name is popular among both Jews and Gentiles.

**Danielle** /dæn'jɛl/ (*f.*) French feminine form of DANIEL. The Latinate form **Daniela** is rather less common.

**Danny** /'dæni:/ (*m.*) Diminutive of DAN, with the hypocoristic suffix -y.

**Daphne** /'dæfni:/ (*f.*) From Greek mythology: name
of a nymph who was changed into a laurel by her
father, a river god, to enable her to escape the attentions of Apollo, who was pursuing her. The name
means 'Laurel' in Greek. According to legend the
nymph gave the name to the shrub, but in fact it was
the other way about; her name was taken from the
vocabulary word (which seems to be of pre-Greek
origin, and may therefore have been thought to need
explaining). The name was not used in England until
the end of the 19th cent., when it seems to have been
adopted as part of the vogue for flower names.

**Darcy** /'dɑ:si:/ (*m.*) From the English surname, originally a Norman baronial name (*d'Arcy*) borne by a
family who came from Arcy in Northern France. It
has always retained a somewhat aristocratic air which
has enhanced its popularity as a given name. It is the
surname of the hero of Jane Austen's novel *Pride and
Prejudice* (1813).

**Darrell** /'dærəl/ (*m.*) From the English surname, originally a Norman baronial name (*d'Airelle*) borne by a
family who came from Airelle in Calvados. It was
first used as a given name towards the end of the 19th
cent., and has enjoyed a considerable vogue in the
latter part of the 20th cent. The spellings **Darrel** and
**Darell** are also found.

**Darren** /'dærən/ (*m.*) Recently coined name of uncertain derivation. It may well have been an arbitrary
coinage, or a surname (of obscure origin) used as a
given name, and seems to have been first borne by the
American actor Darren McGavin (b. 1922). It
came to the attention of the public as the name of a
character in the popular American TV comedy series
*Bewitched* (made in the 1960s). In the spelling *Darin*,
it is associated with the singer Bobby Darin
(1936–73), who was originally called Walden Robert

Cassotto and who chose the name that he made famous from a telephone directory.

**Dave** /deɪv/ (*m.*) Short form of DAVID.

**David** /ˈdeɪvɪd/ (*m.*) Old Testament: name of the greatest of the Israelite kings, whose history is recounted in the first book of Samuel and elsewhere. As a boy he killed the giant Philistine Goliath with his slingshot; as king of Judah, and later of all Israel, he expanded the power of the Israelites and established their security. He was also noted as a poet, the Psalms being attributed to him. He had many sons and, according to the gospels, Jesus was descended from him. The Hebrew derivation of the name is uncertain; it is said by some to represent a nursery word meaning 'Darling'. In the U.S. this is mainly a Jewish name, but it has no such restriction in Britain, where it is particularly common in Wales and Scotland, having been borne by the patron saint of Wales (see DEWI) and by two medieval kings of Scotland.

**Davina** /dəˈviːnə/ (*f.*) Latinate feminine form of DAVID, which originated in Scotland. It is occasionally elaborated to **Davinia**, on the model of LAVINIA. The more straightforward feminine **Davida** is considerably less frequent.

**Dawn** /dɔːn/ (*f.*) From the English vocabulary word for daybreak, no doubt originally bestowed because of the connotations of freshness and purity of this time of day. It may have originated as a vernacular translation of AURORA. According to Dunkling, it was first used in 1928, after which it quickly became popular. Twin girls are sometimes given the names *Dawn* and EVE, although the latter name does not in fact have anything to do with the time of day.

**Dean** /diːn/ (*m.*) From the English surname, which represents two medieval surnames that have fallen

together: a topographic name for someone who lived
in a valley (Middle English *dene*, Old English *denu*),
and an occupational name for someone who served as
a dean, i.e. ecclesiastical supervisor (Latin *decanus*).
It also sometimes represents Italian *Dino*, as in the
case of the American actor and singer Dean Martin
(b. 1917).

**Deanna** /diː'ænə/ (*f.*) Originally a fanciful respelling
of DIANA, now often taken as a feminine form of
DEAN. It was made popular by the singing actress
Deanna Durbin (b. 1922), whose original given name
was EDNA; she may have derived *Deanna* from a par-
tial anagram of this.

**Debbie** /'dɛbi:/ (*f.*) Pet form of DEBORAH. The spelling
**Debby** is rather less common; **Debbi** is also found.

**Deborah** /'dɛbərə/ (*f.*) Old Testament: name (meaning 'Bee' in Hebrew) of the nurse of Rebecca (Gen.
35:8) and of a female prophet (Judges 4–5). It was
not used in the Middle Ages, but was taken up by the
Puritans in the 17th cent., no doubt because the bee
was a symbol of industriousness. It has been moderately popular ever since. The spelling **Debora** is now
becoming increasingly common, together with the
contraction **Debra**.

**Declan** /'dɛklən/ (*m.*) Irish and Scottish: an old Celtic
name (Gaelic **Deaglán** /'djegla:n/) of uncertain derivation. It was borne by a 5th-cent. disciple of St Col-
man, who became a bishop in the district of
Ardmore. In recent years the name has been widely
revived in both Scotland and Ireland.

**Dee** /di:/ (*f.*, *m.*) Pet form of any of the given names
beginning with the letter *D-* (cf. *Kay*), especially DOR-
OTHY. It is also used as an independent name, and
may in some cases be associated with the River Dee
(cf. CLYDE).

**Deirdre** /ˈdɪədri:/ (f.) Irish: borne in Celtic legend by a tragic heroine who was betrothed to Conchobar, King of Ulster, but who eloped with her beloved, Naoise, instead. Eventually the jilted king murdered Naoise and his brothers, and Deirdre herself died of sorrow. The name has become popular in Ireland and elsewhere since the treatments of this story by the poet W. B. Yeats (1907) and the playwright J. M. Synge (1910). It is of uncertain derivation; the earliest Celtic forms are very variable.

**Delia** /ˈdi:lɪə/ (f.) From classical Greek: epithet of the goddess Artemis, referring to her birth on the island of Delos (cf. CYNTHIA). It was taken up by the pastoral and romantic poets of the 17th and 18th cents., and has been moderately popular ever since.

**Delilah** /dɪˈlaɪlə/ (f.) Old Testament: name (meaning 'Delicate' in Hebrew) of Samson's mistress, who wheedled him into revealing the secret of his strength and then betrayed him to the Philistines (Judges 16:4–20). Although the biblical Delilah was deceitful and treacherous, the name was taken up quite enthusiastically by the Puritans in the 17th cent., perhaps because she was also beautiful and clever. The name fell out of use in the 18th cent., but has been occasionally revived as an 'exotic' name. The spelling **Delila** is also occasionally found.

**Dell** /dɛl/ (m.) From the English surname, which was originally a topographic name for someone who lived in a *dell* or hollow. However, recently it has also come to be taken as a pet form of DEREK, and in this use is also found, rather more commonly in the spelling **Del**.

**Della** /ˈdɛlə/ (f.) This name first appeared in the 1870s and has continued to grow steadily in popularity ever since. Its derivation is not clear; if it is not simply an arbitrary creation, it may be an altered form of DELIA or DELILAH, or a short form of ADELA. In modern use it is sometimes taken as a feminine form of DELL.

**Delmar** /'dɛlmɑː/ (*m.*) Of uncertain derivation, possibly an arbitrary alteration of ELMER (cf. DELROY and ELROY). In form it coincides with Spanish *del mar* 'of the sea', which occurs in various place names as a distinguishing epithet. It is popular chiefly among Blacks in the U.S.

**Delphine** /dɛl'fiːn/ (*f.*) French: from Latin *Delphīna* 'Woman from Delphi'. The Blessed Delphina (1283–1358) was a Provencal nun, who may herself have been named in honour of the 4th-cent. St Delphinus of Bordeaux. In modern times the name seems often to have been chosen for its association with the *delphinium* flower.

**Delroy** /'dɛlrɔɪ/ (*m.*) Apparently an altered form of LEROY, perhaps representing the Old French phrase *del roy* '(son, servant) of the king'. It is used chiefly among West Indians in Britain.

**Demelza** /dɪ'mɛlzə/ (*f.*) Modern Cornish name that has no history as a Celtic personal name, but derives from a place in the parish of St Columb Major. The given name began to be used in the 1950s and was given a boost by the serialization on British television of the 'Poldark' novels by Winston Graham, in which it is the name of the heroine.

**Dena** /'diːnə/ (*f.*) Probably a respelling of *Dina*, which was originally a variant of DINAH. The name may also be taken as a feminine form of DEAN.

**Denis** /'dɛnɪs/ (*m.*) Variant of DENNIS, reflecting the usual French spelling of the name.

**Denise** /də'niːz/ (*f.*) French feminine form of DENIS, now widely used in the English-speaking world.

**Dennis** /'dɛnɪs/ (*m.*) Medieval vernacular (French and English) form of the Greek name *Dionysios*, which was borne by several early Christian saints, including St Denis, a 3rd-cent. evangelist who converted the Gauls and became patron saint of Paris. It was on his account that the name was popular among the Normans. In classical times, the word originally denoted a devotee of the god Dionysos. This deity was a relatively late introduction to the classical pantheon; his orgiastic cult seems to have originated in Persia or elsewhere in Asia. His name is of uncertain derivation, although the first part seems to reflect the name of the supreme god *Zeus* (gen. *Dios*).

**Denzil** /'dɛnzəl/ (*m.*) From the Cornish surname, the original spelling of which was *Denzell*, a local name from a place in Cornwall. It came to be used as a given name in the Hollis family in the 16th cent., when the Hollis family and the Denzell family became connected by marriage, and spread from there into more general use.

**Derek** /'dɛrɪk/ (*m.*) Low German form of *Theodoric* (see TERRY), introduced to Britain during the Middle Ages by Flemish settlers connected with the cloth trades. It is a comparatively rare name in the U.S.

**Dermot** /'dɜːmət/ (*m.*) Irish: from Gaelic **Diarmait** /'djɪərmɪdj/. An earlier Gaelic form is *Diarm(u)it*, and it is recorded in the 7th-cent. Latin *Life of St Columba* as *Diormitius*. The derivation is uncertain, but it seems to be composed of the elements *di* without + *airmit* injunction or + *hairmait* envy. The name is confined in the main to families conscious of their Irish descent. It is also used in Scotland, in the forms **Diarmuid**, **Diarmid**, and **Dermid**.

**Derrick** /'dɛrɪk/ (*m.*) Variant spelling of DEREK; this is ꞏꞏ usual U.S. spelling of the given name, but in

Britain it is more common as a surname than as a given name.

**Desdemona** /dɛzd'məʊnə/ (*f.*) Of Shakespearian origin: chosen occasionally by parents in search of an unusual name, who are no doubt attracted by the sweet nature and innocence of Shakespeare's character and not deterred by her tragic fate. She was murdered by her husband Othello in an ill-founded jealous rage, and her name is in fact particularly appropriate to her destiny, as it probably represents a Latinized form of Greek *dysdaimōn* ill-starred.

**Desirée** /də'zɪərɛɪ; *French* dɛzi're/ (*f.*) French (now occasionally used in the English-speaking world): from Latin *Desiderāta* 'Desired'. This name was given by early Christians to a longed-for child, but the French form is now often taken as suggesting that the bearer will grow up into a desirable woman.

**Desmond** /'dɛzmənd/ (*m.*) Of Irish origin: apparently originally a local name for someone who came from south Munster (Gaelic *Deas Mumhán*). The form has been influenced by the Norman (Germanic) given name ESMOND.

**Dewi** /*Welsh* 'dewi/ (*m.*) Welsh form of DAVID, traditionally associated with the patron saint of Wales; the name is now quite common in Wales, but rare elsewhere. St Dewi was born in south Wales in the 5th cent. and became the first bishop of Menevia, the town now known as St Davids.

**Dexter** /'dɛkstə/ (*m.*) From the English surname. Although this is now a boy's given name, the word that gave rise to the surname originally denoted a female dyer, from OE *dēag* dye + -*estre* feminine suffix of agent nouns. However, the distinction of gender was already lost in Middle English. The name coincides in form with Latin *dexter* right(-handed), auspicious, and may sometimes have been chosen because of this.

**Di** /daɪ/ (*f.*) Short form of DIANA.

**Diana** /daɪˈænə/ (*f.*) From classical mythology: name of the Roman goddess of the moon and of hunting, equivalent to the Greek Artemis. She was believed to be both beautiful and chaste. Her name is of ancient and uncertain derivation; it seems to be connected ultimately with that of the supreme god *Jupiter* and with Greek *Dionysos* (see DENNIS). It was adopted in Britain as a Tudor learned given name, a borrowing from Latin influenced by the French form DIANE. It was not particularly popular until the end of the 19th cent., when its increased frequency may have been due in part to George Meredith's novel *Diana of the Crossways* (1885), although Dunkling asserts that this is not the case. Priests have been known to be reluctant to baptize girls with this pagan name, remembering the riots against St Paul stirred up by worshippers of Diana of the Ephesians (Acts 19:24–41).

**Diane** /daɪˈæn/ (*f.*) French version of DIANA, especially popular among the Renaissance aristocracy, who loved hunting and were therefore proud to name their daughters after the classical goddess of the chase. The spelling **Dianne** is also found (originating by association with *Anne*).

**Dick** /dɪk/ (*m.*) Short form of RICHARD; cf. RICK. The alteration of the initial consonant is supposed to result from the difficulty that English speakers in the Middle Ages had with the trilled Norman *R*-.

**Dickie** /ˈdɪkiː/ (*m.*) Diminutive of DICK, with the originally Scottish and Northern English hypocoristic suffix *-ie*. This has replaced the medieval diminutive *Dickon*, with the Old French suffix *-on*.

**Dilys** /ˈdɪlɪs/ (*f.*) From Welsh: of modern origin as a

given name, being derived from the vocabulary word
*dilys* genuine. It was not used as a name before the
mid 19th cent.

**Dinah** /'daɪnə/ (*f.*) Old Testament: the name (meaning
'Vindicated' in Hebrew) borne by a daughter of
Jacob, who was raped by Shechem but avenged by
her brothers Simeon and Levi (Gen. 34). In modern
times it has often been taken as a variant of the much
more common DIANA.

**Dirk** /dɜːk/ (*m.*) Low German, Flemish, and Dutch
form of DEREK. Its use in the English-speaking world
since the 1960s is largely due to the fame of the actor
Dirk Bogarde (b. 1921; originally Derek Niven Van
Den Bogaerde). He is of Dutch descent, although he
was actually born in Scotland. The manly image of
the name has been reinforced by its coincidence in
form with the Scots vocabulary word *dirk* dagger (of
unknown origin, first recorded as *dork* and *durk*).

**Dodie** /'dəʊdiː/ (*f.*) Unusual pet form of DOROTHY,
derived from a child's unsuccessful attempts to pronounce the name.

**Dolly** /'dɒliː/ (*f.*) Originally (from the 16th cent.
onwards) a pet form of DOROTHY, but now more commonly used as a pet form of DOLORES or as an independent name (taken as being the vocabulary
word *doll*, although in fact this was derived from the
pet name in the 17th cent.).

**Dolores** /də'lɔːrɪz/ (*f.*) Of Spanish origin, now sometimes borne in English-speaking countries, mainly by
Roman Catholics. It is abbreviated from *Maria (de
los) Dolores* 'Mary of Sorrows', a reference to the
Seven Sorrows of the Virgin in Christian belief. The
feast of Our Lady's Dolours was established in 1423.

**Dominic** /'dɒmɪnɪk/ (*m.*) English form of the Latin
name *Dominicus* (from *dominus* lord; cf. CYRIL). It is

used mainly by Roman Catholics, in honour of St
Dominic (1170–1221), founder of the Dominican
order of monks. The medieval form **Dominick** is
also still in occasional use.

**Dominique** /dɒmɪnˈiːk/ (f.) French feminine form of
DOMINIC and its Latin source, *Dominica*. It is now
widely used as a given name in the English-speaking
world as well as in France. In Britain it is popular
chiefly among Roman Catholics.

**Domitilla** /dɒmɪˈtɪlə/ (f.) Rare name, occasionally
used by Roman Catholics in honour of a 2nd-cent.
saint, Flavia Domitilla, who was a member of the
Roman imperial family. She was the great-niece of
the Emperor Domitianus, and her name represents a
diminutive form of *Domitius*, the old Roman family
name of which *Domitiānus* is a derivative. It is probably derived from the nickname *Domitus* 'Tamed'.

**Don** /dɒn/ (m.) English: short form of DONALD.

**Donagh** /ˈdɒnə/ (m.) Irish Anglicization of *Donnchadh*; see DUNCAN.

**Donal** /ˈdɒnəl/ (m.) Irish form of DONALD, in Irish
Gaelic spelled and pronounced *Dónall* /ˈdoːnəl/.

**Donald** /ˈdɒnəld/ (m.) A popular name throughout
the English-speaking world, of Scottish origin. The
Scottish Gaelic form is **Domhnull** /ˈdɔːəl/. The name
is very ancient, and is derived from an old Celtic
name composed of the elements *dubno* world + *val*
rule. In the Highlands of Scotland it ranked second
only to IAN (the Gaelic form of JOHN) during the
Middle Ages. *Donald* is now quite common among
people with no Scottish connections.

**Donna** /ˈdɒnə/ (f.) Of recent origin (not found before
the 1920s). It is taken from the Italian word *donna*
lady, no doubt influenced by *Madonna* ('My Lady'),
a title of the Virgin Mary which frequently occurs as

part of the title of Renaissance and other paintings of
her, usually represented as a beautiful and saintly-
looking young woman with the Christ child. *Donna*
does not occur as a given name in Italy, and the English name does not seem to have any particularly
Roman Catholic associations. In recent times it has
come to be used occasionally as a feminine of DON.

**Donovan** /ˈdɒnəvən/ (*m.*) From the Irish surname,
Gaelic Ó *Donndubháin* 'Descendant of Donndub-
hán', a personal name composed of the elements
*donn* brown, dark + *dubh* black, dark, with the
addition of the diminutive suffix -*án*. Its use as a given
name dates from the early 1900s. The folk-rock
singer Donovan may have had some influence on its
increase in popularity in the 1960s. It is now also used
by people with no Irish connections.

**Dora** /ˈdɔːrə/ (*f.*) A 19th-cent. English coinage: short
form of ISIDORA, THEODORA, DOROTHY, and any other
name containing the Greek element *dōron* gift.
Wordsworth's daughter (b. 1804), christened Dorothy, was always known in adult life as Dora. In some
cases, it seems to have been taken as actually meaning 'Gift', presumably as a Latinate version of the
Greek word. Its popularity was enhanced by the
character Dora Spenlow in Dickens's novel *David
Copperfield* (1850).

**Dorcas** /ˈdɔːkəs/ (*f.*) From Greek *dorkas* doe or
gazelle. It does not actually seem to have been used
as a given name by the ancient Greeks, but is offered
in the Bible as an 'interpretation' of the Aramaic
name TABITHA (Acts 9:36), and was taken up by the
early Christians. It was much used among the Puritans in the 17th cent., and has remained in occasional
use ever since.

**Doreen** /ˈdɔːriːn/ (*f.*) Derivative of DORA, with the

addition of the productive suffix *-een* (in origin an Irish diminutive). The name came into use at the beginning of the 20th cent., when there was a particular vogue for such names. The spellings **Dorene** and **Dorine** are occasionally found.

**Dorian** /'dɔːrɪən/ (*m.*) An early 20th-cent. coinage: apparently invented by Oscar Wilde, as no evidence has been found of its existence before he used it for the central character in *The Portrait of Dorian Gray* (1891). Dorian Gray is a dissolute rake who retains unblemished youthful good looks; in the attic of his home is a portrait which does his ageing for him, gradually acquiring all the outward marks of his depravity. The name would seem to be from Late Latin *Dōriānus* 'man from *Dōria*' (a region of Greece). It would thus be a masculine version of DORIS.

**Doris** /'dɒrɪs/ (*f.*) From classical Greek: ancient ethnic name meaning 'Dorian woman'. The Dorians were one of the tribes of Greece; their name was traditionally derived from an ancestor *Dōros* (son of Hellen, who gave his name to the Hellenes), but it is more likely that Doros (whose name could be from *dōron* gift), was invented to account for a tribal name of obscure origin. In Greek mythology, Doris was a minor goddess of the sea, the consort of Nereus and the mother of his daughters, the Nereids or seanymphs, who numbered fifty (in some versions, more). The name was especially popular from about 1880 to about 1930, and was borne by the American film star Doris Day (b. 1924).

**Dorothea** /dɒrə'θiːə/ (*f.*) Post-classical Greek name, composed of the elements *dōron* gift + *theos* god (the same elements as in THEODORA). The masculine form *Dorotheus* was borne by several early Christian saints, the feminine only by two minor ones, but it is

only the latter that is used in the English-speaking
world today. In modern use it represents a 19th-cent.
Latinization of DOROTHY or a learned re-borrowing of
the name.

**Dorothy** /ˈdɒrəθiː/ (*f.*) Usual English form of DOR-
OTHEA. The name was not used in the Middle Ages,
but was taken up in the 16th cent. and became common thereafter.

**Dot** /dɒt/ (*f.*) Short form of DOROTHY.

**Dottie** /ˈdɒtiː/ (*f.*) Diminutive of DOT, with the hypocoristic suffix -*ie*. The form **Dotty** is also used, and its
popularity does not seem to have been adversely
affected by the fact that it coincides in form with the
slang word meaning 'crazy'.

**Dougal** /ˈduːɡəl/ (*m.*) Of Gaelic origin (**Dubhgall**,
**Dughall** /ˈduːəl/), now sometimes used as a given
name in Scotland and elsewhere. It is composed of
the elements *dubh* black, dark + *gall* stranger, and
was originally a byname applied to Danish settlers or
raiders, in contrast to the fairer Scandinavians of
Norse origin (compare FINGAL). The Irish surname
*Doyle* is derived from this epithet.

**Douglas** /ˈdʌɡləs/ (*m.*) From the Scottish surname
borne by one of the most powerful families in Scotland, earls of Douglas and of Angus. Today it is often
taken to be somehow connected with DOUGAL, but in
fact it was originally a local name, from a place
named with Gaelic elements meaning 'black, dark'
and 'water'.

**Drew** /druː/ (*m.*) Scottish aphetic short form of
ANDREW, well established as an independent name in
Scotland, and in recent years increasingly popular
elsewhere in the English-speaking world.

**Drusilla** /druːˈsɪlə/ (*f.*) Latin name, a feminine diminutive of the old Roman family name *Dr(a)usus*,

which was first taken by a certain Livius, who had killed in single combat a Gaul of this name and, according to a custom of the time, took his victim's name as a cognomen. Of the several women in the Roman imperial family who were called Livia Drusilla, the most notorious was Caligula's sister and mistress. The name is borne in the Bible by a Jewish woman, wife of the Roman citizen Felix, who was converted to Christianity by St Paul (Acts 24:24). In England it was taken up as a given name in the 17th cent. as a result of the biblical mention.

**Duane** /dweɪn/ (*m.*) A 20th-cent. coinage from the Irish surname *Duane*, Gaelic *Ó Dubháin* 'Descendant of Dubhán', a personal name or byname meaning 'little dark one'. It has enjoyed considerable popularity since the mid 1950s, due largely to the fame of the guitarist and singer Duane Eddy. The spellings **Dwane** and **Dwayne** are also found.

**Dud** /dʌd/ (*m.*) Short form of DUDLEY, in fairly common use (although not normally as an independent name) in spite of its coincidence in form with the modern slang term *dud* 'useless'.

**Dudley** /'dʌdli/ (*m.*) From the surname of a noble English family, who came originally from Dudley in the West Midlands, named in Old English as the 'wood or clearing of Dudda'. Their most famous member was Robert Dudley, Earl of Leicester (?1532–88), who came closer than any other man to marrying Queen Elizabeth I. In America this given name is much less common than in England.

**Duke** /djuːk/ (*m.*) In modern use this normally represents a nickname parallel to EARL and KING, but it is also a short form of MARMADUKE. It is especially popular in the U.S.

**Dulcie** /'dʌlsi/ (*f.*) Learned re-creation in the 19th

cent. of the medieval name *Dowse*, *Duce* (forms that have given rise to surnames), from Late Latin *Dulcia*, a derivative of *dulcis* sweet.

**Duncan** /'dʌnkən/ (*m.*) Of Scottish and Irish origin, from the Gaelic name **Donnchadh**, composed of old Celtic elements meaning 'brown' and 'battle'. The name was borne by a 7th-cent. Scottish saint, abbot of Iona, and a 10th-cent. Irish saint, abbot of Clonmacnoise. The Anglicized form of the final syllable seems to be the result of confusion with the Gaelic element *ceann* head.

**Dunstan** /'dʌnstən/ (*m.*) From an Old English personal name composed of the elements *dun* dark + *stān* hill, borne most notably by a 10th-cent. saint who was archbishop of Canterbury. The name is now used mainly by Roman Catholics.

**Dustin** /'dʌstɪn/ (*m.*) From the English surname, which is of uncertain origin, probably a Norman form of the Old Norse personal name *Đórstéinn*, composed of elements meaning 'Thor's stone'. It is now used fairly commonly as a given name as a result of the fame of the film actor Dustin Hoffman (b. 1937), who seems to have been named in honour of the lesser-known silent film actor Dustin Farman.

**Dusty** /'dʌsti:/ (*f.*) Apparently a feminine version of DUSTIN, made popular in the 1960s by the singer Dusty Springfield.

**Dwight** /dwaɪt/ (*m.*) From the English surname, which probably comes from the medieval English girl's given name *Diot*, a pet form of *Dionysia* (see DENNIS). It is especially common in America, where its increase in popularity since World War II is mainly a result of the fame of the American general and president Dwight D. Eisenhower (1890–1969). He was apparently named in honour of the New England

thinker Timothy Dwight (1752–1817) and his brother
Theodore Dwight (1764–1846).

**Dyan** /daɪˈæn/ (*f.*) Modern variant spelling of DIANE,
especially popular in the U.S.

**Dylan** /ˈdɪlən/ (*m.*) From Welsh: of uncertain origin,
probably connected with a Celtic element meaning
'sea'. It is the name, in the *Mabinogion*, of the miraculously born son of Aranrhod, who became a minor
divinity of the sea. In the second half of the 20th cent.
the name has become fairly popular outside Wales as
a result of the fame of the Welsh poet Dylan Thomas
(1914–53) and the American singer Bob Dylan (b.
1941), who changed his surname from Zimmerman
out of admiration for the poet.

**Dymphna** /ˈdɪmpfnə/ (*f.*) Of Irish origin: apparently
from the Gaelic name **Damhnait** /ˈdaʊnɪd/, a feminine diminutive form of *damh* poet. Little is known
of the saint of this name, who is regarded as the pro-
tector of the deranged and lunatic; her relics are preserved at Gheel, near Antwerp in Belgium. The form
**Dympna** /ˈdɪmpnə/ is also found.

# E

**Eamonn** /*Irish* 'e:mən/ (*m.*) Irish: the Gaelic form of EDMUND. The Anglicized spelling **Eamon** is also sometimes found.

**Earl** /ɜːl/ (*m.*) Mainly American, from the English aristocratic title, originally a nickname parallel to DUKE, KING, etc. The title was first used in England in the 12th cent., as an equivalent to the French *comte* count; it is from Old English *eorl* warrior, nobleman, prince. In some cases the first name may have been taken from the surname *Earl*, which was given originally to someone who worked in the household of an earl.

**Ebenezer** /ɛbə'niːzə/ (*m.*) Old Testament: originally the name (meaning 'Stone of Help' in Hebrew) of a place where the Israelites were defeated by the Philistines (I Sam. 4:1). When they took their revenge Samuel set up a memorial stone with this same name (I Sam. 7:12). It was taken up as a given name by the Puritans in the 17th cent., and has been in occasional use ever since. The name now has unfortunate associations because of the miserly character of Ebenezer Scrooge in Charles Dickens's *A Christmas Carol* (1843).

**Ed** /ɛd/ (*m.*) Short form of the various boys' names with the first syllable *Ed-*, especially EDWARD. See also TED.

**Eddie** /'edi/ (*m.*) Diminutive of ED, with the hypocoristic suffix *-ie*.

**Edgar** /'ɛdgə/ (*m.*) From an Old English personal name composed of the elements *ēad* prosperity, fortune + *gār* spear. This was the name of an English king and saint, Edgar the Peaceful (d. 975), and of Edgar Atheling (?1060–?1125), who should have succeeded Harold as king, but instead lived on uneasy terms with the new Norman rulers.

**Edith** /'iːdɪθ/ (f.) From an Old English personal name composed of the elements *ēad* prosperity, fortune + *gȳð* battle. This was the name of a daughter (961–84) of Edgar the Peaceful, in accordance with the common practice of repeating name elements within a family. She spent her short life in a convent, and is regarded as a saint.

**Edmond** /'ɛdmənd/ (m.) Variant of EDMUND, reflecting Norman influence, or rather the influence of scribes in Middle English who used *o* for *u* when it occurred with *m* or *n*, since all these letters were written with almost identical downward strokes.

**Edmund** /'ɛdmənd/ (m.) From an Old English personal name composed of the elements *ēad* prosperity, fortune + *mund* protection. It was borne by several early royal and saintly figures, including a 9th-cent. king of East Anglia killed by invading Danes, allegedly for his adherence to Christianity.

**Edna** /'ɛdnə/ (f.) Probably of Irish origin, an Anglicization of EITHNE. However, it also occurs in the Bible in the Apocryphal Book of Tobit, where it is the name of the mother of Sarah and stepmother of Tobias. This is said to be from Hebrew *ednah* rejuvenation, pleasure, or delight, and if so it is connected with the name of the Garden of Eden. The earliest known uses of the given name in England are in the 18th cent., when it was probably imported from Ireland.

**Edward** /'ɛdwəd/ (m.) From an Old English personal name composed of the elements *ēad* prosperity, fortune + *weard* guard. This has been one of the most successful of all Old English names, surviving from before the Conquest to the present day, and even being exported into other European languages (French *Edouard*, Italian, Spanish *Eduardo*, Portuguese *Duarte*, etc). It has been borne by eight kings of England since the Norman Conquest, and is the name of the youngest son of Queen Elizabeth II.

**Edwin** /ˈɛdwɪn/ (*m.*) From an Old English personal name composed of the elements *ēad* prosperity, fortune + *wine* friend. It was borne by a 7th-cent. king of Northumbria, who was converted to Christianity by St Paulinus and was killed in battle against pagan forces, which led to his being venerated as a martyr.

**Edwina** /ɛdˈwiːnə/ (*f.*) Latinate feminine form of EDWIN; a 19th-cent. coinage.

**Effie** /ˈɛfɪ/ (*f.*) Pet form of EUPHEMIA, now as little used as the full form.

**Egbert** /ˈɛgbɜːt/ (*m.*) From an Old English personal name composed of the elements *ecg* edge (of a sword) + *beorht* bright, famous. It was borne by two English saints of the 8th cent. and by a 9th-cent. king of Wessex. It survived for a while after the Conquest, possibly reinforced by a continental form brought in by the Normans, but fell out of use by the 16th cent. It was briefly revived in the 19th cent., but is now again completely out of favour.

**Eileen** /ˈaɪliːn/ (*f.*) Of Irish origin: from the Gaelic name **Eibhlin** /ailjiːnj/ or /ˈɛvjiljiːnj/, which is probably derived from EVELYN. The combination *bh* is normally pronounced as *v*, but sometimes dropped, as reflected in the Anglicized spelling.

**Eireen** /ˈaɪriːn/ (*f.*) Of recent origin: probably a re-spelling of IRENE under the influence of EILEEN.

**Eithne** /*Irish* ˈɛhinjə/ (*f.*) Irish: feminine form of AIDAN, Anglicized variously as EDNA, *Ethna*, *Etna*, and ENA.

**Elaine** /ɪ'leɪn/ (*f.*) From Old French: originally a version of HELEN, but now generally regarded as an independent name in its own right. The Greek and Latin forms of the name had a long vowel in the second syllable, which produced this form (as opposed to ELLEN) in Old French. Elaine was one of the women who fell in love with Lancelot in the Arthurian romances. The name occurs in this form in the 15th-cent. English *Morte Darthur* of Thomas Malory, and in the 19th cent. was popularized by the first part of Tennyson's *Idylls of the King* (1859). Most of the characters in this body of legends have names that are Celtic in origin, although subjected to heavy French influence, and it has been suggested that *Elaine* may ultimately be connected with a Welsh element meaning 'hind, fawn'.

**Eleanor** /'ɛlɪnə/ (*f.*) From an Old French respelling of the Old Provençal name *Alienor*, which has been supposed to be a derivative of HELEN, but is probably of Germanic derivation (with a first element *ali* other, foreign). The name was introduced to England by Eleanor of Aquitaine (1122–1204), who came from south-west France to be the wife of King Henry II. It was also borne by Eleanor of Provence, the wife of Henry III, and Eleanor of Castile, the wife of Edward I.

**Eleonora** /ɛlɪ'nɔːrə/ (*f.*) Latinate or Italian form of ELEANOR, sometimes shortened to LEONORA.

**Elfreda** /ɛl'friːdə/ (*f.*) Latinized form of an Old English personal name, *Ælfþryð*, composed of the elements *ælf* elf, supernatural being + *þryð* strength. This form may also have absorbed the originally distinct *Æðelþryð* (see AUDREY). The name was not used in the Middle Ages, but was revived in the 19th cent.

**Eli** /'iːlaɪ/ (*m.*) Old Testament: from a Hebrew word

meaning 'height', or else derived from an element *el* 'God', in origin a short form of the numerous names containing this element, such as *Elijah* and *Elisha*. It was the name borne in the Old Testament by the high priest who was entrusted with bringing up the future prophet Samuel. It was especially popular among Puritans in the 17th cent.

**Eliot** /ˈɛlɪət/ (*m.*) Variant spelling of ELLIOT.

**Elisabeth** /ɪˈlɪzəbəθ/ (*f.*) The spelling of ELIZABETH used in the Authorized Version of the New Testament, and in most modern European languages. This was the name of the mother of John the Baptist (Luke 1:60). Etymologically, the name was originally the same as that of *Elisheba* ('God is my Oath'), the wife of Aaron, mentioned in an Old Testament genealogy (Exod. 6:23). The final element seems to have been altered by association with Hebrew *shā-bath* rest.

**Elise** /ɛˈliːz/ (*f.*) French short form of ELISABETH. The name was introduced into the English-speaking world in the late 19th cent., but has not been much used.

**Eliza** /ɪˈlaɪzə/ (*f.*) Short form of ELIZABETH, first used in the 16th cent., which became popular, sometimes as an independent name, in the 18th and 19th cents. The name was used by George Bernard Shaw for the main female character, Eliza Doolittle, in his play *Pygmalion* (1913), which was the basis for the film *My Fair Lady*.

**Elizabeth** /ɪˈlɪzəbəθ/ (*f.*) The usual present-day spelling of ELISABETH in the English-speaking world. It was first made popular by being borne by Queen Elizabeth I of England (1533–1603). In the 20th cent. it became tremendously fashionable, partly because it was bestowed both on Elizabeth Bowes-Lyon

(b. 1900), who in 1936 became Queen Elizabeth as the wife of King George VI, and, even more influentially, on her daughter Queen Elizabeth II (b. 1926).

**Ella** /ˈɛlə/ (f.) A Norman French name, of Germanic origin, probably a short form of several compound names containing the first element *ali* other, foreign (cf. ELEANOR and ELVIRA). It is now often taken to be a variant or pet form of ELLEN.

**Ellen** /ˈɛlɪn/ (f.) Originally a variant of HELEN, although now very rarely associated with that name. In the Middle Ages initial *H*- was added and dropped capriciously, leading to many doublets (cf., e.g., ESTHER and *Hester*; ELOISE and *Heloise*).

**Ellie** /ˈɛliː/ (f.) Pet form of any of the numerous girls' names beginning with the syllable *El*-, in particular ELEANOR.

**Elliot** /ˈɛlɪət/ (m.) From the English surname, which is itself derived from a medieval (Norman French) given name. This was a diminutive of *Elie*, the Old French version of *Elias* (see ELLIS). The surname variants **Elliott** and **Eliot(t)** are also occasionally found as given names.

**Ellis** /ˈɛlɪs/ (m.) In Wales this is now generally taken as an Anglicization of the Old Welsh name *Elisud*, from *elus* kind, benevolent. It has also been influenced by the English surname, which is derived from *Elias*, the Greek version (used in the New Testament) of the name of the Old Testament prophet *Elijah* (whose Hebrew name means 'Jehovah is God').

**Elmer** /ˈɛlmə/ (m.) From the English surname, which is from an Old English personal name composed of the elements *æðel* noble + *mær* famous. This has been used as a given name in the U.S. since the 19th cent., in honour of the brothers Ebenezer and Jonathan Elmer, leading supporters of the American Revolution, and is still relatively common in America.

**Eloise** /ɛlu:ˈiːz; *French* eˈlwaːz/ (*f.*) Old French: introduced to Britain by the Normans, and presumably of Germanic origin, although the elements of which it is composed are not clear. Éloise or Héloïse was the name of the learned and beautiful wife (d. *c.* 1164) of the French philosopher and theologian Peter Abelard (1079–1142), whom she married secretly. A misunderstanding with her uncle and guardian, the powerful and violent Canon Fulbert of Notre Dame, led to Abelard being set upon, beaten up, and castrated. He became a monk, and Héloïse spent the rest of her days as abbess of a nunnery, but they continued to write to each other. Her name has been occasionally revived in modern times in allusion to her fidelity and piety.

**Elroy** /ˈɛlrɔɪ/ (*m.*) Variant of LEROY. The initial syllable seems to have resulted from the simple transposition of the first two letters of that name; it may also have been influenced by the Spanish definite article *el* and by the associated name DELROY.

**Elsa** /ˈɛlsə/ (*f.*) German pet form of ELISABETH. The name was given public prominence by the English-born film actress Elsa Lanchester (b. 1902), whose original name was Elizabeth Sullivan. It is now to a large extent associated with the lioness named Elsa featured in the film *Born Free*.

**Elsie** /ˈɛlsiː/ (*f.*) Scottish: simplified form of **Elspie**, a pet form of ELSPETH. This came to be used as an independent name, and in the 20th cent. has proved more popular than *Elspeth*.

**Elspeth** /ˈɛlspəθ/ (*f.*) Scottish contracted form of ELISABETH.

**Elton** /'ɛltən/ (*m.*) From the English surname, a local name from any of numerous places in England so called (mostly from the Old English masculine personal name *Ella* + Old English *tūn* enclosure, settlement). In England it is largely associated with the pop-singer Elton John; born Reginald Dwight, he took his adopted given name in honour of the saxophonist Elton Dean.

**Eluned** /ɛ'lɪnɛd/ (*f.*) Welsh: of uncertain origin, perhaps a derivative of *eilun* image.

**Elvira** /ɛl'viːrə/ (*f.*) Spanish: of Germanic (Visigothic) origin, very common in the Middle Ages and still in use today. The original form and meaning of the elements of which it is composed are far from certain (probably *ali* other, foreign + *wēr* true). The name was not used in the English-speaking world until the 19th cent., when it was made familiar as the name of the long-suffering wife of Don Juan, both in Mozart's opera *Don Giovanni* (1789) and Byron's satirical epic poem *Don Juan* (1819–24).

**Elvis** /'ɛlvɪs/ (*m.*) Of obscure derivation: made famous by the American singer Elvis Presley (1935–78). It may be derived from the surname of an ancestor, or it may have been made up, but it was certainly not chosen for the singer in anticipation of a career in show business, for his father's name was Vernon Elvis Presley.

**Emerald** /'ɛmrəld/ (*f.*) See ESMERALDA.

**Emily** /'ɛmɪliː/ (*f.*) Medieval form of the Latin name *Aemilia*, the feminine version of the old Roman family name *Aemilius* (probably from *aemulus* rival). It was nevertheless not common in the Middle Ages, and when it was revived in the 19th cent. there was much confusion between the originally distinct AMELIA and the Latinate form of this name, *Emilia*.

**Emlyn** /ˈɛmlɪn/ (*m.*) Welsh: apparently from Latin *Aemiliānus*, a derivative of *Aemilius* (see EMILY). On the other hand it may have a Celtic origin; there are Breton and Irish saints recorded as *Aemilianus*, which may be a Latinized form of a lost Celtic name.

**Emma** /ˈɛmə/ (*f.*) Norman: of Germanic origin, a short form of any of various compound names, such as *Ermintrude* and *Ermingarde*, containing the element *erm(en)*, *irm(en)* entire (cf. IRMA). The name is now often taken as a pet form of EMILY, but this is etymologically unjustified.

**Emmanuel** /ɪˈmænjuːəl/ (*m.*) Old and New Testaments: the name (meaning 'God with us' in Hebrew) of the promised Messiah, as prophesied by Isaiah (7:14; reported in Matt. 1:23). The Authorized Version of the Bible uses the form *Immanuel* in the Old Testament, *Emmạnuel* in the New. Both forms have been used as given names in England. However, it has always been a comparatively rare name in the English-speaking world, whereas the Hispanic form MANUEL is one of the commonest Spanish given names.

**Emmeline** /ˈɛməliːn/ (*f.*) Norman: of Germanic origin. Even in the Middle Ages it was not clear whether this name was a derivative of EMMA or of AMELIA (the spellings are very varied), and when it was revived in the 19th cent. there was further confusion with EMILY. A famous bearer was the suffragette Emmeline Pankhurst (1858–1928), mother of Christabel and Sylvia.

**Emrys** /ˈɛmrɪs/ (*m.*) Welsh: originally a form of AMBROSE. The name has been much revived in the 20th cent.

**Ena** /ˈiːnə/ (*f.*) One of several Anglicizations of Irish EITHNE. However, in the case of Queen Victoria's granddaughter Princess Ena (Victoria Eugénie Julia Ena, 1887–1969) it had a different origin: it was apparently a misreading by the minister who baptized her of a handwritten note of the originally intended name EVA. The name is currently out of favour, and is remembered principally as that of the fearsome Ena Sharples in the television soap opera *Coronation Street*.

**Enid** /'iːnɪd/ (*f.*) Celtic name borne by a virtuous character in the Arthurian romances; it is apparently connected with Welsh *enaid* soul, life. It came into use as a modern given name in the second half of the 19th cent., and was at its most popular in the 1920s.

**Enoch** /'iːnɒk/ (*m.*) Old Testament: name (possibly meaning 'Experienced' in Hebrew) of the grandson of Adam, son of Cain, father of Methuselah, grandfather of Lamech, and great-grandfather of Noah (Gen. 4:17). He is said to have lived for 365 years, and the supposed story of his life is narrated in detail in the Apocryphal 'Book of Enoch'.

**Eoghan** /*Scottish* 'eoːun, *Irish* oːn/ (*m.*) Irish and Scottish Gaelic: a name of great antiquity and of disputed derivation, possibly a form of EUGENE, or composed of old Celtic elements meaning 'yew' and 'born'. It is variously Anglicized as EWAN and OWEN.

**Ephraim** /'iːfreɪm/ (*m.*) Old Testament: name of one of the twelve sons of Jacob, who gave his name to one of the twelve tribes of Israel. The name probably means 'Fruitful' in Hebrew; certainly it is so explained in the Bible (Gen. 41:52 'and the name of the second called he Ephraim: For God hath caused me to be fruitful in the land of my affliction'). Unlike many Old Testament names, this was not particularly popular with the Puritans, and was used more in the 18th and 19th cents. than the 17th.

**Eric** /'ɛrɪk/ (*m.*) Of Old Norse origin, composed of the elements *ei*, *ey* forever + *rík* power. It was introduced into Britain by Scandinavian settlers before the Conquest and was occasionally used during the Middle Ages. The surname *Herrick* derives from it. As a modern given name it was revived in the mid-19th cent.

**Erica** /'ɛrɪkə/ (*f.*) Latinate feminine form of ERIC, coined towards the end of the 18th cent. It has no doubt been reinforced by the fact that *erica* is the Latin word for heather.

**Ermintrude** /'ɜːmɪntruːd/ (*f.*) Norman: of Germanic origin, composed of the elements *erm(en)*, *irm(en)* entire + *traut* beloved. It did not survive long into the Middle Ages, but was occasionally revived in the 18th and 19th cents. It is now completely out of favour.

**Ernest** /'ɜːnɪst/ (*m.*) Of Germanic origin, from the vocabulary word *eornost* seriousness, battle (to the death). The name was introduced into England in the 18th cent. by followers of the Hanoverian Elector who became George I of England. The Modern German form *Ernst* has also been introduced more recently, and an English form *Earnest* has arisen from the Modern English adjective *earnest*, which is ultimately connected with the name.

**Ernestine** /ɜːnɪs'tiːn/ (*f.*) Feminine diminutive of ERNEST, formed on the French model with the *-ine* suffix, but not actually used in France.

**Errol** /'ɛrəl/ (*m.*) From the Scottish surname, which itself derives from a place name. It has been made famous by the film actor Errol Flynn (1909–59), noted for his 'swashbuckling' roles. It is now very popular among Blacks, influenced by such figures as the jazz pianist Errol Garner.

**Erskine** /'ɜːskɪn/ (*m.*) From the Scottish surname,

which itself derives from a place name. The surname has also been taken to Ireland by Scottish settlers, and was first brought to public attention as a given name by the half-Irish writer and political activist Erskine Childers (1870–1922).

**Esau** /ˈiːsɔː/ (*m.*) Old Testament: name of the fractionally elder twin brother of Jacob, who sold his birthright for a bite to eat. The name seems to have meant 'Hairy' in Hebrew (Gen. 25:25 'and the first came out red, all over like an hairy garment; and they called his name Esau'); it is now rarely used as a given name in the English-speaking world.

**Esmé** /ˈɛzmeɪ; *French* ɛzˈme/ (*m.*) French: from the past participle of the Old French verb *esmer* to love (Latin *aestimāre* to value, esteem). In French this verb was absorbed by *amer* (see AMY) in the modern French form *aimer*, but it has survived in a different sense in English *aim* (originally 'estimate, reckon'). The name was introduced to Scotland in the 16th cent., and thence to the English-speaking world, where it is sometimes spelled without the accent.

**Esmée** /ˈɛzmeɪ; *French* ɛzˈme/ (*f.*) French: feminine form of ESMÉ.

**Esmeralda** /ˌɛsməˈrældə/ (*f.*) From the Spanish vocabulary word *esmeralda* emerald. Its occasional modern use as a given name seems to date from Victor Hugo's *Notre Dame de Paris* (1831), in which it is the nickname of the gypsy girl loved by the hunchback Quasimodo; she was given the name because she wore an amulet containing an artificial emerald. **Emerald** itself is a rare given name, taken from the gemstone.

**Esmond** /ˈɛsmənd/ (*m.*) From the English surname, which is of disputed origin. It may be a variant of

*Eastman*, from Old English *ēastman* 'man living to the east of the main settlement', or it may be from an Old English or Norman personal name, composed of the Germanic elements *anst* beauty + *mund* protection. It was not common in medieval times, and later died out completely, but was revived in the 1890s.

**Estelle** /ɛ'stɛl/ (*f.*) Old French name meaning 'Star' (Latin STELLA), which was comparatively rare in the Middle Ages. It was revived in the 19th cent., together with the Latinate form **Estella**, which was used by Dickens for the ward of Miss Havisham in *Great Expectations* (1861).

**Esther** /'ɛstə, 'ɛsθə/ (*f.*) Old Testament: name of an Israelite captive of the Persian king Ahasuerus, who became his favourite concubine and managed to save large numbers of the Jews from the evil machinations of the royal counsellor Haman by her perception and persuasion (Esther ch. 7). Her Hebrew name was *Hadassah* 'Myrtle', and the form *Esther* is said to be a Persian translation of this.

**Estrild** /'ɛstrɪld/ (*f.*) From an Old English personal name, composed of the divine name *Eastre* (a goddess of spring, whose name lies behind modern English 'Easter') + the element *hild* battle. The name is rare in modern use.

**Ethan** /'iːθæn/ (*m.*) Old Testament: name (meaning 'Firmness' in Hebrew) of an obscure figure, Ethan the Ezrahite, mentioned as a wise man whom Solomon surpassed in wisdom (I Kings 4:31). The name was sparingly used even among the Puritans, but has become famous in America since it was borne by Ethan Allen (1738–89), leader of the 'Green Mountain Boys', a group of Vermont patriots who fought in the American Revolution.

**Ethel** /ˈɛθəl/ (*f.*) Of Germanic origin: short form of any of various girls' names with a first element meaning 'noble' that were revived in the 19th cent., such as *Ethelburga* 'noble fortress', *Ethelfleda* 'noble beauty', *Ethelgitha* 'noble battle', and *Ethelgiva* 'noble gift'. All of these are now very rare (and were never common), but *Ethel* soon came to be used as an independent name, and has survived as such, although it is now somewhat out of favour.

**Ethna** /ˈɛtnə/ (*f.*) One of several Anglicizations of the Irish girl's name EITHNE, also found in the spelling **Etna**. See also EDNA, ENA.

**Eugene** /ˈjuːdʒiːn, juːˈdʒiːn/ (*m.*) Old French form of the Greek name *Eugenios* (from *eugenēs* well-born, noble). This was the name of various early saints, notably a 5th-cent. bishop of Carthage, a 7th-cent. bishop of Toledo, and a 7th-cent. pope.

**Eugenia** /juːˈdʒiːnɪə/ (*f.*) Feminine form of Greek *Eugenios* or Latin *Eugenius*; see EUGENE.

**Eugenie** /juːˈdʒiːniː, *French* yʒəˈni/ (*f.*) French form of EUGENIA, introduced to England as the name of the Empress Eugénie (Eugénia Maria de Montijo de Guzmán, 1826–1920), wife of Napoleon III.

**Eunice** /ˈjuːnɪs/ (*f.*) Greek: composed of the elements *eu* well, good + *nīkē* victory. It is mentioned in the New Testament as the name of the mother of Timothy, who introduced him to Christianity (2 Tim. 1:5). This reference led to the name being taken up by the Puritans in the 17th cent.

**Euphemia** /juːˈfiːmɪə/ (*f.*) Greek: composed of the elements *eu* well, good + *phēnai* to speak. This is the name of various early saints, most notably a virgin martyr supposedly burnt at the stake at Chalcedon in 307. It was particularly popular in the Victorian period, especially in the pet form EFFIE.

**Ezra** /ˈɛzrə/ (*m.*) Old Testament: name (meaning 'Help' in Hebrew) of a prophet, author of the book of the Bible that bears his name. It was taken up by the Puritans in the 17th cent., and has remained in occasional use ever since, especially in the U.S., where it was borne, for example, by the poet Ezra Pound (1885–1972).

# F

**Fabian** /ˈfeɪbɪən/ (*m.*) English form of the Late Latin name *Fabiānus*. This was originally a family name, a derivative of the old Roman family name *Fabius*, itself a nickname from *faba* bean. It was borne by an early pope (236–250), who was martyred under the Emperor Decius. The name was introduced into Britain by the Normans in the forms *Fabian* and *Fabien*, but it has never been much used in the English-speaking world. Forms of it, such as French *Fabien* and Italian *Fabiano*, are much more common in Catholic countries.

**Faith** /feɪθ/ (*f.*) From the English abstract noun denoting the quality of believing and trusting (in God). The name began to be used in the 16th cent., and was strongly popular among the Puritans of the next century.

**Fanny** /ˈfænɪ/ (*f.*) Pet form of FRANCES and an independent name in its own right. It was very popular in the 19th cent., but is now rarely found, no doubt due to the vulgar senses of the slang term *fanny*. These are of uncertain origin, not found before the 20th cent.

**Fatima** /ˈfætɪmə/ (*f.*) Usually a Muslim name, but occasionally borne by Catholics in honour of 'Our Lady of the Rosary of Fatima', who in 1917 appeared to three shepherd children from the village of Fatima, near Leiria in western Portugal.

**Fay** /ˈfeɪ/ (*f.*) Late 19th cent. coinage: it seems to represent the archaic word *fay* fairy, and may have been chosen as a result of the revival of interest in the Arthurian legends, in which Morgan le Fay plays a role. The name is also spelled **Faye**.

**Fearghus** /ˈfɛːrɡɪs/ (*m.*) Scottish Gaelic form of the

name normally Anglicized as FERGUS. The Irish Gaelic form is **Fearghas** /'fjærɪ:s/.

**Felicia** /fə'lɪsɪə/ (f.) Latinate feminine form of FELIX that seems to have originated in the Middle Ages.

**Felicity** /fə'lɪsɪtɪ/ (f.) From the English abstract noun denoting luck or good fortune (via Old French from Latin *felicitas*; cf. FELIX). The name was first used in the 17th cent. It also represents the English form of the Late Latin personal name *Felicitas*, which was borne by several early saints, most notably a slave who was martyred in AD 203 together with her mistress Perpetua and several other companions.

**Felix** /'fi:lɪks/ (m.) Latin name meaning 'Lucky'. It was first used as a byname of the Roman dictator Sulla (138–78 BC), and was a very popular name among the early Christians, being borne by a large number of saints.

**Fenella** /fə'nɛlə/ (f.) Of Irish origin (Gaelic **Fionnghuala** /'fjinuələ/): composed of the Gaelic elements *fionn* white, fair + *gualainn* shoulder.

**Ferdinand** /'fɛ:dɪnənd/ (m.) Germanic: of Visigothic origin, composed of elements meaning 'journey' (or possibly 'peace') and 'ready, prepared'. The name was originally confined to the Iberian peninsula, where its most famous bearer was King Ferdinand V of Aragon (1452–1516), who expelled the Moors, gave financial backing to Columbus, and was responsible for setting up the Inquisition. During the early Middle Ages, the name was occasionally borrowed into French and Italian. The Old French contracted form *Ferrand* was sometimes used in England in the Middle Ages, but has not survived. The current form seems to have been introduced from Italian (*Ferdinando*) in the 16th cent. The usual Spanish forms of this name are *Hernando* and *Fernando*.

**Fergus** /'fɜːgəs/ (*m.*) Of Gaelic origin (see FEARGHUS), from a name composed of Celtic elements meaning 'man' (or 'best') and 'choice'. It is still mainly confined to Scotland and Ireland and to families elsewhere who remain conscious of their Irish or Scottish ancestry.

**Fern** /fɜːn/ (*f.*) From the name of the family of plants, selected perhaps because of their delicate fronds or their modesty, being found in cool and shaded places. Its use as a given name is of recent origin, but seems to be increasing.

**Fiammetta** /fjæ'mɛtə/ (*f.*) Italian: from a diminutive form of the vocabulary word *fiamma* flame, fire, which is also used as a term of endearment. The name is rarely used in the English-speaking world.

**Fifi** /'fiːfiː/ (*f.*) French nursery form of JOSEPHINE, very rarely used as an independent given name. In some cases it may be associated with the term of endearment *ma fille* my daughter. In the English-speaking world it now has definite connotations of frivolity.

**Finbar** /'fɪnbɑː/ (*m.*) Irish (Gaelic **Fionnbharr** /'fjɪnbɑːr/): composed of the elements *fionn* white, fair + *barr* head. This was the name of at least three early Irish saints, one of whom became the first bishop of Cork in the 6th cent.

**Fingal** /'fɪŋgəl/ (*m.*) Scottish (Gaelic **Fionnghall**): composed of the elements *fionn* white, fair + *gall* stranger. It was originally a byname applied to Norse settlers; cf. DOUGAL. The spelling **Fingall** is also used.

**Finlay** /'fɪnleɪ/ (*m.*) Scottish (Gaelic **Fionnlagh** /'fiwnla/): composed of old Celtic elements meaning 'white, fair' and 'warrior, hero'. In many cases the modern given name represents the surname derived from this name in the Middle Ages. The spelling **Finley** is also found.

**Fiona** /fiːˈəʊnə/ (*f.*) Latinate derivative of the Gaelic element *fionn* white, fair. It was first used as the penname of the Scottish poet William Sharp (1855–1905), who produced many romantic works under the name of Fiona Macleod. It has since become extremely popular.

**Fionola** /fiːəˈnəʊlə/ (*f.*) Irish: a less thoroughly Anglicized form than FENELLA or **Fionnghuala**. It is now sometimes taken as an elaboration or a diminutive of FIONA, and the form **Finola** is also occasionally used.

**Flavia** /ˈfleɪvɪə/ (*f.*) Latin: feminine form of the old Roman family name *Flavius* (from *flavus* yellowhaired, golden). This was the name of at least five saints, most notably Flavia DOMITILLA, and the given name is relatively common in Italy, whence it has occasionally been introduced into England.

**Fleur** /flɜː/ (*f.*) Old French name meaning 'Flower', occasionally used in the Middle Ages. Modern use, however, seems to derive mainly from the character of this name in John Galsworthy's *The Forsyte Saga* (1922). The English form *Flower* has been very occasionally used.

**Flo** /fləʊ/ (*f.*) Short form of FLORENCE and FLORA, common in the early part of the 20th cent., but now generally considered somewhat old-fashioned (in contrast to most other short forms in *-o*, e.g. CARO).

**Flora** /ˈflɔːrə/ (*f.*) From Roman mythology: Latin name of the goddess of flowers and the spring (a derivative of *flōs* flower, genitive *flōris*). It is also the feminine form of the old Roman family name *Flōrus*, likewise derived from *flōs*. It was little used in England before the 18th cent., when it was imported from Scotland; its use there seems to have been the result of French influence.

**Florence** /ˈflɒrəns/ (*f.*) Medieval form of the Latin names *Florentius* (a derivative of *florens* blossoming, flourishing) and its feminine *Florentia*. In the Middle Ages the name was commonly borne by men (as for example the historian Florence of Worcester), but it is now exclusively a girl's name. In the late 19th cent. it was revived, being given in honour of Florence Nightingale (1820–1910), who herself received the name because she was born in the Italian town of Florence (Latin *Florentia*, Italian *Firenze*).

**Florrie** /ˈflɒri/ (*f.*) Pet form of FLORENCE and FLORA, now little used.

**Flossie** /ˈflɒsi/ (*f.*) Pet form from a contraction of FLORENCE. The popularity of the name was no doubt enhanced by association with the soft downy material known as *floss* (Old French *flosche*).

**Floyd** /flɔɪd/ (*m.*) Variant of LLOYD. This form of the name represents the nearest approach to the sound of the Welsh initial *Ll-* that is possible using standard English pronunciation and orthography. In the 20th cent. it has been particularly common in the southern states of the U.S. and among American Blacks.

**Fran** /fræn/ (*f.*, *m.*) Short form of FRANCES, or less commonly (in Britain at least) of FRANCIS.

**France** /frɑːns/ (*m.*) Short form of FRANCIS, often used in America as an independent name.

**Frances** /ˈfrɑːnsɪs/ (*f.*) Feminine form of FRANCIS. In the 16th cent. the two spellings were used indiscriminately for both sexes, the distinction in spelling not being established until the 17th cent.

**Francesca** /frænˈtʃeskə/ (*f.*) Italian form of FRANCES,

now quite well established in the English-speaking world.

**Francine** /fræn'siːn, *French* frã'siːn/ (*f.*) From a French pet form of FRANCES (French *Françoise*). The name is sometimes spelled **Francene** and **Franceen**.

**Francis** /'frɑːnsɪs/ (*m.*) Old French form of Italian *Francesco*, Late Latin *Franciscus* 'Frenchman' (cf. FRANK). This was in origin a nickname given to St Francis of Assisi (1181–1226) because of his father's business connections in France; his baptismal name was *Giovanni*, the Italian form of JOHN. In his honour the various vernacular forms of *Francis* became common given names almost immediately on the Continent, but did not reach England until the late 15th cent.

**Frank** /fræŋk/ (*m.*) Germanic: name referring originally to a member of the tribe of the Franks, who may have got the name from a characteristic type of spear that they used (as the Saxons did from a characteristic knife). When the Franks migrated into Gaul in the 4th cent., the country received its modern name of France (Late Latin *Francia*) and the tribal term Frank came to mean 'Frenchmen'. The name *Frank* is now sometimes taken, especially in America, as a more 'manly' short form of FRANCIS.

**Frankie** /'fræŋkiː/ (*m.*, *f.*) As a boy's name this is a diminutive of FRANK. As a girl's name it is a diminutive of FRANCES, FRANCESCA, or FRANCINE. It is perhaps most familiar as the name of the heroine of *The Ballad of Frankie and Johnny*, who ended up in the electric chair, 'with the sweat running through her hair'.

**Franklin** /'fræŋklɪn/ (*m.*) From the English surname, which derives from Middle English *frankeleyn* free-

man, from Norman French *frank* free or Frankish +
the Germanic suffix *-lin(g)*, denoting persons. The
connection between freemen and Franks is reflected
in the Late Latin term *francālia*, originally denoting
lands held by Franks, which came to mean lands that
were not subject to taxes. The given name is now
quite common, having been so used at first probably
in honour of the American statesman and scientist
Benjamin Franklin (1706–90), and more recently
President Franklin D. Roosevelt (1882–1945).

**Fraser** /ˈfreɪzə/ (*m.*) Scottish: from the surname of a
leading Scots family. The surname is undoubtedly of
Norman origin, but its exact derivation is uncertain.
The earliest forms are *de Frisselle* and *de Fresel(iere)*,
but the name seems to have been altered by association with Old French *fraise* strawberry. The alternative spelling of the surname, **Frazer**, is also used as a
given name.

**Fred** /fred/ (*m.*) Short form of FREDERICK or, occasionally, of ALFRED. It has also been used as an independent given name (cf. BERT).

**Freda** /ˈfriːdə/ (*f.*) Short form of various names such
as ELFREDA and WINIFRED, also occasionally of FRE-
DERICA. The name is sometimes spelled **Frieda**
under the influence of German forms.

**Freddie** /ˈfredɪ/ (*m.*, *f.*) As a boy's name, this is a
diminutive of FRED, also spelled **Freddy**. As a girl's
name, it is a rather rare pet form of FREDA or FREDER-
ICA.

**Frederica** /fredəˈriːkə/ (*f.*) Latinate feminine form of
FREDERICK. The French **Frédérique** and German
**Frederike** are also occasionally used in the English-
speaking world.

**Frederick** /ˈfredrɪk/ (*m.*) Of Germanic origin, composed of the elements *fred, frid* peace + *ric* power. It

was introduced into Britain by the Normans at the time of the Conquest, but did not survive long. Modern use dates from its reintroduction in the 18th cent. by followers of the Elector of Hanover who became George I of England, and was reinforced by the vogue for Germanic names in Victorian times. The variant spelling **Frederic** is also found, no doubt under the influence of French *Frédéric*.

**Fulk** /fʊlk/ (*m.*) Norman: of Germanic origin, a short form of various compound names containing the element 'people, tribe' (cf. Modern English *folk*). It has gradually died out of general use, but is still used in certain families, such as the Grevilles. Fulke Greville, 1st Baron Brooke, was a leading figure at the court of Elizabeth I. The spelling **Fulke** is still sometimes found.

# G

**Gabriel** /'geɪbrɪəl/ (*m.*) Biblical: name (meaning 'man of God' in Hebrew) of one of the archangels, who appeared to Daniel in the Old Testament (Dan. 8:16, 9:21), and in the New Testament to Zacharias (Luke 1:19, 26:27) and most famously to Mary, to announce the impending birth of Christ (Luke 1:2). *Gabriel* has occasionally been used as a given name in the English-speaking world, mainly as a result of continental European influence (rather more commonly than RAPHAEL, but much less so than MICHAEL, the names of the two other chief archangels).

**Gabriella** /gæbrɪˈɛlə/ (*f.*) Italian feminine form of GABRIEL.

**Gabrielle** /gæbriˈɛl/ (*f.*) French feminine form of GABRIEL.

**Gaby** /'gæbiː/ (*f.*) French pet form of GABRIELLE. The spelling **Gabi** is also sometimes found.

**Gaenor** /'geɪnə/ (*f.*) Variant spelling of GAYNOR.

**Gail** /geɪl/ (*f.*) Short form of ABIGAIL, now very commonly used as an independent given name, but apparently not in existence before the middle of the 20th cent.

**Gareth** /'gærəθ/ (*m.*) Of Celtic origin, but uncertain ultimate derivation. It first occurs as the name of the lover of Eluned in Malory's *Morte Darthur*, and seems to have been heavily altered from its original form, whatever that may have been. It may have been originally the same name as GERAINT, or it may have some connection with Welsh *gwared* gentle, benign. It is now very common in Wales, partly because GARY, which is actually an independent name, is now often taken to be a pet form of it.

**Garret** /'gærət/ (*m.*) From an English surname

derived in the Middle Ages from GERALD and GERARD.
The change of *-er-* to *-ar-* is a regular medieval development. The spelling **Garrett** is also found.

**Garth** /gɑːθ/ (*m.*) From an English surname, but often
taken to be a contracted form of GARETH. As a surname it originated in the North of England, and was
originally given to someone who lived beside some
sort of enclosure (Old Norse *garðr*). In modern times
its popularity may have been influenced by the strong
and virile character of this name, hero of a long-
running strip cartoon in the *Daily Mirror* newspaper.

**Gary** /ˈgæri/ (*m.*) From an English surname, which is
probably derived from a Norman given name of Germanic origin, a short form of any of the various compound names with *gar* spear as a first element. One
bearer of this surname was the American industrialist
Elbert Henry Gary (1846–1927), who gave his name
to the steel town of Gary, Indiana (chartered in
1906). In this town was born the theatrical agent Nan
Collins, who suggested *Gary* as a stage name for her
client Frank Cooper, who thus became Gary Cooper
(1901–61). His film career caused the name to
become enormously popular from the 1930s to the
present day. Its popularity has been maintained by
the cricketer Gary Sobers (b. 1936; in his case it is in
fact a pet form of *Garfield*) and the pop singer Gary
Glitter. It is now often taken as a pet form of GARETH.
The spelling **Garry** is also used.

**Gavin** /ˈgævɪn/ (*m.*) Of Celtic origin, but uncertain
ultimate derivation. It is borne in the Arthurian
romances by one of the knights of the Round Table
(more familiar in English versions as Sir *Gawain*),
and seems to have originally meant 'white hawk',
composed of elements represented in Welsh by
*gwalch* hawk + *gwyn* white (or possibly 'hawk of the
plain', *gwalch* + *mai* plain, field). The name died out

in the 16th cent. except in Scotland, whence it has been reintroduced in the past couple of decades. It is now popular in Wales, and is also encountered elsewhere in the English-speaking world.

**Gay** /geɪ/ (*f.*) From the English vocabulary word meaning 'blithe, cheerful' (from Old French, of Germanic origin), chosen as a given name because of its well-omened meaning (cf. HAPPY and MERRY). It was not used before the 20th cent., and has fallen out of favour again since the 1960s, since *gay* has become a vocabulary word meaning 'homosexual'. The spelling **Gaye** is also found.

**Gayle** /geɪl/ (*f.*) Variant spelling of GAIL.

**Gaylord** /'geɪlɔ:d/ (*m.*) From an English surname, which is a form, altered by folk etymology, of the Old French nickname *Gaillard* 'Dandy'. It may have been chosen as a given name because parents liked the idea of their son living as a fine lord, but it now seems likely to suffer the same fate as the girl's name GAY.

**Gaynor** /'geɪnə/ (*f.*) A medieval form of the name of Arthur's queen, GUINEVERE. It has recently been reintroduced from Wales, but does not enjoy the same popularity as the Cornish form JENNIFER.

**Ged** /gɛd/ (*m.*) Short form of GERARD or GERALD.

**Gemma** /'dʒɛmə/ (*f.*) From Italian: introduced into England in the mid-20th cent. It was in origin a medieval nickname meaning 'Gem, Jewel', and has normally been chosen in modern times because of its transparent etymology. Among Irish Catholics it was in use somewhat earlier, in honour of Gemma Galgani (1878–1903), who was apparently the subject of many extraordinary signs of grace, such as ecstasies and the appearance of the stigmata.

**Gene** /dʒi:n/ (*m.*) Short form of EUGENE, now quite common in America. It has been made popular especially by film stars such as Gene Autry, Gene Hackman, and Gene Wilder.

**Genevieve** /ˈdʒɛnəviːv/ (*f.*) From French: the name of the patron saint of Paris, a 5th-cent. Gallo-Roman nun who encouraged the people of Paris in the face of the occupation of the town by the Franks and threatened attacks by the Huns. Her name seems to have been composed of Celtic elements meaning 'people, tribe' and 'woman', but if so it has been heavily altered by its transmission through French sources. The name does not seem to have been used much in England in the Middle Ages, but was introduced from France in the 19th cent.

**Geoff** /dʒef/ (*m.*) Short form of GEOFFREY, sometimes used as an independent name in Britain (although not so commonly as JEFF is in America).

**Geoffrey** /ˈdʒefri/ (*m.*) Norman: of Germanic origin, although the original form and meaning of the elements of which it is composed are disputed. According to one theory the name is merely a variant of GODFREY; others wish to derive the first part from the Germanic elements *gawia* territory, *walah* stranger, or *gisil* pledge. Medieval forms can be found to support all these theories, and it is possible that several names have fallen together, or that the name was subjected to reanalysis by folk etymology at an early date. The spelling *Geoffrey* was at first merely a variant of JEFFREY, but in Britain it has become the more usual form.

**George** /dʒɔːdʒ/ (*m.*) Derivative, via Old French and Latin, of the Greek name *Geōrgios* (from *geōrgos* farmer, a compound of *gē* earth + *ergein* to work). This was the name of several early saints, including the shadowy figure who is now the patron of England (as well as of Germany and Portugal). If he existed at all, he was perhaps martyred in Palestine in the persecutions instigated by the Emperor Diocletian at the beginning of the 4th cent.; the popular legend in which the hero slays a dragon is a medieval Italian invention. He was for a long time a more important saint in the Orthodox Church than in the West, and the name was not much used in England during the Middle Ages, even after St George came to be regarded as the patron saint of England in the 14th cent. The real impulse for its popularity was the accession of the first king of England of this name, who came from Germany in 1714 and brought many German retainers with him. It has been one of the most popular English boys' names ever since.

**Georgette** /dʒɔː'dʒɛt/ (*f.*) French feminine diminutive of GEORGE (French *Georges*). It is occasionally used in the English-speaking world. The crepe material so called derives its name from that of the early 20th-cent. French dressmaker Mme Georgette de la Plante.

**Georgia** /'dʒɔːdʒɪə/ (*f.*) Latinate feminine form of GEORGE. It was borne by a 5th-cent. saint who became a recluse near Clermont in the Auvergne.

**Georgie** /'dʒɔːdʒi/ (*m.*, *f.*) Occasionally used as a diminutive of GEORGE, but more commonly as a pet form of GEORGIA or GEORGINA.

**Georgina** /dʒɔː'dʒiːnə/ (*f.*) Latinate feminine derivative of GEORGE, which originated in Scotland in the 18th cent., when *George* itself became common.

**Geraint** /'ɡeraɪnt/ (*m.*) Welsh: of uncertain origin. It is borne by a character in the Arthurian legends, the husband of Enid, and seems to have been a Celtic form of the Greek name *Gerontios*, a derivative of *gerōn* old man. In recent years it has become very popular in Wales.

**Gerald** /'dʒerəld/ (*m.*) Norman: of Germanic origin,

composed of the elements *gar* spear + *wald* rule. This was not particularly widely used in the Middle Ages and soon died out. It was revived in the 19th cent., along with other long-extinct names of Germanic origin.

**Geraldine** /'dʒɛrəldiːn/ (*f.*) Feminine derivative of GERALD invented in the 16th cent. by the English poet the Earl of Surrey, in a poem praising Lady Fitzgerald. However, it remained very little used until the 18th cent.

**Gerard** /'dʒɛrɑːd/ (*m.*) Norman: of Germanic origin, composed of the elements *gar* spear + *hard* brave, hardy, strong. In the Middle Ages this was a much more common name than GERALD, with which it was sometimes confused, but it is nowadays rare, and may often (especially in the spelling **Gerrard**) be a transferred use of the surname derived from the medieval name.

**Gerda** /'gɜːdə/ (*f.*) From Scandinavian mythology: the name of a goddess who was the wife of Frey. The pair seem to have been originally fertility gods, and her name is probably connected with the Old Norse word *gjorðr* earth. It was revived in Scandinavia in the 19th cent., and is now also sometimes used in the English-speaking world.

**Germaine** /dʒɜː'meɪn/ (*f.*) French: feminine form of the rarer masculine name *Germain* (Late Latin *Germānus*, which originated either as a nickname meaning 'Brother (in Christ)' or as an ethnic name for a 'German'). Germaine Cousin (*c.* 1579–1601) was a Provençal saint, the daughter of a poor farmer. Her canonization in 1867 gave an additional impulse to the use of the name in Europe and the English-speaking world. It is now particularly known as the name of the Australian feminist writer Germaine Greer (b. 1939).

**Gerry** /'dʒɛrɪ/ (*f.*, *m.*) As a girl's name this is a pet form of GERALDINE; as a boy's name it is a short form of GERALD or GERARD. It is also sometimes used as an independent given name, especially for girls.

**Gert** /gɜ:t/ (*f.*) Short form of GERTRUDE.

**Gertie** /'gɜ:tɪ/ (*f.*) Diminutive of GERT.

**Gertrude** /'gɜ:tru:d/ (*f.*) From a Germanic personal name composed of the elements *gar* spear + *traut* beloved. The name does not appear in England immediately after the Conquest, but only in the later Middle Ages, and it is probable that it was introduced by migrants from the Low Countries, who came to England in connection with the cloth trade. It was popular in the 19th cent., at the time of the revival of many Germanic names, but has now fallen from favour.

**Gervaise** /'dʒɜ:veɪz/ (*m.*) Norman: of uncertain derivation. It has been explained as a Germanic name, with the first element *gar* spear, but it is difficult to suggest a satisfactory second element. The use of the name seems to be due entirely to the fame of a certain St Gervasius, who was martyred together with Protasius in one of the early persecutions of Christians. It seems possible that his name was of Greek origin, like that of his fellow martyr, but if so, the elements remain unidentified. The spelling **Gervase** is also used. See also JARVIS.

**Gethin** /'gɛθɪn/ (*m.*) Welsh: derived from a mutated form (originally used after a personal name) of the nickname *Cethin* 'Dusky, Swarthy'. The spelling **Gethen** is also used.

**Ghislain** /gɪz'leɪn/ (*f.*) Of recent origin, or at any rate a recent introduction to the English-speaking world. It is apparently a revival of the Old French oblique case of GISELLE. The spelling indicates some Low German influence.

**Gib** /gɪb/ (*m.*) Medieval and modern short form of GIL-BERT.

**Gideon** /ˈgɪdɪən/ (*m.*) Old Testament: name (which means 'One who cuts down' in Hebrew) of the Israelite leader appointed to deliver his people from the Midianites (Judges 6:14). He did this by getting his army to creep up on them with their torches hidden in pitchers. The name was popular among the 17th-cent. Puritans, and is still used in America.

**Gilbert** /ˈgɪlbət/ (*m.*) Norman: of Germanic origin, composed of the elements *gisil* pledge + *berht* bright, famous. It was borne by the founder of the only native British religious order (abolished at the Dissolution of the Monasteries), St Gilbert of Sempringham (?1083–1189).

**Giles** /dʒaɪlz/ (*m.*) From an Old French form of the Greek name *Aigidios* (a derivative of *aigidion* kid, young goat). The name was very popular in the Middle Ages as the result of the fame of the 8th-cent. St Giles. According to tradition he was an Athenian citizen who fled to Provence because he could not cope with the fame and adulation caused by his power to work miracles. The spelling **Gyles** is also found.

**Gill** /dʒɪl/ (*f.*) Short form of GILLIAN, rather less common than JILL.

**Gillian** /ˈdʒɪlɪən, ˈgɪlɪən/ (*f.*) In origin a variant of JULIAN, not clearly differentiated in spelling until the 17th cent.

**Gilroy** /ˈgɪlrɔɪ/ (*m.*) From the Irish and Scots surname, now occasionally used as a given name, perhaps in part under the influence of the names ELROY, DELROY, and LEROY. The surname (Irish *Mac Giolla Ruaidh*,

Scots *Mac Gille Ruaidh*) meant originally 'son of the red-haired lad'.

**Gina** /ˈdʒiːnə/ (*f.*) Short form of GEORGINA, made famous by the Italian actress Gina Lollobrigida (b. 1927).

**Ginger** /ˈdʒɪndʒə/ (*m.*, *f.*) Nickname for someone with red hair (or, occasionally, with a violent temper). It is sometimes used as a given name for a baby born with red hair. As a girl's name it may also represent a pet form of VIRGINIA (as in the case of the musical actress Ginger Rogers, born in 1911 as Virginia McMath).

**Ginny** /ˈdʒɪni/ (*f.*) Aphetic pet form of VIRGINIA.

**Giselle** /French ʒiˈzɛl/ (*f.*) French: of Germanic origin, from a short form of any of several compound girls' names containing the element *gisil* pledge. Use of the name in English-speaking countries seem to derive from the ballet *Giselle* (first performed in 1841).

**Gladys** /ˈglædɪs/ (*f.*) From the Welsh name **Gwladys** /ˈɡulædɪs/, which is of uncertain derivation, perhaps an Old Welsh version of CLAUDIA. It has been widely used outside Wales in the 20th cent.

**Glen** /glɛn/ (*m.*) From the Scottish surname, which was originally a local name from any of various places named with the Celtic element *gleann* valley. The spelling **Glenn** is also used. There has probably been some confusion with the Welsh name GLYN.

**Glenda** /ˈglɛndə/ (*f.*) Welsh: derived from the element *glân* clean, pure, holy, + a suffix of uncertain meaning (probably *da* good).

**Glenys** /ˈglɛnɪs/ (*f.*) Welsh: of uncertain derivation, probably a variant of GLYNIS or a blend of GLADYS and GLENDA.

**Gloria** /ˈglɔːrɪə/ (*f.*) From the Latin word meaning 'Glory', not used as a given name before the 20th cent. It first occurs as the name of a character in George Bernard Shaw's play *You Never Can Tell* (1898).

**Glyn** /glɪn/ (*m.*) Welsh: from the Welsh place-name element *glyn* valley. This seems to have been transferred directly from a place name to a given name in the 20th cent., as the result of a desire to bestow on Welsh children specifically Welsh names. The spelling **Glynn** is also used.

**Glyndwr** /ˈglɪndʊːr, glɪnˈdʊːr/ (*m.*) Welsh: adopted in the 20th cent. in honour of the medieval Welsh patriot Owain Glyndwr (*c.* 1359–1416; known in English as Owen Glendower). In his case it was a byname referring to the fact that he came from a place named as the 'Black Valley', from Welsh *glyn* valley + *dwr* black.

**Glynis** /ˈglɪnɪs/ (*f.*) Welsh: of recent origin and uncertain derivation, possibly a combination of the elements *glyn* valley (see GLYN) + *-is* (extracted from GLADYS).

**Godfrey** /ˈgɒdfriː/ (*m.*) Norman: of Germanic origin, composed of the elements *god* god (or *gōd* good) + *fred*, *frid* peace. It was borne by a Norman saint (*c.* 1066–1115) who became bishop of Amiens.

**Goldie** /ˈgəʊldiː/ (*f.*) Mainly Jewish: an Anglicized form of Yiddish *Golde* (borne, for example, by the former Israeli Prime Minister Golda Meir, 1898–1978, who Hebraicized her name from Golde Meyer). It was originally a nickname from German (and Yiddish) *Gold* gold. Occasionally it is an English name, derived from a nickname for a fair-haired person.

**Gordon** /ˈgɔːdən/ (*m.*) From the Scottish surname, which is derived from a place name. It is a matter of dispute whether it referred originally to the Gordon in the Scottish Borders region (in the former county of Berwickshire) or to a similarly named place in Normandy. As a given name it seems to have been taken up in honour of Charles George Gordon (1833–85), the British general who died at Khartoum.

**Grace** /greɪs/ (*f.*) From the English abstract noun (from Latin *grātia*), first used as a given name by the Puritans in the 17th cent., and still moderately popular (and to a large extent dissociated from the vocabulary word). Its popularity has increased in the 20th cent. owing to the fame of the late wife of Prince Rainier of Monaco, the actress Grace Kelly. It has always been common in Scotland (borne, for example, by Grace Darling, the lighthouse keeper's daughter whose heroism in 1838, saving sailors in a storm, caught popular imagination).

**Gracie** /ˈgreɪsi:/ (*f.*) Diminutive of GRACE, with the hypocoristic suffix *-ie*. It was made famous by the Lancashire singer Gracie Fields (1898–1979), whose original name was Grace Stansfield.

**Graham** /ˈgreɪəm/ (*m.*) From the Scottish surname, which derives from a place that is in neither Scotland nor Normandy, but Lincolnshire. *Grantham*, near the border with Leicestershire and Nottinghamshire, is recorded in the Domesday Book not only in its current form but also as *Grandham*, *Granham*, and *Graham*; it seems to have been originally named as the 'gravelly place', from Old English *grand* gravel (unattested) + *hām* homestead. The alternative spellings of the surname **Grahame** and **Graeme** are also used as given names.

**Grainne** /*Irish* ˈgrɑːnjə/ (*f.*) Irish: of uncertain origin (probably a derivative of the element *gráidhte* loved). In Irish legend Grainne was a daughter of King Cormac; she was beloved by the hero Finn, who pursued her over long distances after she eloped with Diarmait.

**Grant** /grɑːnt/ (*m.*) From the Scottish surname, which was originally a Norman nickname meaning 'Large' (Anglo-Norman *grand*). In America the name has sometimes been given in honour of the Civil War general and 18th president, Ulysses S. Grant (1822–85).

**Granville** /'grænvɪl/ (*m.*) From one of the Norman baronial names that subsequently became aristocratic English surnames and are now used intermittently as boys' given names. It derives from any of several places in Normandy named with the Old French elements *grand* large + *ville* settlement.

**Greg** /greg/ (*m.*) Short form, mainly Scottish, of GREGOR and GREGORY. The spelling **Gregg** is also used.

**Gregor** /'gregə/ (*m.*) Scots (and central European) form of GREGORY. This name gave rise to the Highland patronymic surname *Macgregor*, and is currently undergoing a revival in popularity.

**Gregory** /'gregəri/ (*m.*) From the post-classical Greek name *Gregōrios* 'Watchful' (a derivative of *gregōrein* to watch or be vigilant). The name was a popular one with the early Christians, who were mindful of the instruction 'Be sober, be vigilant' (I Peter 5:8), and was borne by a number of early saints. The most important, in honour of whom the name was often bestowed from medieval times onwards, were Gregory of Nazianzen (*c.* 329–90), Gregory of Nyssa (d. *c.* 395), Gregory of Tours (538–94), and Gregory the Great (*c.* 540–604).

**Greta** /'griːtə/ (*f.*) Short form of *Margareta*, the Swedish version of MARGARET, introduced to the English-speaking world by the Swedish-born actress Greta Garbo (b. Greta Louisa Gustafsson in 1905).

The German form **Grete** is also occasionally used in the English-speaking world.

**Griff** /grɪf/ (*m.*) Short form of GRIFFITH, now also established as an independent given name.

**Griffith** /'grɪfɪθ/ (*m.*) Welsh: Anglicized spelling of **Gruffydd** or **Gryffydd**, a name attested from the Middle Ages but of uncertain derivation. Its popularity in the 20th cent. has probably been influenced by the common surname *Griffith(s)*, which is in fact derived from it.

**Griselda** /grɪ'zɛldə/ (*f.*) Of uncertain origin, possibly composed of the Germanic elements *gris* grey + *hild* battle. It became popular in the Middle Ages with reference to the tale of 'patient Griselda' (told by Boccaccio and Chaucer), who was taken as a model of the patient, long-suffering wife.

**Grizel** /'grɪzəl/ (*f.*) Scottish vernacular form of GRISELDA, which has waned in popularity, no doubt in part because of its similarity to the vocabulary word meaning to grumble or whine.

**Guinevere** /'gwɪnəvɪə/ (*f.*) From an Old French form of the Old Welsh name *Gwenhwyfar*, which is composed of the elements *gwen* white, fair, holy + *hwyfar* smooth, soft. It is famous as the name of King Arthur's unfaithful wife. See also GAYNOR and JENNIFER.

**Gus** /gʌs/ (*m.*) Short form of AUGUSTUS, ANGUS, or GUSTAVE.

**Gustave** /'gusta:v/ (*m.*) French form of the Swedish name *Gustav* or *Gustaf*, composed originally of the Old Norse tribal name *Gaut* (or *goð* god) + *stafr* staff. In the forms *Gustavus* or *Gustaf* it was borne by various kings of Sweden, beginning with Gustavus Vasa (?1496–1560), who was elected king in 1523 after freeing Sweden from Danish occupation.

**Guy** /gaɪ/ (*m.*) Norman: from a short form of a compound Germanic name having as its first element *witu* wood or *wīt* wide. In Norman French initial *w-* was regularly changed to *gu-*, and the usual Norman forms of the name were *Gy* or *Guido*. In medieval Latin the same name occurs as *Wido*.

**Gwen** /gwɛn/ (*f.*) Short form of GWENDOLEN, or an independent name from Welsh *gwen*, the feminine form of *gwyn* white, fair, holy (see GWYN). It was borne by a 5th-cent. saint, aunt of St David and mother of the minor saints Cyby and Cadfan.

**Gwendolen** /'gwɛndəlɪn/ (*f.*) Welsh: composed of the elements *gwen* white, fair, holy + *dolen* ring, bow. The name is borne by one of the principal characters in Oscar Wilde's play *The Importance of Being Earnest* (first performed in 1895). The spellings **Gwendolin**, **Gwendolyn**, and **Gwendoline** are now also common.

**Gwilym** /'gwɪlɪm/ (*m.*) Welsh version of WILLIAM, currently undergoing a revival of popularity among Welsh people conscious of their national identity.

**Gwyn** /gwɪn/ (*m.*, *f.*) Welsh: as a boy's name this is from *gwyn* white, fair, holy. As a girl's name it is a short form of GWYNETH or a variant of GWEN, used by non-Welsh speakers.

**Gwyneth** /'gwɪnɪθ/ (*f.*) Welsh (spelled **Gwynaeth** in Welsh): from the vocabulary word meaning 'luck, prosperity'. It has sometimes been taken as associated with *Gwynedd*, a region of North Wales.

**Gwynfor** /'gwɪnvɔːr/ (*m.*) Welsh: coined in the 20th cent., apparently from the elements *gwyn* white, fair, holy + *iôr* lord.

# H

**Hal** /hæl/ (*m.*) Short form of HARRY, of medieval origin, used for example by Shakespeare in *King Henry IV* as the name of the king's son, the future Henry V. Similar substitution of *l* for *r* has occurred in derivatives of *Terry* (*Tel*), *Derek* (*Del*), and in girls' names such as *Sally* (from *Sarah*).

**Hale** /heɪl/ (*m.*) From the English surname, originally a topographic name for someone living in a nook or recess (Old English *halh*).

**Hamish** /'heɪmɪʃ/ (*m.*) Scottish: derived from the vocative case, *Sheumais*, of the Gaelic version of JAMES; see SEUMAS.

**Hank** /hæŋk/ (*m.*) Pet form of JOHN, of medieval origin, a back-formation from *Hankin*, which is composed of *Han*, a short form of *Jehan*, and the Middle English diminutive suffix *-kin*, which seems to be of Dutch origin. The suffix was, however, taken to be the Anglo-Norman diminutive *-in*, hence the form *Hank*. This is now sometimes used as an independent name in America, where it is usually taken as a pet form of HENRY. It has more or less died out in Britain.

**Hannah** /'hænə/ (*f.*) Old Testament: the name of the mother of the prophet Samuel (I Sam. 1:2), Hebrew *Chana*, from a Hebrew word meaning 'He (i.e God) has favoured me' (see ANNE). This form of the name taken up as a given name by the Puritans in the 16th–17th cents.

**Happy** /'hæpi:/ (*f.*) Occasionally used in the 20th cent. for the sake of the good omen contained in the vocabulary word (Middle English *happy* fortunate, from *hap* (lucky) chance; cf. MERRY and GAY.

**Harold** /'hærəld/ (*m.*) of Old English origin, composed of the elements *here* army + *weald* rule, re-

inforced before the Norman Conquest by the
Scandinavian cognate *Haraldr*, introduced by Norse
settlers. The name was not common in the later
Middle Ages, perhaps because it was associated with
King Harold, the loser at the Battle of Hastings in
1066. It was revived in the 19th cent., along with a
number of other Old English names.

**Harriet** /'hærɪət/ (*f.*) Anglicized form of French *Henriette*, a feminine diminutive of HENRY (French
*Henri*), coined in the 17th cent. The form **Harriot**,
which is also found in the 17th cent., is a feminine
diminutive of HARRY, and may have influenced this
name. It was particularly common in England in the
18th and early 19th cents. The spelling **Harriette** is
also found.

**Harry** /'hærɪ/ (*m.*) Pet form of HENRY, sometimes
used as an independent name. This was the usual
English form of HENRY in the Middle Ages and later,
and was the form used by Shakespeare for the familiar name of the mature King Henry V (compare
HAL). The intermediate form *Herry* probably arose
from the French pronunciation with a nasalized
vowel, or it may be the result of straightforward assimilation; the change of *-er-* to *-ar-* was a regular
feature of Middle English.

**Harvey** /'hɑːvi:/ (*m.*) From the English surname,
which was introduced by the Normans, but is of Breton origin, being composed of the elements *haer*
battle + *vy* worthy.

**Hattie** /'hæti:/ (*f.*) Pet form of *Harriet*, now rarely
used either as such or as an independent name.

**Hayley** /'heɪli:/ (*f.*) From the English surname, which
derives from a place name, probably from *Hailey* in
Oxfordshire, which was originally named from Old
English *hēg* hay + *lēah* clearing. Its use as a given

name began only in the 1960s, inspired by the actress Hayley Mills. The variant **Haley** has already established itself.

**Hazel** /'heɪzəl/ (*f.*) From the name of the plant (Old English *hæsel*), perhaps sometimes given with reference to the *hazel*, i.e. reddish-brown, colouring of a baby's hair. The name was first used in the late 19th cent.

**Heather** /'hɛðə/ (*f.*) From the name of the plant (Middle English *hather*, the spelling of which was altered in the 18th cent. as a result of popular etymological association with *heath*). The name was first used in the late 19th cent., but has been particularly popular since about 1950.

**Hebe** /'hiːbiː/ (*f.*) From classical mythology: name (from Greek *hēbos* young) of a minor goddess who was a personification of youth. She was a daughter of Zeus and the wife of Hephaistos; it was her duty to act as cup-bearer to the gods. The name was taken up in the late 19th cent., but has not been much used.

**Hector** /'hɛktə/ (*m.*) From classical legend: name of the Trojan champion who was killed by the Greek Achilles. His name (Greek *Hektōr*) seems to be an agent derivative of Greek *ekhein* to check, restrain. In Scotland the given name has sometimes been used as an Anglicized form of the somewhat similar-sounding Scots Gaelic name *Eachdonn*, composed of elements meaning 'horse' and 'brown'.

**Heidi** /'haɪdiː/ (*f.*) Swiss pet form of *Adelheid*, the German version of ADELAIDE. It has been used in the English-speaking world in the 20th cent. as a result of the fame of Johanna Spyri's popular children's classic *Heidi* (1881).

**Helen** /'hɛlɪn/ (*f.*) From classical legend: name (Greek *Hēlēnē*) of the famous beauty whose seizure sparked off the Trojan War. Her name is of uncertain origin; it may be connected with an element meaning 'ray, beam of the sun' (cf. Greek *hēlios* sun). It has sometimes been taken as connected with the Greek word for 'Greek', *Hellēn*, but there does not seem to be any etymological justification for this. In the post-classical period the name was borne by the mother of the Emperor Constantine, who is credited with having found the True Cross. She was probably born in Bythinia rather than Britain; nevertheless the latter version was believed in the Middle Ages, which made the name a popular one in England. The Latinate form **Helena** is also used, and occasionally the French **Hélène**.

**Helga** /'hɛlgə/ (*f.*) Scandinavian: from an Old Norse word meaning 'holy'. It was introduced to England before the Conquest, but did not survive long. It has been reintroduced to the English-speaking world in the 20th cent. from Scandinavia and Germany.

**Héloïse** /'ɛluːɪːz; *French* elo'iz/ (*f.*) French variant of ELOISE, which enjoyed a revival of popularity in the 18th cent. after publication of Rousseau's philosophical novel *La Nouvelle Héloïse* (1761).

**Henrietta** /hɛnri'ɛtə/ (*f.*) Latinized version of French *Henriette*, a feminine diminutive of HENRY (French *Henri*). This form of the name has enjoyed a vogue since the late 19th cent.

**Henry** /'hɛnri/ (*m.*) Norman: of Germanic origin, composed of the elements *haim* home + *ric* power. It has been steadily popular since the time of the Conquest, and has been borne by eight kings of England. It was not until the 17th cent. that this form of the name (rather than HARRY) began to become regular, as a result of comparison with French *Henri*.

**Herb** /hɜːb/ (*m.*) Short form of HERBERT.

**Herbert** /ˈhɜːbət/ (*m.*) Norman: of Germanic origin, composed of the elements *heri* army + *berht* famous. A form of this (*Herebeorht*) existed in England before the Conquest, when it was replaced by the continental form introduced by the Normans, which gave rise to an important surname. By the end of the Middle Ages it was little used, and its greater frequency in the 19th cent. owed something to the trend for the revival of medieval names of Germanic origin and something to the trend for the use of surnames as given names.

**Hercules** /ˈhɜːkjuːliːz/ (*m.*) From classical mythology: the Latin form of the name of the Greek hero *Herakles*, whose name means 'Glory of Hera'. (Hera was the chief goddess in the Greek pantheon.) Herakles was a son of Zeus and Alkmene, noted for his exceptional physical strength; after completing a daunting series of twelve labours he was made a god. The name has occasionally been used, under European influence, in the English-speaking world.

**Herman** /ˈhɜːmən/ (*m.*) Of Germanic origin, composed of the elements *heri* army + *man* man. The name was in use among the Normans, and enjoyed a limited revival in Britain in the 19th cent., when it also became common in America, probably in part as the result of the influence of German settlers, among whom the German form *Hermann* was common.

**Hermione** /hɜːˈmaɪəniː/ (*f.*) From classical mythology: name of a daughter of Helen and Menelaus, who grew up to marry her cousin Orestes. The name is a derivative of *Hermes*, the messenger god, but the formation is not clear. The name was used by Shakespeare in *A Winter's Tale*, and has been occasionally chosen in the 20th cent.

**Hester** /ˈhɛstə/ (*f.*) Variant of ESTHER, of medieval origin. For a long while the two forms were interchangeable, the addition or dropping of *h-* being commonplace in a whole range of words, but now they are generally regarded as two distinct names.

**Hettie** /'heti:/ (*f.*) Pet form of HENRIETTA, now rarely used either as such or as an independent name.

**Hilary** /'hɪləri:/ (*m.*, *f.*) Medieval form of the (postclassical) Latin name *Hilarius* (a derivative of *hilaris* cheerful) and its feminine form *Hilaria*. From the Middle Ages onwards, the name was borne principally by men (in honour of the 4th-cent. theologian St Hilarius of Poitiers). Now, however, it is more commonly given to girls.

**Hilda** /'hɪldə/ (*f.*) Norman: of Germanic origin, originally a short form of any of various names containing the element *hild* battle, which were also found in Old English. Before the Norman Conquest and during the early Middle Ages this was one of the most common girl's names in England. It never quite died out, and was strongly revived in the 19th cent.

**Hiram** /'haɪrəm/ (*m.*) Old Testament: name of a king of Tyre who is repeatedly mentioned in the Bible (II Sam. 2:11, I Kings 5, 9:11, 10:11, I Chron. 14:1, II Chron 2:11) as supplying wood, craftsmen, and money to enable David and Solomon to construct various buildings. It was also the name of a craftsman of Tyre who worked in brass for Solomon (I Kings 7:13). It is presumably of Semitic origin, but is not immediately explicable in terms of Hebrew elements. The name was taken up by the Puritans in the 17th cent., and is still used in America.

**Holly** /'hɒli:/ (*f.*) From the name of the plant (Middle English *holi(n)*, Old English *holegn*). The name was first used at the beginning of the 20th cent., and has been particularly popular since about 1960. It is bestowed especially on girls born around Christmas.

**Homer** /ˈhəʊmə/ (*m.*) Usual English form of the name of the Greek epic poet *Homēros*, now regularly used as a given name in the U.S. (cf. VIRGIL). Many theories have been put forward to explain the name of the poet; it is identical in form with the Greek vocabulary word *homēros* hostage.

**Honoria** /ɒˈnɔːriːə/ (*f.*) Feminine form of the Late Latin male name *Honorius* (a derivative of *honor* honour), which was borne by various early saints, including a 7th-cent. archbishop of Canterbury. *Honoria* is rarely used as a given name in the English-speaking world, although its French form *Honore* is relatively common in France.

**Honour** /ˈɒnə/ (*f.*) From the English vocabulary word *honour* (via Old French from Latin *honor*). The name was popular with the Puritans in the 17th cent. and has survived to the present day. In America both vocabulary word and name are now usually spelled with *-or*.

**Hope** /həʊp/ (*f.*) From the abstract noun *hope* (Old English *hopa*), denoting the quality, especially of Christian expectation in the resurrection and eternal life. The name was created by the Puritans and has been one of their most successful inventions. The name is now to a large extent dissociated from the vocabulary word, and has been reinforced by the surname *Hope*, which is derived from the dialect term *hope* enclosed valley.

**Hopkin** /ˈhɒpkɪn/ (*m.*) From the surname, now found mainly in Wales, derived from a medieval given name. This is a diminutive (with the diminutive suffix *-kin*, of Dutch origin) of *Hob*, which is a rhyming short form of ROBERT.

**Horace** /ˈhɒrɪs/ (*m.*) Usual English form (via Old French) of the old Roman family name *Horatius* (of

obscure, possibly non-Roman, origin; see also HORA-
TIO). *Horatius* was the name of the early Roman hero
whose exploit is recounted in one of Macaulay's *Lays
of Ancient Rome*, which tells 'How Horatius kept the
bridge'. In later Roman times, the name was borne
by the poet Quintus Horatius Flaccus, generally
known in English as Horace.

**Horatia** /həˈreɪʃɪə/ (*f.*) Feminine form of Latin *Horatius*; see HORACE. It has never been common in the
English-speaking world, but was borne, for example,
by the daughter of Horatio, Lord Nelson.

**Horatio** /həˈreɪʃɪəʊ/ (*m.*) Variant of HORACE,
influenced by the Italian version *Orazio*. This form
has occasionally been used in the English-speaking
world, for example by the admiral Horatio Nelson
(1758–1805).

**Hortense** /hɔːˈtɛns; *French* ɔrˈtɑ̃s/ (*f.*) French form of
Latin *Hortensia*, the feminine version of the old
Roman family name *Hortensius*. This is of uncertain
origin, but may be derived from Latin *hortus* garden.
The given name was not used in the English-speaking
world before the 19th cent., and is not common
today.

**Howard** /ˈhaʊəd/ (*m.*) From the surname of an English noble family, now regularly used as a given
name. The surname has a large number of possible
origins, but in the case of the noble family early forms
often have the spelling *Haward*, and it is probably
from a Scandinavian name composed of the elements
*hā* high + *ward* guard. (The traditional derivation
from the Old English name *Hereward* 'army guard' is
untenable.)

**Howell** /ˈhaʊəl/ (*m.*) Anglicized form of the Welsh
name HYWEL, or a transferred use of the surname
derived from that name.

**Hubert** /'hjuːbət/ (*m.*) Norman: of Germanic origin, composed of the elements *hug* heart, mind, spirit + *berht* famous. The popularity of the name in medieval Britain was reinforced by settlers from the Low Countries. An 8th-cent. St Hubert succeeded St Lambert as bishop of Maastricht and is regarded as the patron of hunters, since, like St Eustace, he is supposed to have seen a vision of Christ crucified between the antlers of a stag.

**Hugh** /hjuː/ (*m.*) Norman: of Germanic origin, derived from the element *hug* heart, mind, spirit. Originally the name was probably a short form of various compound names containing this element. Hugh of Lincoln was a child supposed in the Middle Ages to have been murdered by Jews, a legend responsible for several outbursts of anti-Semitism at various times. In spite of this, it has been a perennially popular given name. In Ireland it is sometimes used as an Anglicization of AODH.

**Hugo** /'hjuːgəʊ/ (*m.*) Latinized form of *Hugh*, used occasionally in the English-speaking world.

**Humbert** /'hʌmbət/ (*m.*) Norman: of Germanic origin, composed of the elements *hun* bear-cub, warrior + *berht* famous. It was not common in the Middle Ages, and modern use seems to stem from a recent reintroduction from Germany.

**Humphrey** /'hʌmfri/ (*m.*) Norman: of Germanic origin, composed of the elements *hun* bear-cub, warrior + *fred*, *frid* peace. A form (*Hunfrith*) of this name seems to have existed in England before the Conquest, but it was replaced by the Norman continental version *Hunfrid*. The spelling with *-ph-* reflects classicizing influence. The spelling **Humphry** is also used.

**Hyacinth** /'haɪəsɪnθ/ (*m.*, *f.*) From classical mythology: name of a beautiful youth, *Hyakinthos*, who was accidentally killed by Apollo and from whose blood sprang the flower that bore his name (not the modern hyacinth, but a type of dark lily). The name was later borne by various early saints, principally one martyred in the 3rd cent. with his brother Protus. Occasionally used from the Middle Ages onwards as a boy's name, in its rare modern use it is normally given to girls, and must be regarded as a special use of the vocabulary word for the flower.

**Hyam** /ˈhaɪəm/ (*m.*) Jewish: derived from a Hebrew element meaning 'life'. A large number of transliterations are in use; another common one is CHAIM.

**Hyman** /ˈhaɪmən/ (*m.*) Jewish: altered form of HYAM, influenced by the common Yiddish name element *man* man. The spelling **Hymen** is also found, which is identical in form to the name in classical mythology of the Greek and Roman god of marriage.

**Hymie** /ˈhaɪmi:/ (*m.*) Jewish: pet form of HYMAN.

**Hywel** /*Welsh* ˈhəwɛl/ (*m.*) Welsh name meaning 'Eminent'. It was common in the Middle Ages and lies behind the Anglicized surname *Howell*. In the 20th cent. it has been revived as a result of increased interest in the Welsh language and Welsh culture.

# I

**Ian** /'ɪən/ (*m.*) Scottish version of JOHN, now very widely used in the English-speaking world, having largely lost its connection both with Scotland and with *John*. The Gaelic form **Iain** is now also comparatively popular in Scotland.

**Ida** /'aɪdə/ (*f.*) Originally a Norman name, of Germanic origin, derived from the element *id* work. This died out during the later Middle Ages. It was revived in the 19th cent., mainly as a result of its use in Tennyson's *The Princess* (1847) as the name of the heroine, who devotes herself to the cause of women's rights and women's education in a thoroughly Victorian way. The name is also associated with Mount Ida in Crete, which was connected in classical times with the worship of Zeus, king of the gods, who was supposed to have been brought up in a cave on the mountainside.

**Idris** /'ɪdrɪs/ (*m.*) from Welsh: composed of the elements *iud* lord + *ris* ardent. It was common in the Middle Ages and earlier, and has been strongly revived since the late 19th cent. as a result of increased interest in the Welsh language and Welsh culture.

**Ieuan** /'ju:ən/ (*m.*) Welsh version of JOHN.

**Ignatius** /ɪg'neɪʃəs/ (*m.*) Late Latin: derived from the old Roman family name *Egnatius* (of uncertain, probably Etruscan, origin), altered in the early Christian period by association with Latin *ignis* fire. It was borne by various early saints, and more recently by St Ignatius Loyola (1491–1556), who founded the Society of Jesus (Jesuits). It is occasionally used in the modern English-speaking world, mainly by Roman Catholics.

**Igor** /'i:gɔ:/ (*m.*) Russian name of Scandinavian origin, from *Ingvar*, which is composed of the name of an Old Norse fertility god, *Ing*, + the element *var* warrior. This name was taken to Russia at the time of the first Scandinavian settlement of Kiev in the 9th cent., and introduced to the English-speaking world in the 20th cent.

**Ike** /aɪk/ (*m.*) Pet form of ISAAC, but made famous in the 20th cent. as the nickname of the American general and president Dwight D. Eisenhower (1890–1969).

**Ilona** /ɪˈləʊnə/ (*f.*) Hungarian form of HELEN, now regularly used in the English-speaking world.

**Immanuel** /ɪˈmænjʊəl/ (*m.*) Variant of EMMANUEL, used in the Old Testament. In the English-speaking world this spelling in particular is generally a Jewish name.

**Imogen** /ˈɪmədʒən/ (*f.*) Of Shakespearian origin: the name owes its existence to a character in *Cymbeline*, but in earlier accounts of the events on which the play is based this character is named as *Innogen*. The modern form of the name is thus due to a misreading of these sources by Shakespeare or of the play's text by his printer. The name *Innogen* is of Celtic origin, probably connected with Gaelic *ingean* girl, maiden.

**Ina** /ˈiːnə/ (*f.*) Short form of any of the various girls' names ending in this syllable (often a Latinate feminine diminutive suffix), for example CHRISTINA, GEORGINA, and KATRINA; also a variant of ENA.

**Inez** /ˈinɛz/ (*f.*) Spanish version of AGNES (in Spanish written with a tilde, *Iñez*). It is also spelled **Ines** and **Innes**, the latter probably as a result of confusion with the Scottish surname *Innes* (derived from places named with the Gaelic element *innis* island).

**Inga** /ˈɪŋə/ (*f.*) Respelled version of the German and Scandinavian name *Inge*. This is a short form of various girls' names, such as INGRID and *Ingeborg*, which have as their first element the name of an Old Norse fertility god, *Ing*.

**Ingram** /'ɪŋgrəm/ (*m.*) From an English surname, derived from a medieval Norman given name. This was probably a contracted form of the Norman name *Engelram*, composed of the Germanic tribal name *Engel* Angle + the element *hramn* raven. It is also possible that in some cases the first element was the name of an Old Norse fertility god, *Ing*.

**Ingrid** /'ɪŋgrɪd/ (*f.*) Of Scandinavian origin: composed of the name of an Old Norse fertility god, *Ing*, + the element *friðr* fair, beautiful. It was introduced into the English-speaking world in the 20th cent., and became popular in large part because of the fame of the Swedish film actress Ingrid Bergman (1915–82).

**Inigo** /'ɪnɪgəʊ/ (*m.*) Of Spanish origin (in Spanish written *Iñigo*): vernacular derivative of the Late Latin name IGNATIUS. In the English-speaking world it is mainly associated with the architect Inigo Jones (1573–1652). The name had previously been borne by his father, and the architect passed it on to his son, but later occurrences are rare.

**Ione** /aɪˈəʊniː/ (*f.*) A 19th-cent. coinage, apparently with reference to the glories of Ionian Greece in the 5th cent. BC. No such name exists in classical Greek.

**Ira** /'aɪrə/ (*m.*) Old Testament: name (meaning 'Watchful' in Hebrew) of a character mentioned very briefly in the Bible (II Sam. 20:26). It was taken up by the Puritans in the 17th cent., and is still occasionally used, mainly in America.

**Irene** /'aɪriːn, aɪˈriːn; *formerly* aɪˈriːniː/ (*f.*) From Greek mythology: name (from Greek *eirēnē* peace) of a minor goddess who personified peace. The name was taken up in the English-speaking world at the end of the 19th cent., and has become popular in the 20th, partly as a result of being used as the name of a character in John Galsworthy's *The Forsyte Saga* (1922). It was formerly pronounced in three syllables, now usually in two.

**Iris** /ˈaɪrɪs/ (*f.*) From Greek mythology: name (from Greek *iris* rainbow) of a minor goddess, one of the messengers of the gods, who was so named because the rainbow was thought to be a sign from the gods to men. In English her name was given in the 16th cent. to both the flower and the coloured part of the eye, on account of their varied colours. In modern use the name seems often to be taken as being from the flower name, but it is also in use in Germany, where there is no such pattern of naming.

**Irma** /ˈɜːmə/ (*f.*) German pet form of various names beginning with the element *erm(en)*, *irm(en)* entire, such as *Irmgard* and *Irmentraut*. Its origins are thus the same as those of EMMA. It was introduced to the English-speaking world at the end of the 19th cent.

**Irving** /ˈɜːvɪŋ/ (*m.*) From a Scottish surname, originally a local name from a place in the former county of Dumfriesshire. The surname variant **Irvine** (which in most cases comes from a place in the former county of Ayrshire) is also used as a first name.

**Irwin** /ˈɜːwɪn/ (*m.*) From an English surname, which is derived from the medieval personal name *Erwin*. This is composed of the Old English elements *eofor* boar + *wine* friend. There has also been some confusion with IRVING.

**Isaac** /ˈaɪzək/ (*m.*) Old Testament: name of the son of Abraham, who was about to be sacrificed by his father when he was miraculously saved by the discovery of a ram caught in a thicket, which was sacrificed instead (Gen. 21:3). He lived on to marry

Rebecca and become the father of Esau and Jacob. The interpretation of the name is not certain; it has traditionally been connected with the Hebrew verb meaning 'to laugh'. In the Middle Ages it seems to have been borne only by Jews, but it was taken up by the Puritans in the 17th cent. and has continued in use since then among Christians, although it is still more common among Jews.

**Isabel** /ˈɪzəbɛl/ (*f.*) Originally a Spanish version of ELI-SABETH, this has long been used in the English-speaking world as a distinct name. The Spanish form arose as a result of the loss of the first syllable (helped by the fact that it was identical to the masculine form of the definite article, *el*) and the alteration of the final consonant to one that can end a word in Spanish. The name was common in England in the late Middle Ages and seems never to have fallen out of use.

**Isabella** /ɪzəˈbɛlə/ (*f.*) Italian form of ISABEL, which came into use in England in the 18th cent.

**Isaiah** /aɪˈzaɪə/ (*m.*) Old Testament: name (meaning 'God is Salvation' in Hebrew) of the most important of the Old Testament prophets. The name has never been common in the English-speaking world, apart from a brief flicker in the 17th cent., and in modern use is usually an Anglicized version of European forms such as Italian *Isaia* or French *Isaïe*, or else a Jewish name.

**Iseabail** /ˈɪʃɪpɛl, ˈɪʃəbɛl/ (*f.*) Gaelic form of ISABEL. The Anglicized spelling **Ishbel** is occasionally used, supposedly representing the Gaelic pronunciation.

**Iseult** /ɪzˈəʊlt/ (*f.*) Variant of ISOLDE, from the medieval French form of the name.

**Isidora** /ɪzɪˈdɔːrə/ (*f.*) Feminine form of ISIDORE. This name was little used in the Middle Ages, but has recently become more popular and is sometimes spelled **Isadora**, as a result of the fame of the American dancer Isadora Duncan (1878–1927).

**Isidore** /'ızıdɔ:/ (*m.*) English form (via Old French and Latin) of the Greek name *Isidoros*, composed of the name of the goddess *Isis* (who was Egyptian in origin) + the Greek element *dōron* gift. In spite of its pagan connotations the name was a common one among early Christians, and was borne for example by St Isidore of Seville (*c.* 560–636). By the late Middle Ages, however, it had come to be considered a typically Jewish name (although originally adopted as a Christianized version of ISAIAH). It is now seldom borne by anyone.

**Isla** /'aılə/ (*f.*) Scottish: of recent origin, apparently taken directly from the name of a river.

**Isobel** /'ızəbəl/ (*f.*) Variant of ISABEL, found mainly in Scotland. The contracted form **Isbel** also occurs.

**Isolde** /ı'zɒldə/ (*f.*) From Celtic legend: name of the tragic mistress of Tristram in the Arthurian romances. It was relatively common in Britain in the Middle Ages, but is much rarer today. It probably originally meant 'of fair aspect' (Welsh **Esyllt**).

**Israel** /'ızreıəl/ (*m.*) Old Testament: byname (meaning 'Soldier of God' in Hebrew) given to Jacob after he had wrestled with an angel. 'Thy name shall be called no more Jacob, but Israel: for as a prince hast thou power with God and with men, and hast prevailed' (Gen. 32:28). It was used by the Puritans in the 17th cent., but is now almost exclusively a Jewish name.

**Ivan** /'aıvən/ (*m.*) The Russian version of JOHN, sometimes used in the English-speaking world.

**Ivor** /'aıvə/ (*m.*) Of Scandinavian origin, composed of the Norse elements *ýr* yew, bow + *herr* army. The name has now become particularly popular in Wales (although it is not clear why this should be so) and is often respelled **Ifor**.

**Ivy** /'aɪvi:/ (*f.*) From the name of the plant (Old English *ifig*). This given name was coined at the end of the 19th cent. together with a large number of other girls' names derived from flowers and plants.

# J

**Jacinta** /dʒə'sɪntə; *Spanish* xa'θɪnta/ (*f.*) Spanish feminine form of HYACINTH. The French cognate **Jacinthe** is also found occasionally in the English-speaking world, but is much less common.

**Jack** /dʒæk/ (*m.*) Although now generally taken to be an Anglicized form of *Jacques* (the French version of JAMES), *Jack* in fact originated as a pet form of JOHN. It derives from Middle English *Ja(n)kin*, introduced by migrants from the Low Countries, from Low German *Jan* + the diminutive suffix *-kin*. This led in England to the back-formation *Jack*, as if the name had contained the Old French diminutive suffix *-in*.

**Jackie** /'dʒæki:/ (*f.*, *m.*) Originally a boy's name, a diminutive of JACK, but now more commonly a girl's name, to be taken as a pet form of JACQUELINE.

**Jackson** /'dʒæksən/ (*m.*) From an English surname, meaning originally 'son of JACK', now used occasionally as a given name. In the U.S. it is sometimes bestowed in honour of the American president Andrew Jackson (1767–1845) or the Confederate general Thomas 'Stonewall' Jackson (1824–63).

**Jacob** /'dʒeɪkəb/ (*m.*) Old Testament: name of an Israelite patriarch, the son of Isaac and Rebecca. According to the story in Genesis, he was the clever younger twin who persuaded his fractionally older brother Esau to part with his right to his inheritance in exchange for a bowl of soup when he was hungry. Later, he tricked his blind and dying father into blessing him in place of Esau. The derivation of the name has been much discussed, and no certainty is possible. It was traditionally explained as 'Supplanter', and indeed Esau remarks, 'Is he not rightly named Jacob? For he has supplanted me these two times' (Gen. 27:36). This remark is, however, better inter-

preted as a pun on a name that already existed.
Another derivation with biblical authority is that the
name comes from the Hebrew word for 'heel', and
that the child was so named because when he was
born 'his hand took hold of Esau's heel' (Gen.
25:26).

**Jacqueline** /ˈdʒækəlɪn, -liːn/ (*f.*) French feminine
diminutive of *Jacques* (the French version of JAMES).
The name is widely used in the English-speaking
world. It has also been respelled as **Jacquelyn**
(under the influence of the productive suffix -*lyn*; see
LYNN) and **Jacklyn** (a further simplification, based
on the male name JACK). In the 1960s it became very
popular in the U.S. and elsewhere, no doubt under
the influence of Jacqueline Kennedy, wife of President John F. Kennedy.

**Jacquetta** /dʒəˈkɛtə/ (*f.*) Respelling (influenced by
JACQUELINE) of the Italian name *Giachetta*, a femi-
nine diminutive of *Giac(om)o*, the Italian version of
JAMES.

**Jacqui** /ˈdʒæki:/ (*f.*) Variant spelling of JACKIE, reflecting the influence of the full form JACQUELINE and
the increasing tendency to use -*i* as a distinctively
feminine suffix (cf., e.g., TONI).

**Jade** /dʒeɪd/ (*f.*) From the name of the precious stone,
a word that reached English from Spanish (*piedra de*)
*ijada*, which literally means '(stone of the) bowels'. It
was so called because it was believed to have the
magical power of providing protection against dis-
orders of the intestines. The vogue for this word as a
given name developed later than that for other gemstone names, possibly because of the unfortunate etymological associations, or more probably because it
sounds the same as a word for a broken-down old
horse or a nagging woman. Its popular appeal
received a considerable boost in the early 1970s,

when the daughter of the English rock singer Mick Jagger was so named.

**Jago** /ˈdʒeɪɡəʊ/ (*m.*) Cornish form of JAMES or JACK, which has increased in popularity recently, perhaps as a result of transferred use of the surname *Jago*, which itself derives from the Cornish given name.

**Jake** /dʒeɪk/ (*m.*) Variant of JACK, of Middle English origin, which has now come back into fashion as an independent name. It is also sometimes used as a short form of JACOB.

**James** /dʒeɪmz/ (*m.*) New Testament: borne by two of Christ's disciples, James son of Zebedee and James son of Alphaeus. In origin a form of JACOB, it has for many centuries now been thought of as a distinct name. *Jacob* appears in Greek (in the New Testament and elsewhere), as *Iakobos*, which in Latin became *Iacobus* and *Iacomus*, hence *James*.

**Jamie** /ˈdʒeɪmi:/ (*m.*, occasionally *f.*) Pet form of JAMES, used especially among Lowland Scots, in contrast to the Highland (Gaelic) form HAMISH. It is also bestowed occasionally on girls, like most other boy's names ending in *-ie*.

**Jan** /*m.* dʒæn, jæn; *f.* dʒæn/ As a boy's name, a variant of JOHN, perhaps in many cases in Britain a revival of the medieval English *Jan*, which is usually said to have been an importation from Low German or Dutch, although there is some evidence to suggest that it was a native coinage. In the U.S. and elsewhere, the name is more commonly an Anglicization, pronounced with a soft *J*, of the Dutch and Central European forms of JOHN (also spelled *Jan*, but pronounced *Yan*). As a girl's name it is a shortened form, now quite common, of JANET and JANICE.

**Jana** /ˈjɑːnə/ (*f.*) Distinctively feminine variant of JAN; in the English-speaking world a 20th-cent. importation from eastern Europe, where it is well established.

**Jane** /dʒeɪn/ (*f.*) Originally a feminine form of JOHN, from the Old French form *Je(h)anne*. Since the 17th cent. it has proved the most common of the feminine forms of *John*, ahead of JOAN and JEAN. It now also commonly occurs as the second element in combinations such as *Sarah-Jane*.

**Janet** /'dʒænət/ (*f.*) From a Middle English diminutive of JANE. Towards the end of the Middle Ages the name largely died out except in Scotland. It was revived at the end of the 19th cent. to much wider use, but still retains something of a Scottish flavour.

**Janette** /dʒə'nɛt/ (*f.*) Either an elaborated version of JANET, emphasizing the feminine form of the suffix, or an altered form of JEANETTE.

**Janey** /'dʒeɪnɪ/ (*f.*) Pet form of JANE. The spellings **Janie** and, occasionally, **Jayni** are also found.

**Janice** /'dʒænɪs/ (*f.*) Derivative of JANE, with the addition of the suffix *-ice*, extracted from girls' names such as CANDICE and BERNICE. It seems to have been first used as the name of the heroine of the novel *Janice Meredith* by Paul Leicester Ford, published in 1899.

**Janine** /dʒə'niːn/ (*f.*) A simplified spelling of French *Jeanine*, feminine diminutive of *Jean* (the French version of JOHN). The latinate form **Janina** is also used.

**Janis** /'dʒænɪs/ (*f.*) Variant spelling of JANICE, made popular mainly by the U.S. rock singer Janis Joplin (1943–70).

**Jarvis** /'dʒɑːvɪs/ (*m.*) From an English surname, itself from a given name derived in the Middle Ages from the Norman name GERVAISE. Modern use of the name may in part represent an antiquarian revival of the medieval given name.

**Jasmine** /ˈdʒæzmɪn/ (*f.*) From the name of the flower (taken via Old French from Persian *yasmin*). The spelling **Jasmin** is also found, as is the variant **Yasmin**, which represents either a restoration of the Persian form or an alteration inspired by the German and Dutch pronunciation of names beginning in *J-*.

**Jason** /ˈdʒeɪsən/ (*m.*) From Greek mythology: name of the leader of the Argonauts, who sailed in search of the Golden Fleece and endured a stormy relationship with the sorceress Medea. His name probably derives from Greek *iasthai* to heal. It is also the name of an early Christian mentioned in the Bible (Acts 17:5, Rom. 16:21), where it seems to be a classicized form of JOSHUA, which gave it respectability among the Puritans in the 17th cent., although it did not become common until the late 20th cent.

**Jasper** /ˈdʒæspə/ (*m.*) From Christian legend: usual English form of the name of one of the three magi, who brought gifts to the infant Christ at His birth. The name has no biblical authority, but first appears in medieval tradition. It seems to be ultimately of Persian origin, from a word meaning 'treasurer'. There is probably no connection with the English vocabulary word for the gemstone, which is of Semitic origin. The form CASPAR is a Central European variant. The names assigned by tradition to the other Magi, *Balthazar* and *Melchior*, have also been used as given names in Europe, but only very rarely in the English-speaking world.

**Jay** /dʒeɪ/ (*m.*, *f.*) Pet form of any of the given names beginning with the letter *J-* (cf. DEE and KAY), but also used as an independent name.

**Jayne** /dʒeɪn/ (*f.*) Variant spelling of JANE.

**Jean** /dʒiːn/ (*f.*) Like JANE and JOAN, a medieval variant of Old French *Je(h)anne*. Towards the end of the Middle Ages this form became largely confined to Scotland. In the 20th cent. it has been more widely used in the English-speaking world, but still retains a Scottish flavour.

**Jeanette** /dʒəˈnɛt/ (*f.*) French feminine diminutive of *Jean*, the French version of JOHN.

**Jeanie** /ˈdʒiːniː/ (*f.*) Pet form of JEAN, which is even more strongly associated with Scotland than *Jean* itself, and occasionally used as an independent given name. It is also spelled **Jeannie**.

**Jed** /dʒɛd/ (*m.*) Mainly American: now frequently used as an independent name, although originally a short form of the Old Testament name *Jedidiah*, which was an alternative name of King Solomon (II Sam. 12:25), meaning 'Beloved of God'. This was a favourite with the Puritans, who considered themselves too to be loved by God, but the full form fell out of favour along with other unwieldy Old Testament names.

**Jeff** /dʒɛf/ (*m.*) Short form of JEFFREY or GEOFFREY. It is now commonly used as an independent given name in the U.S.

**Jefferson** /ˈdʒɛfəsən/ (*m.*) From an English surname, meaning originally 'son of Jeffrey', now used as a given name. It has sometimes been chosen in honour of the American president Thomas Jefferson (1743–1826), who was principally responsible for the text of the Declaration of Independence. It has also occasionally been chosen for their sons by fathers themselves named JEFFREY or GEOFFREY.

**Jeffrey** /ˈdʒɛfriː/ (*m.*) Variant spelling of GEOFFREY, common in the Middle Ages (as reflected in surnames such as *Jefferson*). The spelling **Jeffery** is also found.

**Jem** /dʒem/ (*m.*) From a Middle English vernacular form of JAMES. In modern use, however, it is often taken as a pet form of JEREMY.

**Jemima** /dʒə'maɪmə/ (*f.*) Old Testament: name (meaning 'Dove' in Hebrew) of the eldest of the daughters of Job, born to him towards the end of his life when his prosperity had been restored (Job 42:14). The name was common in the first part of the 19th cent., and has continued in modest use since then. Recently the name of Job's second daughter, KEZIA, has been taken up by parents looking for an unusual name, but that of the youngest, *Keren-happuch*, meaning 'Horn of paint', has remained intractable.

**Jenkin** /'dʒenkɪn/ (*m.*) From the English surname, which is derived from the medieval English given name *Jankin*. This was a pet form of JOHN, probably introduced by migrants from the Low Countries and composed of Low German *Jan* and the diminutive suffix *-kin* (cf. JACK). The modern given name is comparatively popular in Wales, where the surname *Jenkins* also predominates.

**Jenna** /'dʒenə/ (*f.*) Fanciful alteration, with the Latinate feminine ending *-a*, of JENNY.

**Jennifer** /'dʒenɪfə/ (*f.*) Of Celtic (Arthurian) origin: Cornish form of the name of King Arthur's unfaithful wife (see GUINEVERE). At the beginning of the 20th cent., the name was merely a Cornish curiosity, but since then it has become enormously popular all over the English-speaking world. One factor in its rise was probably Bernard Shaw's use of it for the character of Jennifer Dubedat in *The Doctor's Dilemma* (1905). See also GAYNOR.

**Jenny** /'dʒɛni:/ (*f.*) Although now universally taken as
a short form of JENNIFER, this name in fact existed
during the Middle Ages as a pet form of JEAN. It is
also often spelled **Jennie** and occasionally **Jenni**.

**Jeremy** /'dʒɛrəmi:/ (*m.*) Old Testament: Anglicized
form (used once in the Authorized Version of the
Bible) of the name (meaning 'Appointed by God' in
Hebrew) *Jeremiah* (Greek *Iēremaias*). This was the
name of the great biblical prophet whose history is
told in the book of Jeremiah.

**Jerome** /dʒə'rəum/ (*m.*) From early Christian tradition: Anglicized form of the Greek name *Hieronymos*, composed of the elements *hieros* holy + *onoma*
name. St Jerome (c. 342–420) was a citizen of the
Eastern Empire of Rome who bore the Greek names
Eusebios Hieronymos Sophronios; he was chiefly
responsible for the translation into Latin of the Bible,
on which he also wrote many works of commentary
and exposition.

**Jerrold** /'dʒɛrəld/ (*m.*) From an English surname,
derived from the Norman given name GERALD, or a
fanciful respelling of the latter.

**Jerry** /'dʒɛri:/ (*m., f.*) As a boy's name, a pet form of
JEREMY and GERALD, and occasionally of GERARD and
JEROME. It is occasionally found as a girl's name, a
variant of GERRY.

**Jess** /dʒɛs/ (*f., m.*) Usually a girl's name, a short form
of JESSIE or JESSICA. As a boy's name, it is a simplified
form of JESSE, or occasionally an independent name.

**Jesse** /'dʒɛsi:/ (*m.*) Old Testament: name (apparently
meaning 'Gift' in Hebrew) of the father of King
David (I Sam. 16), from whose line (according to the
New Testament) Jesus was ultimately descended. It
was popular among the Puritans and is still used fairly
frequently in America, more rarely in Britain.

**Jessica** /ˈdʒɛsɪkə/ (*f.*) Apparently of Shakespearian origin: name of the daughter of Shylock in *The Merchant of Venice*. Shakespeare's source has not been discovered, but he presumably intended it as a typically Jewish name. It may be from the biblical name (of obscure origin) which appeared in the translations available in Shakespeare's day as *Jesca* (later as *Iscah* in the Authorized Version; Gen. 11:29).

**Jessie** /ˈdʒɛsi/ (*f.*) Apparently originally a Scottish pet form of JEAN, although the derivation is not clear. It is now sometimes used as a given name in its own right, or as a short form of JESSICA.

**Jethro** /ˈdʒɛθrəʊ/ (*m.*) Old Testament: name of the father of Moses's wife Zipporah (Exod. 3:1, 4:18). It seems to be a variant of the name *Ithra* (apparently meaning 'Excellence' in Hebrew), which also occurs in the Bible (II Sam. 18:25). It was popular with the Puritans, but then fell out of general use and was mainly associated with the agricultural reformer Jethro Tull (1674–1741). In 1968 a 'progressive rock' group in Britain adopted the name 'Jethro Tull', and shortly afterwards the given name *Jethro* enjoyed a revival of popularity.

**Jill** /dʒɪl/ (*f.*) Short form (respelled) of GILLIAN, also often used as an independent name. It was already used as a typical girl's name in the phrase 'Jack and Jill' by the 15th cent.

**Jim** /dʒɪm/ (*m.*) Short form of JAMES, already common in the Middle Ages.

**Jimmy** /ˈdʒɪmi/ (*m.*) Pet form of JIM, also found in the spelling **Jimmie**.

**Jo** /dʒəʊ/ (*f., m.*) Usually a girl's name, a short form of JOANNA, JOANNE, JODY, or JOSEPHINE, sometimes used in combination with other names, for example *Nancy Jo* and *Jo Anne* (see JOANNE). Its popularity as

a girl's name was influenced by the character of Jo
March in Louisa M. Alcott's *Little Women* (1868).
Occasionally it is a boy's name, a variant of JOE.

**Joachim** /ˈdʒəʊəkɪm/ (*m.*) Of Jewish origin: derived,
directly or indirectly, from Hebrew *Johoiachin* or
*Jehoiahim* 'Established by God', the name of a king
of Judah mentioned in the Old Testament. In medieval Christian tradition, this is the name commonly
ascribed to the father of the Virgin Mary. (Other
names assigned to him include *Cleopas*, *Eliachim*,
*Heli*, *Jonahir*, and *Sadoc*.) He is not named at all in
the Bible, but with the growth of the cult of Mary
many legends grew up about her early life, and her
parents came to be venerated as saints under the
names *Joachim* and ANNE. It has always been more
popular as a given name in Europe than in the English-speaking world.

**Joan** /dʒəʊn/ (*f.*) The usual feminine form of JOHN in
Middle English, representing a contracted form of
Old French *Jo(h)anne*, Late Latin *Johanna*, which
was coined as a feminine equivalent of *Johannes*. In
the 17th cent. it was largely replaced by JANE, but was
revived in the 20th cent.

**Joanna** /dʒəʊˈænə/ (*f.*) Latinate form of JOAN, regularly found in medieval documents, but only used as a
given name in its own right since the 19th cent.

**Joanne** /dʒəʊˈæn/ (*f.*) Old French feminine form of
JOHN, which gave rise to the simplified English spelling JOAN. This form, with its more markedly feminine
spelling, was revived in the early 20th cent. It has to
some extent been influenced by the independently
formed combination *Jo Anne*.

**Job** /dʒəʊb/ (*m.*) Old Testament: name of the eponymous hero of the book of Job, a man of exemplary
patience, whose faith was severely tested by God's

apparently motiveless maltreatment of him. His name, appropriately enough, means 'Persecuted' in Hebrew. His story was a favourite one in the Middle Ages and formed the subject of miracle plays.

**Jocasta** /dʒɔ'kæstə/ (*f.*) From classical legend: name of the mother of Oedipus, King of Thebes. As the result of a series of misunderstandings, she also became his wife and the mother of his children. The derivation of her name is not known. In spite of its tragic associations, the name has enjoyed a certain vogue in recent years. The names of her daughters, *Antigone* and *Ismene*, have been occasionally used since the Middle Ages, but there has been no move to take up those of her sons, *Eteocles* and *Polynices*.

**Jocelyn** /'dʒɒsəlɪn/ (*f.*, *m.*) Now normally a girl's name, but in earlier times more often given to boys. It represents a transferred use of the English surname, which in turn is derived from a masculine personal name introduced to Britain by the Normans in the form *Joscelin*. This was of Germanic origin, ultimately derived from the name of a Germanic tribe, the *Gauts*. The form was altered because it was taken as a double diminutive of a personal name *Josce* (see JOYCE).

**Jock** /dʒɒk/ (*m.*) Variant of JACK, now generally associated with Scotland to the extent that it stands as an archetypal nickname for a Scotsman.

**Jodie** /'dʒəʊdi:/ (*f.*) Variant of JODY, occasionally also spelt **Jodi**.

**Jody** /'dʒəʊdi:/ (*f.*, *m.*) Of uncertain origin. It may be a pet form of JUDITH and JUDE, but if so the reason for the change in the vowel is not clear. Alternatively, it may be a playful elaboration of JO and JOE, with -*d*-introduced for euphony before the diminutive suffix -*ie*.

**Joe** /dʒəʊ/ (*m.*) Short form of JOSEPH.

**Joel** /'dʒəʊəl/ (*m.*) Old Testament: name of a minor prophet, composed of two different elements in Hebrew, *Yah* and *El*, both of which mean 'God'. This was very popular among the Puritans, and is still occasionally used in America. In Britain it seems to have dropped out of common use at present.

**John** /dʒɒn/ (*m.*) New Testament: from Greek *Ioannes*, Latin *Johannes*, contracted forms of the Hebrew name *Johanan* 'God is gracious'. *John* is the spelling used in the Authorized Version of the Bible. The name has been borne by John the Baptist, John the Evangelist, and several hundred other Christian saints. In its numerous European forms, including French *Jean*, Italian *Giovanni*, Spanish *Juan*, German *Hans*, Dutch *Jan*, and Russian *Ivan*, the name has for centuries been the commonest of all boys' names in the Christian world.

**Johnny** /'dʒɒnɪ/ (*m.*, *f.*) Pet form of JOHN. It is not often used as a genuinely independent boy's given name, except in America, where it is occasionally also used as a girl's name.

**Jolene** /dʒəʊ'liːn, 'dʒəʊlɪn/ (*f.*) Of recent origin: a combination of the short form JO with the productive suffix *-lene*, extracted from names such as MARLENE; it seems to have originated in America in the 1940s and has been made famous by the song with this title, a hit for the country singer Dolly Parton in 1979.

**Jolyon** /'dʒɒlɪ:ən/ (*m.*) Medieval variant spelling of JULIAN. Its occasional use in modern Britain derives from the name of a character in John Galsworthy's sequence of novels *The Forsyte Saga* (1922), serialized on television in the late 1960s.

**Jon** /'dʒɒn/ (*m.*) Variant spelling of JOHN or short form of JONATHAN.

**Jonah** /ˈdʒəʊnə/ (*m.*) Old Testament: name (meaning 'Dove' in Hebrew) of a prophet whose adventures are the subject of one of the shorter books of the Bible. God appeared to Jonah and ordered him to go and preach in Nineveh. When Jonah disobeyed, God caused a storm to threaten the ship in which Jonah was travelling. His shipmates, realizing that Jonah was the cause of their peril, threw him overboard, whereupon the storm subsided. A great fish swallowed Jonah, and delivered him willy-nilly to the coasts of Nineveh. This story was immensely popular in the Middle Ages, and a favourite subject of miracle plays.

**Jonas** /ˈdʒəʊnəs/ (*m.*) New Testament: Greek form of the Old Testament (Hebrew) name JONAH. The spelling **Jona** is also occasional.

**Jonathan** /ˈdʒɒnəθən/ (*m.*) Old Testament: name composed of the same Hebrew elements ('God' and 'gift') as MATTHEW, but in reverse order. It was borne by several biblical characters, most notably by a son of King Saul, who was an inseparable friend of the young David, even when David and Saul were themselves at loggerheads (I Sam. 31; II Sam. 1:19–26).

**Joni** /ˈdʒəʊniː/ (*f.*) Modern respelling of *Joanie*, pet form of JOAN. It is more or less confined to America, and is particularly associated with the Canadian folk singer Joni Mitchell (b. 1943).

**Jonquil** /ˈdʒɒnkwɪl/ (*f.*) From the name of the flower, which was taken into English from French *jonquille* (a diminutive of Spanish *junco*, Latin *juncus* reed). This is one of the latest and rarest of the flower names, which enjoyed a brief vogue during the 1940s and 1950s.

**Jordan** /ˈdʒɔːdən/ (*m.*) From medieval Christian tradition: a name often given to children (of both sexes) who were baptized with water (allegedly) from the River Jordan in the Holy Land. It was in this river, whose Hebrew name means 'Flowing down', that Christ was baptized by John the Baptist, and medieval pilgrims to the Holy Land often brought back a flask of its water as a holy symbol. The modern given name is either a revival of this, or else an application of the surname, itself from the medieval given name.

**José** /'həʊzeɪ; *Spanish* xo'se/ (*m.*) Spanish version of JOSEPH, now occasionally used as a given name in English-speaking countries.

**Joseph** /'dʒəʊzɪf/ (*m.*) Old Testament: name (meaning '(God) shall add (another son)' in Hebrew) of the son of Jacob who became chief steward to Pharaoh in Egypt (Gen. 30). In the New Testament it is the name of the husband of the Virgin Mary. It was also borne by Joseph of Arimathea (Matt. 27:57, Mark 15:43, Luke 23:50, John 19:38), who according to legend brought the Holy Grail to Britain (for the Grail legend, see PERCIVAL).

**Josephine** /'dʒəʊzəfi:n/ (*f.*) French feminine diminutive of JOSEPH.

**Josette** /dʒəʊ'zɛt/ (*f.*) French pet form of JOSEPHINE, occasionally used in the English-speaking world since World War II.

**Josh** /dʒɒʃ/ (*m.*) Short form of JOSHUA, occasionally used as an independent given name.

**Joshua** /'dʒɒʃjuːə/ (*m.*) Old Testament: name (meaning 'God is salvation' in Hebrew) of a major prophet. Other forms of the same name are Hebrew *Jehoshua*(*h*), *Jeshua*, *Hosea*, *Oshea*, and the Greek *Iēsos* (*Jesus*). These are rare or non-existent as given names in the English-speaking world, but *Jesus* is common in Spain and Portugal.

**Josiah** /dʒəʊ'zaɪə/ (*m.*) Old Testament: name (apparently meaning 'God heals' in Hebrew) of a king of Judah, whose story is recounted in II Kings 22–23. It was fairly frequently used as a first name in the English-speaking world from the 18th to the early 20th cent.; the most famous bearer is probably the potter Josiah Wedgwood (1730–95).

**Josie** /'dʒəʊzi:/ (f.) Pet form of JOSEPHINE, occasionally used as an independent given name in the 20th cent.

**Joss** /dʒɒs/ (f., m.) Short form of JOCELYN.

**Joy** /dʒɔɪ/ (f.) From the English vocabulary word (from Old French *joie*, Late Latin *gaudia*). Being 'joyful in the Lord' was a duty that the Puritans took very seriously, so the name became popular in the 17th cent. under their influence. In modern times the name is most often given with the intention of wishing the child a happy life (cf. HAPPY and MERRY).

**Joyce** /dʒɔɪs/ (f.) Norman: of Celtic origin. The Norman form *Josce* was a boy's name, derived from *Jodocus*, a Latinized form of a Celtic name meaning 'Lord', which was borne by a 7th-cent. Breton saint. Though the given name was fairly common in the Middle Ages, its modern use may represent the surname derived from it. The name is now nearly always a girl's name.

**Juan** /'dʒuːən; *Spanish* xwan/ (m.) Spanish version of JOHN, now occasionally used as a given name in English-speaking countries.

**Juanita** /dʒuːə'niːtə; *Spanish* xwa'niːtə/ (f.) Spanish feminine diminutive of JUAN. It is now occasionally used in the English-speaking world, to which it was introduced mainly by Hispanic settlers in the U.S.

**Judah** /'dʒuːdə/ (m.) A popular Jewish name, also used among Christians, of Old Testament origin: possibly meaning 'Praised' in Hebrew. This was the name of the fourth son of Jacob (Gen. 29:35), who gave his name to one of the twelve tribes of Israel and to one of its two kingdoms.

**Judas** /'dʒuːdəs/ (*m.*) New Testament: Greek form of JUDAH. This is borne in the New Testament by several characters, but most notably by Judas Iscariot, the apostle who betrayed Christ in the Garden of Gethsemane. There was another apostle called *Judas* (see JUDE), and the name was also borne by Judas Maccabbaeus, who liberated Judea briefly from the Syrians in 165 BC, but was killed in battle (161). His story was very popular in the Middle Ages. However, the association with Iscariot has ensured that this name has hardly ever been bestowed as a Christian name, and that *Jude* has always been much rarer than other apostles' names.

**Jude** /dʒuːd/ (*m.*) Short form of JUDAS, occasionally adopted in the New Testament and elsewhere in an attempt to distinguish the apostle Jude (Judas Thaddaeus), author of an Epistle in the New Testament, from Judas Iscariot. The name took a further knock from Thomas Hardy's gloomy novel *Jude the Obscure* (1895), but more recently received some support from the Lennon and McCartney song 'Hey Jude' (1968).

**Judith** /'dʒuːdɪθ/ (*f.*) Old Testament: name of one of the Hittite wives of Esau (Gen. 26:34), probably connected etymologically with JUDE. The name was occasionally used on the Continent in the early Middle Ages, at least in aristocratic circles (it was borne by a niece of William the Conqueror), but was not taken up in England until the 17th cent.

**Judy** /'dʒuːdiː/ (*f.*) Pet form of JUDITH, now sometimes regarded as an independent name.

**Jules** (*m.*, now sometimes also *f.*) /*m.* dʒuːlz, *French* ʒyl; *f.* dʒuːlz/ As a boy's name, this is a French version of JULIUS, commonly used as a first name in France and occasionally also in the English-speaking world. It is also used, pronounced with an English *J*-, as a jocular pet form of JULIAN and, as a girl's name, of JULIE.

**Julia** /'dʒuːlɪə/ (*f.*) Latin: feminine form of the old Roman family name JULIUS. The name was borne by various early saints, but was not used in England before the 18th cent.

**Julian** /'dʒuːlɪən/ (*m.*; occasionally *f.*) From the common Late Latin name *Juliānus*, a derivative of JULIUS. For many centuries it was borne in this form by women as well as men, for example by the Blessed Julian of Norwich (*c.* 1342–after 1413), and the formal differentiation of *Julian* and GILLIAN did not occur until at least the end of the Middle Ages. *Julian* is still occasionally used as a girl's name.

**Juliana** /dʒuːlɪˈɑnə/ (*f.*) Latin feminine form of *Juliānus* (see JULIAN), which was revived in the 18th cent. and has been used occasionally ever since.

**Julie** /'dʒuːliː/ (*f.*) French form of JULIA, which has been used in the English-speaking world only since the 1920s, but has now become enormously popular.

**Juliet** /'dʒuːlɪet/ (*f.*) Anglicized form of French *Juliette* or Italian *Giulietta*, diminutives of the national forms of JULIA. The name is most famous as that of the 'star-crossed' young heroine of Shakespeare's tragedy *Romeo and Juliet*.

**Julius** /'dʒuːlɪəs/ (*m.*) Latin: an old Roman family name (of obscure derivation), borne most notably by Gaius Julius Caesar (?102 BC–44 BC). It is now often found as a Jewish name, having on occasions been chosen as a substitute for any of the numerous Hebrew names transliterated with an initial *J*-.

**June** /dʒuːn/ (*f.*) The most successful and enduring of the names coined in the early 20th cent. from the names of months of the year (cf. APRIL and MAY).

**Justin** /'dʒʊstɪn/ (*m.*) Anglicized form of Latin *Justīnus*, a derivative of *Justus*, which means 'Just' or 'Fair'. It was borne by various early saints, notably a 2nd-cent. Christian apologist and a (possibly spurious) boy martyr of the 3rd cent.

**Justine** /dʒʊs'tiːn; *French* ʒys'tiːn/ (*f.*) French feminine form of JUSTIN, whose popularity in Britain since the 1960s is no doubt partly due to the influence of Lawrence Durrell's novel of this name. The Latin form **Justina** is also occasionally used.

# K

**Karen** /'kærən/ (*f.*) Danish and Norwegian short form of KATHERINE, first introduced to the English-speaking world by Scandinavian settlers in America. It has been used in Britain only since the 1950s, but has become very popular.

**Karin** /'kærɪn/ (*f.*) Swedish short form of KATHERINE, found as a less common variant of KAREN in America and Britain.

**Kate** /keɪt/ (*f.*) Short form of KATHERINE (or any of its variant spellings), reflecting the French pronunciation with *t* for *th*, which was also usual in medieval England. This short form has been continuously popular since the Middle Ages. It was used by Shakespeare for two important characters: the daughter of the King of France who is wooed and won by King Henry V, and the 'shrew' in *The Taming of the Shrew*.

**Kath** /kæθ/ (*f.*) Modern short form of KATHERINE (and its variants).

**Katharine** /'kæθrɪn/ (*f.*) Variant of KATHERINE, the preferred form in the U.S. The spelling has been affected by folk-etymological association with Greek *katharos* pure.

**Katherine** /'kæθrɪn/ (*f.*) From early Christian tradition: name of a saint martyred at Alexandria in 307. The earliest sources that mention her are written in Greek and give the name in the form *Aikaterinē* (still the modern Greek form, reflected also in Russian *Yekaterina*). The name is of unknown origin; it may be derived from that of *Hecate*, the classical goddess of magic and enchantment. From an early date, however, it was affected by association with Greek *katharos* pure, leading to spellings with *th* and a change in the middle vowel (see KATHARINE).

**Kathleen** /'kæθliːn/ (*f.*) Of Irish origin: Anglicized form of Gaelic CAITLÍN.

**Kathryn** /'kæθrɪn/ (*f.*) American form of KATHERINE, now the most common spelling in the U.S. It seems to have originated as a deliberate alteration for the sake of distinction, perhaps influenced by the suffix *-lyn* (see LYNN).

**Katie** /'keɪtiː/ Pet form of KATE, with the hypocoristic suffix *-ie*. The spelling **Katy** is also found.

**Katrina** /kə'triːnə/ (*f.*) Anglicized spelling of CATRIONA.

**Katrine** /kə'triːn; *German* kə'triːnə/ (*f.*) German short form of KATHERINE, now occasionally used in Britain.

**Kay** /keɪ/ (*f.*, *m.*) As a girl's name, a pet form of any of the various names beginning with the letter *K-* (cf. DEE and JAY), most notably KATHERINE and its variants. It is comparatively rare as a boy's name; the male use presumably originated in honour of the Arthurian knight so called, although Sir Kay is not a particularly attractive character. His name seems to be a Celticized form of Latin *Gaius*, an old Roman given name of uncertain derivation.

**Keith** /kiːθ/ (*m.*) From a Scottish surname, derived from lands in the former county of East Lothian, which probably get their name from a Gaelic element meaning 'wood'. It is now found as a given name throughout the English-speaking world.

**Kelly** /'kɛliː/ (*m.*, *f.*) A 20th-cent. coinage from the Irish surname *Kelly*, an Anglicized form of Gaelic *Ó Ceallaigh* 'descendant of Ceallach'. *Ceallach* 'Strife' was the name of several shadowy Irish saints; there is a certain amount of confusion and duplication in standard hagiographical accounts of them.

**Kelvin** /ˈkɛlvɪn/ (m.) A modern given name, first found in the 1920s. It is taken from a Scottish river (cf. CLYDE) and its choice may have been influenced by names such as MELVIN and CALVIN.

**Ken** /kɛn/ (m.) Short form of KENNETH, or occasionally of various other boys' names with this first syllable..

**Kendrick** /ˈkɛndrɪk/ (m.) In some cases, from the English surname, derived from the Old English personal name *Cēneric*, composed of the elements *cēne* keen, bold + *rīc* power. In other cases it is a transferred use of the Scottish surname *Kendrick*, a shortened form of *McKendrick* (Gaelic *Mac Eanruig* 'Son of Henry').

**Kenelm** /ˈkɛnɛlm/ (m.) From an Old English personal name composed of the elements *cēne* keen, bold + *helm* helmet, protection. The name was popular in England during the Middle Ages, when a shadowy 9th-cent. Mercian prince of this name was widely revered as a saint and martyr, although his death seems to have been entirely the result of personal and political motives. It has remained in occasional use ever since.

**Kennedy** /ˈkɛnədiː/ (m.) From the common Irish surname, which represents an Anglicized form of Gaelic *Ó Ceanneidigh* 'descendant of Ceanneidigh', a byname meaning 'Armoured head'. In recent years the given name has sometimes been chosen in honour of the assassinated American statesmen President John F. Kennedy (1917–63) and his brother Robert Kennedy (1925–68).

**Kenneth** /ˈkɛnɪθ/ (m.) Of Scottish origin, representing an Anglicized form of the Gaelic name COINNEACH, an ancient personal name meaning 'born of Fire'.

**Kenny** /ˈkɛniː/ (m.) Pet form of KEN, or else a trans-

ferred use of the Irish surname *Kenny*, which is an
Anglicized form of Gaelic *Ó Cionnaidh* 'descendant
of *Cionnadh*'. Cionnadh is an old personal name
meaning 'born of Fire' (cf. KENNETH).

**Kent** /kɛnt/ (*m.*) From the English surname, originally
used to denote people from this county. The county
seems to have got its name from a Celtic element
meaning 'border'. Its use as a given name is of recent
origin.

**Kerr** /kɜː/ (*m.*) From the English surname, originally a
Northern English toponymic name for someone who
lived by a patch of wet brushwood (from Old Norse
*kjarr* brushwood). Its use as a given name is of recent
origin.

**Kerry** /'kɛri/ (*f.*, *m.*) Of Australian origin, but uncertain derivation (perhaps a respelling of CERI or a variant of KELLY). It is now becoming relatively common
in Britain, especially as a girl's name.

**Kevin** /'kɛvɪn/ (*m.*) Of Irish origin: an Anglicized form
of Old Irish **Caoimhghin**, modern **Caoimhín**
/'kiːvjɪnj/, a personal name meaning 'Handsome
born'. This was the name of a 7th-cent. saint who is
one of the patrons of Dublin.

**Kezia** /'kiːzɪə/ (*f.*) Old Testament: name of one of
Job's daughters, born to him towards the end of his
life, after his prosperity had been restored (Job
42:14). It represents the Hebrew word for the *cassia*
tree (named in English, via Latin and Greek, from a
similar Semitic source). The name is used in the English-speaking world rather less frequently than
JEMIMA, but considerably more so than *Keren-
happuch*, the name of Job's third daughter.

**Kieran** /'kɪərən/ (*m.*) Of Irish origin: an Anglicized
form of CIARÁN.

**Kilian** /'kɪlɪən/ (*m.*) Of Irish origin, representing an

Anglicized form of CILLIAN. The name was born by various early Irish saints, including the 7th-cent. author of a Life of St Bridget, and missionaries to Artois and Franconia.

**Kim** /kɪm/ (f., m.) Originally a boy's name, a short form of KIMBERLEY, but now much more common than the latter, and nearly always given to girls. It is now established as an independent name in its own right. The (male) hero of Rudyard Kipling's novel *Kim* (1901) bore the name as a short form of *Kimball* (a surname used as a given name).

**Kimberley** /ˈkɪmbəlɪ/ (f., m.) Not a common name for boys or girls, but still regarded by some as the full form of KIM, of which it is the source. Its history is complicated, in that it is from a place name, from a surname, from a place name. The immediate source is the town in South Africa, the scene of fighting during the Boer War, which brought it to public notice at the end of the 19th cent. The town was named after a certain Lord Kimberley, whose ancestors were associated with one of the places in England called Kimberley. The first part of the place name derives from various Old English personal names; the second (from Old English *lēah*) means 'clearing' or 'meadow'.

**King** /kɪŋ/ (m.) From the vocabulary word for a monarch, bestowed, especially in the U.S., with a hint of the notion that the bearer would have kingly qualities; cf. DUKE and EARL. In some cases it may be a transferred use of the surname (originally a nickname or an occupational name given to someone who was employed in a royal household). Its frequency has increased recently among American Blacks, no doubt partly as a result of its being bestowed in honour of the civil rights leader Martin Luther King (1929–68).

**Kingsley** /ˈkɪŋzlɪ/ (m., f.) From an English surname,

derived from various places (Cheshire, Hampshire, Staffs.), named in Old English as *Cyninglesēah* 'king's wood'. It is not clear what was the first impulse towards use as a given name; the usual pattern in such cases is for the mother's maiden name to be chosen as a given name, but in this case the choice may have been made in honour of the author Charles Kingsley (1819–75).

**Kirk** /kɜːk/ (*m.*) From the surname, originally a Northern English and Scottish topographic name for someone who lived near a church (from Old Norse *kirkjr*). Recent use is probably partly influenced by the adopted name of the film actor Kirk Douglas, born in 1916 as Issur Danielovich Demsky.

**Kirsten** /ˈkɜːstən/ (*f.*) Danish and Norwegian form of CHRISTINE, now well established in English-speaking countries.

**Kirstie** /ˈkɜːstiː/ (*f.*) Scottish pet form of CHRISTINE, now quite commonly used as an independent given name in the rest of the English-speaking world as well as in Scotland. The spelling **Kirsty** is also found.

**Kit** /kɪt/ (*m., f.*) As a boy's name, a pet form of CHRISTOPHER, based on a childish pronunciation. As a girl's name it is a pet form of KATHERINE, derived as an altered form of *Kat* or *Cat*.

**Kitty** /ˈkɪtiː/ (*f.*) Pet form of KATHERINE, derived from the pet form KIT + the diminutive suffix -*y*.

**Krystle** /ˈkrɪstəl/ (*f.*) Fanciful respelling of CRYSTAL.

**Kurt** /kɜːt; *German* kʊrt/ (*m.*) From German: originally a contracted form of *Konrad* (see CONRAD), but now very common as a given name in its own right. It is also spelled **Curt**.

**Kyle** /kaɪl/ (*m., f.*) From a Scottish surname, which originated as a local name from the region so called in the former country of Ayrshire (now part of Strath-clyde region).

**Kylie** /ˈkaili:/ (*f.*) Of Australian origin: said to represent an Aboriginal term for the boomerang, but in view of the inappropriateness of this meaning it seems more likely that the name is an artificial invention influenced by KYLE and KELLY. It is extremely popular in Australia, and is gradually coming into use in the rest of the English-speaking world.

# L

**Lachlan** /'læxlən/ (*m.*) Of Scottish origin, normally used only by those who have some connection with Scotland. The name (Gaelic **Lachla(i)nn** /'laxlɪɲ/, earlier **Lochlann**) referred originally to a migrant from Scandinavia, the 'land of the lochs'.

**Lalage** /'lælədʒi:/ (*f.*) From classical literature: derived from Greek *lalagein* to chatter, babble. It was used by Horace in one of his Odes as the name of his beloved of the moment; presumably it was not her real name, but a literary pseudonym.

**Lally** /'læli:/ (*f.*) Pet form of LALAGE or else simply a name taken from a child's babbling. The forms **Lallie**, **Lalla**, and **Lala** are also found.

**Lambert** /'læmbət/ (*m.*) Of Germanic origin, composed of the elements *land* land, territory + *berht* famous, and first introduced to Britain by the Normans. Its frequency in the Middle Ages, however, was mainly due to its popularity among immigrants from the Low Countries (who came to England in connection with the cloth trades). St Lambert of Maastricht was a 7th-cent. saint who aided St Willibrord in his evangelical work.

**Lana** /'lɑːnə/ (*f.*) Of uncertain origin, perhaps an anagram of ALAN or an aphetic form of ALANA. It seems to have been first used by the film actress Lana Turner (b. 1920), whose original name was *Julia*. Her example has not been much imitated.

**Lance** /lɑːns/ (*m.*) Norman: from Old French *Lance*, from the Germanic name *Lanzo*, a short form of various compound names with the first element *land* land, territory (cf., e.g., LAMBERT), but it was early associated with Old French *lance*, the weapon (from Latin *lancea*). In modern use the given name seems to have originated as a transferred use of the surname derived from the medieval given name, although it is also commonly taken to be a short form of LANCELOT.

**Lancelot** /ˈlɑːnsəlɒt/ (*m.*) From Arthurian romance: the name borne by one of King Arthur's best and most valued knights, who eventually betrayed his trust by becoming the lover of Queen Guinevere. The name is of uncertain origin, probably, like other Arthurian names, of Celtic derivation but heavily distorted by mediation through French sources. The modern given name is in many cases no more than an elaboration of LANCE.

**Lara** /ˈlɑːrə/ (*f.*) Russian short form of *Larissa*, introduced to the English-speaking world in the early 20th cent. and made popular as the name of a character in Boris Pasternak's *Dr Zhivago* (1957). *Larissa* is itself of uncertain derivation; it is the name of an early Greek martyr venerated in the Eastern Church.

**Larry** /ˈlærɪ/ (*m.*) Pet form of LAURENCE or LAWRENCE, frequently used as an independent given name, especially in America.

**Laura** /ˈlɔːrə/ (*f.*) Feminine form of the Late Latin name *Laurus* 'Laurel'. St Laura was a 9th-cent. Spanish nun who met her death in a cauldron of molten lead. Current use of the given name in the English-speaking world dates from the 19th cent., when it was probably imported from Italy. It had long been common there as a result of the fame of Petrarch's sonnets to his beloved Laura.

**Laurel** /ˈlɒrəl/ (*f.*) From the English vocabulary word for the tree (Middle English *lorel*, a dissimilated form of Old French *lorer*), probably influenced by the popularity of LAURA.

**Lauren** /ˈlɒrən/ (*f.*) A name apparently first brought to public attention by the film actress Lauren Bacall (born Betty Joan Perske in 1924). It seems to have been modelled on LAURENCE.

**Laurence** /'lɒrəns/ (*m.*) From a French form of Latin *Laurentius* 'man from Laurentum'. Laurentum was a town in Latium, which may have got its name from Latin *laurus* laurel, or it may alternatively be of pre-Roman origin. The given name was popular in the Middle Ages as a result of the fame of a 3rd-cent. saint allegedly roasted to death on a gridiron. In England it was also associated with the 9th-cent. St Laurence of Canterbury, who fought against pagan backsliding among his flock. See also LAWRENCE.

**Lauretta** /lə'retə/ (*f.*) Italian diminutive form of LAURA; cf. LORETTA.

**Laurie** /'lɒri:/ (*f., m.*) Pet form of LAURA, LAUREL, or LAURENCE. The spelling **Lawrie** (from the full form LAWRENCE) is also found as a male name.

**Lavinia** /lə'vɪnɪə/ (*f.*) From Roman mythology: name of the wife of Aeneas, and thus the mother of the Roman people. According to legend she gave her name to the Latin town of Lavinium, but in fact she was almost certainly invented to explain the place name, which is of pre-Roman origin. She was said to be the daughter of King Latinus, likewise, no doubt, invented to account for the name of *Latium* itself.

**Lawrence** /'lɒrəns/ (*m.*) Anglicized spelling of LAURENCE; the usual spelling of the surname, and now becoming increasingly common as a given name, especially in the U.S.

**Lazarus** /'læzərəs/ (*m.*) New Testament: the name borne by two different characters, the brother of Martha and Mary, who was raised from the dead by Jesus (John 11:1–44), and the beggar who appears in the parable of Dives and Lazarus narrated by Jesus (Luke 16:19–31). The form *Lazarus*, used in the

Authorized Version, is a Latinate version of Greek
*Lazaros*, itself an adaptation of Hebrew *Eleazar*
'God is my help'. Because the beggar Lazarus was
'full of sores' the name was often used in the Middle
Ages as a generic term for a leper, and so came to be
avoided as a given name. It is still not common.

**Leah** /'lɪə/ (f.) Old Testament: name (meaning 'Lan-
guid' in Hebrew) of the elder sister of Rachel (Gen.
29:23). Jacob served her father Laban for seven years
in return for the hand of Rachel but was deceived
into marrying Leah first, and had to labour seven
more years to get Rachel. The name was adopted by
the Puritans in the 17th cent., but has never been particularly common.

**Leander** /lɪ'ændə/ (m.) From classical mythology:
Latin form of Greek *Leandros*, which is composed of
the elements *leōn* lion + *anēr* man (genitive *andros*).
Leander swam across the Hellespont every night to
visit his beloved Hero and back again in the morning,
but was eventually drowned during a violent storm.
In modern times, the name seems sometimes to have
been used as an elaboration of the boy's name LEE.

**Lee** /liː/ (m., f.) From the English surname, derived
from any of numerous places so called from Old English *lēah* wood. It is especially popular now in America, where it has sometimes been bestowed in honour
of the Confederate general Robert E. Lee (1807–70).
As a girl's name, it may also be a variant of LEAH.

**Leighton** /'leɪtən/ (m.) From the English surname,
derived from any of several places named with the
Old English elements *lēac* leek + *tūn* enclosure,
settlement, of which the best known is Leighton Buz-
zard in Beds. The name is sometimes found in the
spelling **Layton**, reflecting its pronunciation.

**Leila** /'liːlə, 'leɪlə, 'laɪlə/ (f.) Of Arabic origin, now fairly common in Britain, having been used both by Byron, in *The Giaour* (1813) and *Don Juan* (1819–24), and by Lord Lytton in his novel *Leila* (1838), as a name for an oriental beauty. It means 'Night', apparently referring to a dark complexion.

**Lemuel** /'lemjuːəl/ (*m.*) Old Testament: name (possibly meaning 'devoted to God' in Hebrew) of an obscure king who was lectured by his mother on the perils of strong drink and the virtues of a dutiful wife (Prov. 31). He is mentioned by Chaucer in *The Canterbury Tales*, where his name is carefully distinguished from the more familiar SAMUEL. Lemuel Gulliver was the unusual name of the hero of Jonathan Swift's *Gulliver's Travels* (1726).

**Len** /lɛn/ (*m.*) Short form of LEONARD, and possibly also occasionally of rarer given names such as LENNOX.

**Lena** /'liːnə/ (*f.*) Abstracted in the 19th cent. from various names ending in *-lena*, such as *Helena* (from HELEN) and *Magdalena* (from MAGDALENE).

**Lennox** /'lɛnəks/ (*m.*) From the Scottish surname, originally a place name, now also sometimes used as a given name. It is borne by the composer Sir Lennox Berkeley (b. 1903).

**Lenny** /'lɛniː/ (*m.*) Normally a diminutive of LEN, also to some extent used as an independent given name. Occasionally, however, it may represent the Scottish surname *Lennie*, *Len(n)y*, derived from the old lands of Leny in the parish of Callander, in the former county of Perthshire.

**Lenora** /lɪ'nɔːrə/ (*f.*) Originally a contracted form of LEONORA, although sometimes chosen as an expanded version of LENA. It is also spelled **Lennora** and occasionally **Len(n)orah**.

**Leo** /'liːəʊ/ (*m.*) From a Latin personal name, meaning

'Lion'. It was borne by a large number of early Christian saints, most notably Pope Leo the Great (?390–461). It is also found as a Jewish name (see LEON). In recent use it seems also to have been given as a kind of nickname by parents who wished for a 'lion-hearted' son.

**Leon** /'liːɒn/ (*m.*) French form of LEO (derived from the oblique form of the Latin name). This form is particularly common as a Jewish name. The lion is an important symbol among Jews because of Jacob's dying pronouncement that 'Judah is a lion's whelp' (Gen. 49:9).

**Leonard** /'lɛnəd/ (*m.*) Norman: of Germanic origin, composed of the elements *leon* lion (a late borrowing from Romance) + *hard* brave, strong. This was the name of a 5th-cent. Frankish saint, who became the patron of peasants and horses. Although it was introduced into Britain by the Normans, this name was not common during the Middle Ages. Its was revived during the 19th cent. and became very popular. It is also common as a Jewish name (cf. LEON).

**Leonie** /'liːəniː; *French* leo'niː/ (*f.*) French form of the Latin name *Leonia*, feminine of *Leonius*, derived from *leo* lion. It is most common among Jews as a feminine equivalent of LEO and LEON.

**Leonora** /liːə'nɔːrə/ (*f.*) Aphetic form of ELEONORA.

**Leopold** /'liːəpɒld/ (*m.*) Of Germanic origin, composed of the elements *liut* people + *bold* bold, brave. The first element was altered by association with Latin *leo* lion. A name of this form may have been introduced into Britain by the Normans, but if so it does not seem to have survived long. It was reintroduced from Germany towards the end of the 19th cent., partly in honour of King Leopold of the Belgians (1790–1865), the uncle of Queen Victoria, who was an influential adviser to her in her youth, and after whom she named one of her sons.

**Leroy** /'liːrɔɪ/ (*m.*) This is now considered a typical Black American given name, but it was formerly also extensively borne by White Americans. It is from a French nickname meaning 'The King', but why it should have become a popular given name in English is not clear. See also DELROY.

**Les** /lez/ (*m.*) Short form of LESLEY or *Leslie*, borne almost exclusively by males.

**Lesley** /'lezli/ (*f.*, *m.*) Of Scottish origin, from the surname or baronial name of the lands of Lesslyn. It is first recorded as a girl's name in a poem by Robert Burns; surnames seem to have been used as given names, and particularly as girls' names, earlier and more readily in Scotland than elsewhere. This form of the name is still generally given to girls, whereas the variant spelling of the surname **Leslie** has been used more for boys.

**Lester** /'lestə/ (*m.*) From the English surname, derived from the name of the city of Leicester. The place name is recorded in the 10th cent. as *Ligora cæster*, representing a British name of obscure origin plus the Old English term *cæster* 'Roman fort'.

**Lettice** /'letɪs/ (*f.*) Medieval English form of the Latin name *Laetitia* 'Happiness'. It was popular among the Victorians, but is now regarded as faintly risible (perhaps because of its similarity to the vocabulary word *lettuce*).

**Letty** /'leti/ (*f.*) Pet form of LETTICE.

**Levi** /'liːvaɪ/ (*m.*) Old Testament: the name seems to have meant 'Associate' in Hebrew, and was given by Jacob's wife Leah to her third son as an expression of her hope, 'Now this time will my husband be joined to me, because I have born him three sons: therefore was his name called Levi' (Gen. 29:34). From Levi descended the priestly caste of the Levites. Levi was also a byname of the Christian apostle and evangelist Matthew. In modern times the name is borne mostly by Jews and occasionally by revivalist Christians.

**Lew** /luː/ (*m.*) Short form of LEWIS or, occasionally, LLEWELLYN.

**Lewis** /ˈluːɪs/ (*m.*) A common English form, since the Middle Ages, of the Norman and French name LOUIS. In modern use it may also in part represent the surname which derives from this given name.

**Liam** /ˈliːəm/ (*m.*) Irish: aphetic shortened form of WILLIAM.

**Libby** /ˈlɪbi/ (*f.*) Pet form of ELIZABETH, based originally on a child's attempts to pronounce the name; it is now also used as an independent name.

**Liese** /ˈliːzə, ˈliːsə/ (*f.*) German short form of ELISABETH, now sometimes used as an independent given name in the English-speaking world. In Germany it is frequently used in the combination *Lieselotte* (with the second element from *Carlotte*).

**Lilian** /ˈlɪliən/ (*f.*) Of uncertain origin, first recorded in the late 16th cent., and probably derived from a nursery form of ELIZABETH. It is now sometimes regarded as a derivative of the flower name LILY, but this was not used as a given name in England until the 19th cent.

**Lillian** /ˈlɪliən/ (*f.*) Variant spelling of LILIAN, common especially in America.

**Lily** /ˈlɪli/ (*f.*) From the name of the flower (Latin *lilium*), regarded in Christian imagery as a symbol of purity.

**Lincoln** /ˈlɪŋkən/ (*m.*) From the English surname, derived from the name of the city of Lincoln. This is found in the 7th cent. as *Lindum colonia*, representing a British name probably meaning 'lake' and the Latin defining term *colonia* colony, settlement. As a given name it has sometimes been bestowed in honour of Abraham Lincoln (1809–65), 16th president of the U.S.

**Linda** /'lɪndə/ (*f.*) Of recent and somewhat uncertain origin. It seems to have arisen in the 19th cent. as an aphetic form of BELINDA. Alternatively, it may be derived from the Latinate forms of other Germanic girls' names ending in the element *lind* which means both 'lime-tree' and 'shield'. It has become enormously popular in the 20th cent.

**Lindon** /'lɪndən/ (*m.*) Variant spelling of LYNDON.

**Lindsey** /'lɪndzi:/ (*f.*, *m.*) From the Scottish surname, originally borne by a family who came from Lindsey in Lincolnshire. This place was named in Old English as the 'wetland (Old English *ey*) belonging to Lincoln'. It was first used as a male name, and this is still often the case in Scotland, but elsewhere it is nearly always now given to girls. The surname has a variant **Lindsay**, which is also used as a given name.

**Linnette** /lɪ'nɛt/ (*f.*) Variant spelling of LYNETTE.

**Linus** /'laɪnəs/ (*m.*) The name of two obscure figures in classical mythology, and at a later date that of the second pope. It is of unknown derivation. It has occasionally been used as a given name in America, but is now chiefly associated with a companion of the cartoon character Charlie Brown.

**Lionel** /'laɪənəl/ (*m.*) From a medieval diminutive of the Old French name LEON or of the Middle English nickname *Lion*.

**Lisa** /'li:sə/ (*f.*) Variant of LIZA, influenced by French *Lise* and German *Liese*.

**Lisette** /liː'zɛt/ (*f.*) French diminutive of *Lise*, which is itself a short form of ELISABETH.

**Livia** /'lɪvɪə/ (*f.*) In modern use often taken as a short form of OLIVIA, but originally a distinct name, a feminine form of the Roman family name *Livius*. This is of uncertain derivation, perhaps connected with *lividus* bluish.

**Liz** /lɪz/ (*f.*) The most common of all the various short forms of ELIZABETH.

**Liza** /'laɪzə, 'liːzə/ (*f.*) Short form of ELIZA (also found as LISA).

**Lizzie** /'lɪzɪ/ (*f.*) Diminutive of LIZ, with the hypocoristic suffix -*ie*. The spelling **Lizzy** is also found.

**Llewellyn** /luː'ɛlɪn/ (*m.*) Welsh: an altered form of *Llywelyn*, a name of uncertain derivation, borne in particular by Llywelyn ap Iorwerth (1173–1240) and his grandson Llywelyn ap Gruffydd (d. 1282), Welsh princes who for a time united the Welsh in North Wales and led opposition to the power of the Norman barons in South Wales and the borders. Various other spellings of the name are also found. It is normally used mainly by people who wish to draw attention to their Welsh nationality or ancestry. In some cases it is taken from the Welsh surname, which is itself from the Welsh first name.

**Lloyd** /lɔɪd/ (*m.*) From the Welsh surname, originally a nickname meaning 'Grey(-haired)' (Welsh *llwyd*); cf. FLOYD, which is more common as a given name.

**Lois** /'ləʊɪs/ (*f.*) New Testament: name of the grandmother of the Timothy to whom St Paul wrote two epistles. Both Timothy and his mother Eunice bore common Greek names, but *Lois* is hard to explain. It certainly has no connection with either LOUISE or ELOISE (which are both of Germanic origin), although it has often been taken to be associated with them in modern times.

**Lola** /'ləʊlə; *Spanish* 'lola/ (*f.*) Spanish: originally a nursery form of DOLORES.

**Lolita** /lə'liːtə/ (*f.*) Diminutive of LOLA. The name has been relatively common in America, with its large Hispanic population, but is now somewhat clouded by its association with Vladimir Nabokov's novel *Lolita* (1955). The Lolita of the title is the pubescent object of the narrator's desires and fantasies, and the name is now used as a generic term for any under-age sex-symbol.

**Lonnie** /'lɒniː/ (*m.*) Of uncertain origin, possibly a pet or Anglicized form of the Spanish name *Alonso*, but just as likely a variant of LENNIE. It is chiefly associated in Britain with the popular singer Lonnie Donegan, famous in the 1950s and 1960s.

**Loretta** /lə'retə/ (*f.*) Variant of LAURETTA, normally borne by Catholics, among whom it is associated with Loreto, a town in central Italy to which the Holy House of the Virgin in Nazareth is supposed to have been miraculously transported by angels in the 13th cent.

**Lori** /'lɒriː/ (*f.*) Pet form of LORRAINE or variant of LAURIE, also found in the spelling **Lorri**.

**Lorna** /'lɔːnə/ (*f.*) Invented by R. D. Blackmore for the heroine of his novel *Lorna Doone* (1869), who is eventually discovered to be in reality Lady Lorna Dugal, daughter of the Earl of Dugal. The name seems to be derived from the place name *Lorn*, ancestral seat of the McDougals.

**Lorraine** /lə'reɪn/ (*f.*) From a surname apparently originating in Scotland and referring to a migrant from the French province of Lorraine, which derives its name from the Germanic tribal name *Lotharingi* 'people of Lothar'. It was first used as a girl's given name in the 19th cent., and has recently become enormously popular, for reasons which are not at all clear.

**Lou** /luː/ (*m.*, *f.*) Pet form of LOUIS or, less commonly, LOUISE.

**Louella** /luːˈɛlə/ (*f.*) Modern coinage from the first element of LOUISE and the productive suffix -*ella* (an Italian or Latinate feminine diminutive and a name in its own right). It is also spelled **Luella**.

**Louis** /ˈluːiː; *French* lwi/ (*m.*) French form of the Germanic name *Ludwig* (composed of the elements *hlod* fame + *wig* war). From the Middle Ages, this was a hereditary name in French noble families who claimed descent from *Clovis* (another form of the same name), King of the Franks (?466–511). Among them were the Bourbons, kings of France from 1589 to 1793. In modern times, *Louis* is occasionally used in Britain, but the Anglicized form LEWIS is more common, whereas in America the reverse is true.

**Louisa** /luːˈiːzə/ (*f.*) Latinate form of LOUISE, first used in the 18th cent.

**Louise** /luːˈiːz/ (*f.*) French feminine form of LOUIS, introduced to England in the 17th cent.

**Lourdes** /lʊəd/ (*f.*) Borne almost exclusively by Roman Catholics, taken from the name of the place in southern France where a shrine was established after a young peasant girl, Bernardette Soubirous, had visions of the Virgin Mary and uncovered a healing spring in 1858. In recent times, Lourdes has become a major centre for pilgrimage, especially by people suffering from various illnesses or physical handicaps.

**Lovell** /ˈlʌvəl/ (*m.*) From the English surname, which originated in the Middle Ages from the Old (Nor-

# Lowell

man) French nickname *Louvel* wolf-cub, a diminutive of *lou* wolf.

**Lowell** /'ləʊəl/ (*m.*) From the surname of a well-known New England family, whose members included the poet Robert Lowell (1917–77). The surname is in fact a variant of LOVELL.

**Lucas** /'luːkəs/ (*m.*) Latin and hence English form of the Greek name *Loukas* 'Man from Lucania'. As a given name it is usually further Anglicized as LUKE. The form *Lucas* was often used in the Middle Ages in written documents in place of the spoken vernacular form *Luke*, hence the common surname *Lucas*. The modern first name may in part represent a transferred use of the surname, as well as a revival of the learned form; it is also found as an Anglicized form of various Eastern European equivalents.

**Lucetta** /luːˈsɛtə/ (*f.*) A fanciful elaboration of LUCIA or LUCY, formed with the productive suffix -*etta*, originally an Italian feminine diminutive suffix. The name seems to have originated in the English-speaking world in the 19th cent., and is not much used in Italy.

**Lucia** /luːˈsiːə/ (*f.*) Feminine form of the old Roman given name *Lucius*, which is probably ultimately a derivative of Latin *lux* light. St Lucia of Syracuse, who was martyred in 304, was a very popular saint in the Middle Ages; she is often represented in medieval art as blinded and with her eyes on a platter, but the tradition that she had her eyes put out seems to be based on nothing more than the association between light and eyes.

**Lucilla** /luːˈsɪlə/ (*f.*) Latin diminutive of LUCIA, borne by various early saints.

**Lucille** /luˈsiːl, *French* ly'si:/ (*f.*) French form of LUCILLA, popular especially in the Southern U.S.

**Lucinda** /luːˈsɪndə/ (*f.*) An early derivative of LUCIA,

with the addition of the productive suffix *-inda*. The
formation is first found in Cervantes's *Don Quixote*
(1605), but may also have been independently made
in English in the 18th cent.

**Lucretia** /luːˈkriːʃə/ (*f.*) Feminine form of the Roman
family name *Lucretius*, of unknown derivation. In
Roman legend, it is the name of a Roman maiden of
the 5th cent. BC who killed herself after being raped
by the King of Rome; the resulting scandal led to the
end of the monarchy. It was also borne by a Spanish
martyr who perished under Diocletian, but is now
chiefly remembered as the name of Lucretia (Italian
*Lucrezia*) Borgia (1480–1519), a demon poisoner in
popular imagination, in reality a generous patron of
the arts.

**Lucy** /ˈluːsiː/ (*f.*) Variant of *Lucie*, the Old French
form of LUCIA.

**Ludmilla** /lʊdˈmɪlə/ (*f.*) From Russian: introduced to
England in the 20th cent. It was borne by a 10th-cent.
Bohemian saint who was responsible for the edu-
cation of St Wenceslas.

**Ludo** /ˈluːdəʊ/ (*m.*) Short form of LUDOVIC.

**Ludovic** /ˈluːdəvɪk/ (*m.*) From Latin *Ludovicus*, the
form used in documents of the Middle Ages to represent the Germanic name *Hlutwig*, which lies behind
English LEWIS, French LOUIS, German *Ludwig*, Italian *Lodovico* and *Luigi*, and various other cognates.
Its occasional use as a first name is the result of a
recent learned revival.

**Luke** /luːk/ (*f.*) English form of the post-classical
Greek name LUCAS. *Luke* is probably best known as
the name of the author of the third gospel in the New
Testament.

**Lulu** /ˈluːluː/ (*f.*) Reduplicated pet form of LOUISE, of
German origin.

**Luther** /'luːθə/ (*m.*) From the German surname, derived from a Germanic personal name composed of the elements *liut* people + *heri* army. It is most commonly bestowed among evangelical Protestants, in honour of the ecclesiastical reformer Martin Luther (1483–1546). In recent times it has become especially popular among American Blacks, in honour of the assassinated civil rights leader Martin Luther King (1929–68).

**Lydia** /'lɪdɪə/ (*f.*) Of Greek origin, meaning 'woman from Lydia', an area of Asia Minor. It is borne in the Bible by a woman of Thyatira who was converted by St Paul and entertained him in her house (Acts 16:14–15).

**Lyndon** /'lɪndən/ (*m.*) From the English surname, derived from the place Lyndon in the former county of Rutland (now part of Leicestershire), so called from Old English *lind* linden, lime tree + *dūn* hill. Its modern use as a given name is partly due to the American President Lyndon Baines Johnson (1908–73). The given name is also spelled **Lindon**.

**Lynette** /lɪ'nɛt/ (*f.*) In modern use, a derivative of LYNN, formed with the French feminine diminutive suffix *-ette*. It first came to public attention, however, in Tennyson's *Idylls of the King* (1859–85), where it is a Gallicized form of Welsh **Eluned**. It is also spelled **Lynnette** and **Lin(n)ette**.

**Lynn** /lɪn/ (*f.*) Apparently a modern short form of LINDA, with the spelling arbitrarily altered. There may also be some connection with the French name *Line*, which originated as a short form of various girls' names ending in this syllable, notably CAROLINE. The element *-lyn(ne)* was also used as a productive suffix around the middle of the 20th cent.

# M

**Mabel** /'meɪbəl; *formerly* 'mæbəl/ (*f.*) Originally a nickname from Old French *amabel*, *amable* lovely (related to modern English *amiable* friendly, good-humoured). The initial vowel began to be lost as early as the 13th cent., but a short vowel after the *M*-seems to have been standard until the 19th cent., when the name began to be pronounced to rhyme with *table*. It is also found occasionally in the spelling **Mable**.

**Madeleine** /'mædəleɪn; *French* mad'len/ (*f.*) Usual modern form, taken from French, of the name that derives from that of Mary *Magdalene* 'Mary of Magdala' in the New Testament. Magdala was a village on Lake Galilee, a few miles north of Tiberias. The woman 'which had been healed of evil spirits and infirmities' (Luke 8:2) was given this name in the Bible to distinguish her from other bearers of the very common name MARY. It was widely accepted in Christian folk belief that she was the same person as the repentant sinner who washed Christ's feet with her tears in the previous chapter (Luke 7), but there is no support in the text for this identification.

**Madge** /mædʒ/ (*f.*) Pet form of MARGARET, representing a palatalized version of *Mag(g)* (see MAGGIE).

**Mae** /meɪ/ (*f.*) Variant spelling of MAY, possibly influenced by MAEVE. It has been most notably borne by the American film actress Mae West (b.1892), whose prominent bust led to her name being given by American troops to a type of inflatable life jacket used in World War II. Possibly as a result of that unfortunate association this spelling of the name is no longer much used.

**Maeve** /meɪv/ (*f.*) Of Irish origin (**Meadhbh**, /'mʲeːwə/ or /mʲau/, in Gaelic): name of the fairy ruler sometimes referred to in English literature as Queen *Mab*. The name is also sometimes spelled **Mave**, and has sometimes been taken as a short form of MAVIS.

**Magda** /'mægdə/ (*f.*) Short form of German MAGDA-LENE, the usual form in that language of MADELEINE.

**Magdalene** /'mægdəlɪn, -liːn; German magda'leːnə/ (*f.*) German form of MADELEINE. As an English name, it is either an Anglicization of this or else a learned respelling taken from the Bible. The name is also found in the spelling **Magdalen**.

**Maggie** /'mægi:/ (*f.*) Pet form of MARGARET. In the Middle Ages the short form *Mag(g)* was common, as a result of the early loss in pronunciation of the English preconsonantal *r*. This is not now used as a given name, but has given rise to the surname *Maggs*; *Maggie* is a diminutive of *Mag(g)* formed with the characteristically Scottish suffix *-ie*, and until recently it was most common in Scotland.

**Magnus** /'mægnəs/ (*m.*) Originally a Latin nickname meaning 'Great', this was first extracted from the name of *Charlemagne* (recorded in Latin chronicles as *Carolus Magnus* 'Charles the Great') and used as a given name by the Scandinavians. It was imported by them to Scotland and Northern England during the Middle Ages, and until recently remained strongly characteristic of that area.

**Maisie** /'meɪzi:/ (*f.*). Scottish diminutive from the Gaelic form (**Marsail**) of MARGARET. The name still retains a Scottish flavour in Britain, although it is used more generally in the U.S.

**Malachy** /'mæləki:/ (*m.*) Irish (Gaelic **Maoileach-lainn** /'mljæxlinj/): the name of an important Irish saint, Malachy O'More (1095–1148), who was a friend and contemporary of St Bernard of Clairvaux. His Gaelic name means 'devotee of St Sechnall', from (*S*)*eachlainn*, genitive case of *Sechnall*. It was early identified with that of the biblical prophet generally known as **Malachi** or *Malachias*. Malachi was the last of the twelve minor prophets of the Old Testament; he foretold the coming of Christ and his name means, appropriately, 'Messenger of God' in Hebrew.

**Malcolm** /'mælkəm; *Scottish* 'mɔːlkəm/ (*m.*) Of Scottish origin, meaning 'Devotee of St Columba' (Gaelic *Mael-Colum*). Columba, whose name means 'Dove' in Latin, was a 6th-cent. monk of Irish origin who played a leading part in the conversion to Christianity of Scotland and Northern England. He has always been one of the most popular saints in Scotland, but in the Middle Ages it was felt to be presumptuous to give the names of saints directly to children; instead their blessing was invoked by prefixing the name with *mael-* 'devotee of' (cf. MARMADUKE) or *gille-* 'servant of'.

**Malvina** /mæl'viːnə/ (*f.*) Apparently a factitious name invented by James Macpherson (1736–96), a Scottish antiquarian poet who published works allegedly translated from the 3rd-cent. Irish bard Ossian. Las Malvinas is the Argentinian name for the Falkland Islands; the origin of this, and its connection, if any, with Macpherson's Ossianic name is disputed.

**Mamie** /'meɪmi/ (*f.*) Short form of MARGARET or MARY, used occasionally as an independent name. It seems to have originated as a nursery name.

**Mandy** /'mændi/ (*f.*) Pet form of AMANDA, now often used as a given name in its own right. (Occasionally it is also found as a Jewish boy's name, an Anglicized version of *Mendel* or *Mandel*, pet forms of the Hebrew name *Menachem*.)

**Manfred** /'mænfrəd/ (*m.*) Norman: of Germanic origin, usually said to be composed of the elements *man* man + *fred*, *frid* peace. However, it is at least as likely that the first element was *magin* strength (the Norman form being normally *Main-*; cf. modern English 'might and *main*') or *manag* much (cf. modern English *many*).

**Manny** /'mæni:/ (*m.*) Pet form of EMMANUEL, in use mainly among British Jews.

**Manuel** /'mænwel; *Spanish* manu'el/ (*m.*) Aphetic short form of EMMANUEL, extremely common in Spain (where it has the pet form *Manolito*).

**Marc** /maːk/ (*m.*) French spelling of MARK, given some currency in England in the 1960s by the fame of the pop singer Marc Bolan.

**Marcel** /maːˈsɛl; *French* marˈsɛl/ (*m.*) French: from the Latin personal name *Marcellus*, originally a diminutive of MARCUS. The name has always been popular in France as it was borne by a 3rd-cent. missionary to Gaul, martyred at Bourges with his companion Anastasius.

**Marcia** /'maːʃə, 'maːsiə/ (*f.*) Often used as a feminine equivalent of MARK, but in fact a feminine form of *Marcius*, itself a derivative of MARCUS. One St Marcia is commemorated in a group with Felix, Luciolus, Fortunatus, and others; another with Zenais, Cyria, and Valeria; and a third with Ariston, Crescentian, Eutychian, Urban, Vitalis, Justus, Felicissimus, Felix, and Symphorosa. None is individually very famous.

**Marcie** /'maːsiː/ (*f.*) Pet form of MARCIA, now regularly used as an independent name, especially in America. It is also sometimes spelled **Marcy**.

**Marcus** /'maːkəs/ (*m.*) Original Latin form of MARK, of unknown derivation. It may possibly be connected with MARIUS. It was rarely used in England until recent years, when it has been seized on by parents seeking to give a distinctive form to a common and popular name. Among American Blacks it is sometimes bestowed in honour of the Black Consciousness leader Marcus Garvey (1887–1940).

**Marganita** /mɑːgəˈniːtə/ (*f.*) Artificial alteration of *Margarita* (a Spanish or Latinate form of MARGARET), by association with the element -*nita* extracted from names of Spanish origin such as ANITA and JUANITA. The spelling **Marghanita** is also found.

**Margaret** /ˈmɑːgrət/ (*f.*) A common medieval English name, from French *Marguerite*, Latin *Margarita*, Greek *Margarītēs*, from *margaron* pearl, a word ultimately of Hebrew origin. The name was always understood to mean 'pearl' throughout the Middle Ages. The first St Margaret was martyred at Antioch in Pisidia during the persecution instigated by the Emperor Diocletian in the early 4th cent. However, there seems to be some doubt about her name, as the same saint is venerated in the Orthodox Church as MARINA. As a given name, *Margaret* received a boost in Britain in 1930 when it was selected by the future King George VI and his wife for their second daughter, Princess Margaret.

**Margery** /ˈmɑːdʒəriː/ (*f.*) The usual English form in the Middle Ages of MARGARET; now also commonly spelled MARJORIE.

**Margot** /ˈmɑːgəʊ; *French* marˈgo/ (*f.*) A relatively recent importation from France, where it was originally a pet form of MARGUERITE, but is now used as an independent name. In England it is still usually pronounced in the French way, but in Eastern Europe the final consonant is sounded, and this has had some influence in America.

**Marguerite** /mɑːgəˈriːt; *French* marˈgriːt/ (*f.*) French form of MARGARET. Its occasional modern use in the English-speaking world seems to be in part an adoption of the French given name, in part a use of the flower name. In French the vocabulary word *marguerite* means 'daisy', but it was borrowed into English as the name of a similar but much larger garden plant in the 19th cent., just in time to catch the vogue for deriving given names from flowers and trees.

**Maria** /məˈriːə, məˈraɪə/ (*f.*) Latin form of MARY, a learned revival dating from the 18th cent. *Maria* seems to have arisen as a back-formation from *Mariam*, which was taken as the accusative case, although in fact it is a variant of MIRIAM, and is indeclinable.

**Mariamne** /mærɪˈæmniː/ (*f.*) A rare name, representing the form of MIRIAM used by the Jewish historian Flavius Josephus, writing in Latin in the 1st cent. BC, as the name of the wife of King Herod.

**Marian** /ˈmærɪən/ (*f.*) Originally a medieval or early modern English variant spelling of MARION. However, in the 18th cent., when combined names began to come into fashion, it came to be understood as a combination of MARY and ANN.

**Marianne** /mærɪˈæn/ (*f.*) Probably an extended spelling of MARIAN, reinforcing the association of its second element with the name ANN(E), but possibly also an assimilated form of MARIAMNE.

**Marie** /məˈriː; *French* maˈriː/ (*f.*) French form of MARIA. When first introduced to England in the Middle Ages, it was Anglicized in pronunciation, and respelled MARY. This French form was revived in the 19th cent. and is now pronounced more or less in the French manner, although sometimes with the accent on the first syllable.

**Marietta** /mærɪˈɛtə/ (*f.*) Italian diminutive of MARIA,

now sometimes used as an independent name in the English-speaking world.

**Marigold** /'mærɪgold/ (*f.*) One of the older of the group of flower names that were especially popular in the early 20th cent. The Old English name of the flower was *golde*, presumably from *gold* (the precious metal), in reference to its colour. At some time before the 14th cent. the flower became associated with the Virgin Mary, and the name was extended accordingly to *marigold*.

**Marilyn** /'mærɪlɪn/ (*f.*) A 20th-cent. elaboration of MARY, with the suffix *-lyn(ne)* (see LYNN).

**Marina** /mə'ri:nə/ (*f.*) From a Late Latin given name, a feminine form of the family name *Marīnus*. This was in fact a derivative of MARIUS, but even during the early cents. AD it was widely assumed to be identical with the Latin adjective *marīnus* 'of the sea'. The early saints of this name are all of extremely shaky historical identification.

**Mario** /'mærɪəʊ; *Italian* 'ma:rɪo/ (*m.*) Italian form of *Marius*, now sometimes used in the English-speaking world, where it normally reflects either Italian origin or else admiration of some particular figure, for example the film star and singer Mario Lanza (1921–59).

**Marion** /'mærɪən/ (*f.*) Originally a medieval French diminutive of MARIE, introduced to Britain in the Middle Ages, and now completely Anglicized in pronunciation.

**Marisa** /mə'ri:sə/ (*f.*) A 20th-cent. elaboration of MARIA using the suffix *-isa*, apparently abstracted from LISA.

**Marius** /'mærɪəs/ (*m.*) From a Latin family name of uncertain derivation. It is probably from *Mars*, the name of the Roman god of war, or from *mas* (geni-

tive *maris*) male, virile. A derivation from *mare* sea
has been assumed by some writers, but is unlikely (cf.
MARINA). In modern times, the name is occasionally
used (especially in Catholic families) as a masculine
equivalent of MARY.

**Marjorie** /'mɑːdʒərɪ/ (*f.*) The usual modern spelling
of MARGERY. It seems to have arisen as the result of
popular etymological association of the name with
that of the herb *marjoram* (cf. ROSEMARY). This word
is of uncertain origin; its Middle English and Old
French form was *majorane*, without the first -*r*-.

**Mark** /mɑːk/ (*m.*) English form of the Latin name
MARCUS, borne by the Evangelist, author of the
second gospel in the New Testament, and by several
other early and medieval saints. This was one of the
extremely limited number of Roman given names in
use in the classical period. There were only about a
dozen of these in general use, with perhaps another
dozen confined to particular families.

**Marlene** /'mɑːliːn, mɑːˈliːn; *German* marˈleːnə/ (*f.*)
German contracted form of *Maria Magdalene* (see
MADELEINE). Probably the first, and certainly the
most famous, bearer of the name is Marlene Die-
trich, born in 1902 as Maria Magdalene von Losch.
The name was further popularized in the 1940s by the
wartime German song, popular among British troops
in North Africa, 'Lili Marlene'.

**Marlon** /'mɑːlɒn/ (*m.*) Apparently first borne by the
American actor Marlon Brando (b. 1924) and now
sometimes used more widely as a result of his fame.
The name was borne also by his father, and is of
uncertain origin, possibly derived from MARC with the
addition of the French diminutive suffix -*lon* (originally a combination of two separate suffixes, -*el* and
-*on*); the family is said to have been of French origin.
In America it is used fairly regularly among Blacks,

but in Britain the most notable bearer is the young go-karting enthusiast in the *Perishers* cartoon.

**Marmaduke** /'maːmədjuːk/ (*m.*) Anglicized form of the Irish name **Mael-Maedoc** 'devotee of Maedoc' (cf. MALCOLM). The name *Maedoc* (which is of uncertain derivation) was borne by various early Irish saints, most notably a 6th-cent. abbot of Clonmore and a 7th-cent. bishop of Ferns. *Marmaduke* is at present out of favour, and indeed has never been common except in a small area of North Yorkshire.

**Marsha** /'maːʃə/ (*f.*) Phonetic spelling of MARCIA, popular especially among Blacks.

**Marshall** /'maːʃəl/ (*m.*) From the English surname, derived from a Norman French occupational term that originally denoted someone who looked after horses, ultimately from the Germanic elements *marah* horse + *scalc* servant. By the time it became fixed as a surname it had the meaning 'shoeing-smith'; later it came to denote an official whose duties were to a large extent ceremonial. The surname is phonetically identical with the English pronunciation of the name of the Roman poet Martial (from Latin *Mars*, genitive *Martis*; cf. MARTIN), and this may possibly have contributed something to its use as a given name.

**Martha** /'maːθə/ (*f.*) New Testament: name borne by the sister of Lazarus and of Mary of Bethany (John 11:1). The name is of Aramaic rather than Hebrew origin, and meant 'Lady'.

**Marti** /'maːtiː/ (*f.*) Short form of MARTINE or MARTINA; its best-known bearer is the English comedienne Marti Caine (b. 1945).

**Martin** /'maːtɪn/ (*m.*) From the Latin name *Martīnus*, probably originally derived from *Mars* (genitive *Martis*), the name of the Roman god of war (and earlier of fertility). *Martin* became very popular in the Middle Ages, especially on the Continent, as a result of the fame of St Martin of Tours. He was the son of a Roman officer, born in Upper Pannonia (now part of Hungary), an outpost of the Roman Empire. He was a leading figure in the 4th-cent. Church, but was later largely remembered for having divided his cloak in two and given half to a beggar. Among Protestants the name is sometimes bestowed in honour of the German theologian Martin Luther (1483–1546), and a further influence, especially among American Blacks, may be its use as the first name of the civil-rights leader Martin Luther King (1929–68).

**Martina** /maː'tiːnə/ (*f.*) Feminine form of the Latin name *Martīnus* (see MARTIN). This was in use as a given name from an early period, being borne by a notorious poisoner mentioned by the historian Tacitus. The 3rd-cent. saint of the same name is of doubtful authenticity. Modern use of the name in the English-speaking world seems to be the result of German or central European influence, as in the case of the tennis player Martina Navratilova (b. 1956), who was born in Czechoslovakia.

**Martine** /maː'tiːn; *French* mar'tiːn; *German* mar'tiːnə/ (*f.*) French or German form of MARTINA. It is now fairly regularly used in the English-speaking world.

**Marty** /'maːtiː/ (*m.*) Short form of MARTIN (or MARTYN), which has come into favour in the latter part of the 20th cent., being associated particularly with the comedian Marty Feldman (1933–83), the 1960s pop singer Marty Wilde (b. 1938 as Reginald Smith), and the country-and-western singer Marty Robbins (b. 1926). It occurs occasionally as a girl's name, but the usual spelling is MARTI.

**Martyn** /'maːtɪn/ (*m.*) Arbitrarily altered spelling of MARTIN, becoming increasingly common in England.

**Marvin** /'mɑːvɪn/ (*m.*) From a medieval variant of
MERVYN, resulting from the regular Middle English
change of *-er-* to *-ar-*. Modern use may represent a
transferred use of the surname derived from this in
the Middle Ages. It is to a large extent borne by
Blacks and has been made famous by the American
singer Marvin Gaye (1939–84).

**Mary** /'meəri/ (*f.*) Anglicized form of French MARIE,
from Latin MARIA. This is a New Testament form of
MIRIAM, which St Jerome derived from elements
meaning 'drop of the sea' (Latin *stilla maris*, later
altered to *stella maris* 'star of the sea'). *Mary* has
been an extremely popular girl's name for centuries,
originally chosen by Christians to honour and invoke
the Virgin Mary, as well as the dozens of other saints
so named.

**Matilda** /mə'tɪldə/ (*f.*) Latin form of a Germanic personal name composed of the elements *maht, meht*
might + *hild* battle. The name was introduced into
England by the Normans, and this Latinized form is
the one that normally occurs in medieval records.
The vernacular form was MAUD. *Matilda* was revived
as a learned form in the 18th cent.

**Matt** /mæt/ (*m.*) Short form of MATTHEW.

**Matthew** /'mæθjuː/ (*m.*) New Testament: from the
name of the apostle and evangelist, author of the first
gospel. His name is a form of the Hebrew name *Mat-
tathia* meaning 'Gift of God', which is fairly common
in the Bible, and is rendered in the Authorized Version in a number of different forms: *Mattan(i)ah,
Mattatha(h), Mattathiah, Mattathias*, and so on. In
the New Testament and elsewhere the evangelist is
regularly referred to as *Matthew*, while the apostle
chosen to replace Judas Iscariot is distinguished as
MATTHIAS.

**Matthias** /məˈθaɪəs/ (*m.*) Greek form of MATTHEW used in the Authorized Version of the New Testament for the disciple who was chosen after the treachery of Judas to make up the twelve (Acts 1:23–26). This form of the name has always had a learned flavour and has been little used in the English-speaking world, although it is more common in Germany.

**Mattie** /ˈmætiː/ (*m.*, occasionally *f.*) Diminutive of MATTHEW (see MATT), with the hypocoristic suffix -*ie*. As a girl's name, it is somewhat rarer, originating as a pet form of MATILDA.

**Maud** /mɔːd/ (*f.*) From the normal medieval English form of MATILDA. It seems to have been characteristically or originally Low German (the wife of William the Conqueror, so named, was the daughter of Baldwin, Count of Flanders), and it is a characteristic of that region to lose the letter *t* between vowels, giving forms such as *Ma(h)auld*. *Maud* became quite common in the 19th cent., when its popularity was influenced in part by Tennyson's poem *Maud*, published in 1855.

**Maureen** /ˈmɔːriːn/ (*f.*) Of Irish origin: from Gaelic **Máirín** /ˈmɑːrjɪŋ/, a diminutive of *Máire*, the Gaelic form of MARY; see MOIRA. The spellings **Maurene** and **Maurine** are also found.

**Maurice** /ˈmɒrɪs/ (*m.*) From the Latin name *Mauritius* meaning 'Moor'. The name was introduced to Britain by the Normans, but did not achieve great popularity except, for some reason, in Wales, in the form **Meurick**. In Ireland it has been used as an Anglicized form of **Muirgheas**, which is composed of Old Celtic elements meaning 'sea' and 'choice'. It is common in France, and in Britain is now sometimes taken as a French name. See also MORRIS.

**Mavis** /ˈmeɪvɪs/ (*f.*) Not found before the last decade

of the 19th cent., this name seems to belong to the
small class of girls' names taken from birds. Mavis is
another word for the song-thrush, first attested in
Chaucer. It is from Old French, and probably ultimately of Breton origin.

**Max** /mæks/ (*m.*) Short form of both MAXIMILIAN and,
now more commonly, MAXWELL. It is also now widely
used as an independent name in its own right.

**Maximilian** /ˌmæksɪˈmɪlɪən/ (*m.*) From the Latin
name *Maximiliānus* (derived from a diminutive of
*Maximus* 'Greatest'). This was borne by a 3rd-cent.
saint numbered among the 'Fourteen Holy Helpers'.
Although already existing, the name was reanalysed
in the 15th cent. by the Emperor Friedrich III, who
bestowed it on his first-born son, as a blend of the
names *Maximus* and *Aemiliānus*, intending thereby
to pay homage to the two famous Roman generals Q.
Fabius Maximus 'Cunctator' and P. Cornelius Scipio
Aemilianus.

**Maxine** /ˈmaksiːn, makˈsiːn/ (*f.*) Modern coinage, first
recorded around 1930. It seems to be a derivative of
MAX, with the addition of the feminine ending *-ine*.

**Maxwell** /ˈmækswəl/ (*m.*) From the Scottish surname,
which is derived from a place name. Maxwell, originally 'the stream (Old English *well(a)*) of Mack (a
form of MAGNUS)', was a minor place on the River
Tweed. It is not known how the surname first came to
be used as a given name; perhaps it was taken as an
expansion of MAX.

**May** /meɪ/ (*f.*) Short form of MARGARET or MARY. The
popularity of this name has been reinforced by the
fact that it fits into the series of month names with
APRIL and JUNE, and also belongs to the group of
flower names, being another word for the hawthorn,

whose white flowers blossom in May. It is at present somewhat out of favour.

**Maynard** /'meɪnɑːd/ (*m.*) From the English surname, which is itself from a Norman given name of Germanic origin, composed of the elements *magin* strength + *hard* hardy, brave, strong.

**Meg** /mɛg/ (*f.*) Pet form of MARGARET, evidently an alteration of the obsolete short form *Mag(g)* (as in MAGGIE). Until recently *Meg* was characteristically Scottish. Its increased popularity owes something to Meg March, one of the four sisters who are the main characters in Louisa M. Alcott's *Little Women* (1868).

**Megan** /'mɛgən/ (*f.*) Welsh pet form of MARGARET, nowadays generally used as an independent name both within and beyond Wales, but nevertheless retaining a strong Welsh flavour.

**Meggie** /'mɛgi/ (*f.*) Pet form of MEG (itself a pet form of MARGARET) or of MEGAN, as in the case of the central character of Colleen McCullough's novel *The Thorn Birds* (1977).

**Mehitabel** /mə'hɪtəbɛl/ (*f.*) Old Testament: from the Hebrew name *Mehetabel* 'God makes happy'. Mehetabel 'the daughter of Matred, the daughter of Mezahab' is mentioned in passing in a biblical genealogy (Gen. 36:39), and the name achieved some currency among the Puritans in the 17th cent. Nowadays, however, the name is chiefly associated with the companion (a cat) of Archy the cockroach in the poems of Don Marquis (pub. 1927).

**Mel** /mɛl/ (*m.*) Short form of MELVIN or MELVILLE.

**Melanie** /'mɛləni/ (*f.*) From an Old French form of Latin *Melania*, the name of two Roman saints of the 5th cent., a grandmother and granddaughter. Their name is a derivative of the feminine form, *melaina*, of the Greek adjective *melas* black, dark. The name was introduced to England in the early Middle Ages, but has become common only in the late 20th cent.

**Melinda** /məˈlɪndə/ (*f.*) Derived from the first syllable of names such as MELANIE and MELISSA, with the addition of the productive suffix -*inda* (cf. LUCINDA).

**Melissa** /məˈlɪsə/ (*f.*) From the Greek word *melissa* 'bee'. The name has recently increased considerably in popularity, together with other girls' names sharing the same first syllable.

**Melody** /ˈmɛlədi:/ (*f.*) Modern transferred use of the vocabulary word (Greek *melōdia* singing of songs, from *melos* song + *aeidein* to sing), chosen partly because of its pleasant associations and partly as a result of the popularity of other girls' names with the same first syllable.

**Melony** /ˈmɛləni:/ (*f.*) Variant of MELANIE, perhaps influenced by MELODY.

**Melville** /ˈmɛlvɪl/ (*m.*) From the Scottish surname, originally a Norman baronial name borne by the lords of a place called *Malleville* 'bad settlement', i.e. settlement on infertile land. The name was taken to Scotland as early as the 12th cent. and became a common surname there; use as a given name seems also to have originated in Scotland.

**Melvin** /ˈmɛlvɪn/ (*m.*) Of uncertain origin, probably a variant of the less common MELVILLE.

**Melvyn** /ˈmɛlvɪn/ (*m.*) Arbitrarily altered form of MEL-VIN; cf. MARTYN.

**Mercedes** /mɜːˈsiːdɪz; *Spanish* mɛrˈθeðɛs/ (*f.*) Of Spanish origin, from the liturgical title *Maria de las mercedes* (literally 'Mary of Mercies', in English 'Our Lady of Ransom'). Latin *mercēdes* originally meant 'wages' or 'ransom'; in Christian theology, Christ's sacrifice is regarded as a 'ransom for the sins of mankind', and hence an 'act of ransom' was seen as identical with an 'act of mercy'. There are special feasts in the Catholic calendar on 10 August and 24 September to commemorate the Virgin under this name. The name is now occasionally used in England, and more commonly in America, but normally only by Roman Catholics.

**Mercy** /'mɜːsɪ/ (*f.*) From the vocabulary word, denoting the quality of magnanimity to offenders much prized in Christian tradition. The word is derived from Latin *mercēs*, which originally meant 'wages' (see MERCEDES). The name was much favoured by the Puritans, but subsequently fell out of use. These days it is commonly an Anglicized form of *Mercedes*.

**Meredith** /'mɛrədɪθ/ (*m.*, *f.*) From the Old Welsh personal name *Maredudd*. This is of uncertain origin, but may be composed of Celtic elements meaning 'great' and 'chief, lord'. In recent years the name has sometimes also been given to girls, presumably being thought of as an expansion of MERRY.

**Meriel** /'mɛrɪˈɛl, 'mɛrɪəl/ (*f.*) Variant of MURIEL; both forms are 19th-cent. revivals of an older Celtic name. Of the two forms, *Meriel* was never as popular as *Muriel*, but has lasted better, and seems to have escaped the somewhat old-fashioned image of the latter name.

**Merle** /mɜːl/ (*f.*) Probably a contracted form of MERIEL, but also associated with the small class of girls' names derived from birds, since it is identical in form with Old French *merle* blackbird (Latin *merula*). The name came to public notice in the 1930s with the actress Merle Oberon (1911–79); she was born Estelle Merle O'Brien Thompson.

**Merlin** /ˈmɜːlɪn/ (*m.*) Usual English form of the Old
Welsh name *Myrddyn* (see MERVYN). It is best known
as the name of the magician in Arthurian legend. It
seems to have originally been composed of old Celtic
elements meaning 'sea' and 'hill, fort', but it has been
distorted by mediation through Old French sources,
which associated the second element with the diminutive suffix -*lin*, and then by association with the vocabulary word *merlin*, denoting a type of small falcon.
The spelling **Merlyn** is also used.

**Merry** /ˈmɛrɪ/ (*f.*) Originally apparently an assimilated form of MERCY. In Dickens's novel *Martin
Chuzzlewit* (1844), Mr Pecksniff's daughters CHARITY
and *Mercy* are known as *Cherry* and *Merry*. Nowadays the name is usually bestowed because of its
association with the adjective denoting a cheerful and
jolly temperament (cf. HAPPY). In the accent of the
central and northern U.S. there is no difference in
pronunciation between MERRY and MARY.

**Mervyn** /ˈmɜːvɪn/ (*m.*) From the Welsh name **Myrddyn** /ˈmɪrðɪn/, of which the English equivalent, at any
rate in Arthurian legend, is MERLIN. It is sometimes
also spelled **Mervin**.

**Meryl** /ˈmɛrəl/ (*f.*) A recent coinage, owing its current
popularity to the fame of the American actress Meryl
Streep (b. Mary Louise Streep in 1949). *Meryl* has
also been influenced in part by the ending -*yl* in
names such as CHERYL.

**Michael** /ˈmaɪkəl/ (*m.*) From a Hebrew personal
name meaning 'Who is like God?', borne by one of the
archangels, who is also regarded as a saint of the
Catholic Church (cf. GABRIEL and RAPHAEL). In the
Middle Ages Michael was regarded as a symbol of the
Church Militant and the patron of soldiers; he was
often depicted bearing a flaming sword.

**Michaela** /mɪˈkeɪlə; *German* mɪçaˈeːla/ (*f.*) German feminine form of MICHAEL. The Spanish form **Micaela** /mikaˈela/ is also used.

**Michelle** /mɪˈʃɛl; *French* mɪˈʃɛl/ (*f.*) French feminine form of MICHAEL (French *Michel*), now quite common in the English-speaking world.

**Mick** /mɪk/ (*m.*) Short form of MICHAEL; now common as a generic and often somewhat derogatory term for an Irishman.

**Micky** /ˈmɪkiː/ (*m.*) Diminutive of MICK, also found in the spelling **Mickey**. The latter spelling is also sometimes used as a girl's name; see MIKKI.

**Mignonette** /*French* mɪnjõˈnɛt/ (*f.*) Probably a direct use of the French nickname *mignonette* 'little darling', a feminine diminutive of *mignon* sweet, cute, dainty. The word *mignonette* is also used in English to denote a species of *Reseda*, and so in some cases this name may be assigned to the class of flower names that became popular at the beginning of the 20th cent.

**Mike** /maɪk/ (*m.*) Usual short form of MICHAEL in the English-speaking world. It is also used as an independent name to a large extent, particularly in America.

**Mikki** /ˈmɪkiː/ (*f.*) Feminine variant of *Micky*, or pet form of MICHAELA, now sometimes used as a given name in its own right. The spellings **Micki** and **Mickie** are also found.

**Mildred** /ˈmɪldrəd/ (*f.*) From the Old English girl's name *Mildþrýð*, composed of the elements *mild* gentle + *þrýð* strength. The 7th-cent. abbess of this name had a less famous but equally saintly elder sister Mildburh and a younger sister Mildgyð; all were daughters of St Ermenburh. Their names illustrate clearly the Old English pattern of reusing and recombining the same small group of name elements within a single family.

**Miles** /maɪlz/ (*m.*) Norman: of uncertain origin. It does not appear to be derived from any known Germanic name element, but there is a frequent Slavic name element *mil* mercy, with which it may have some ultimate connection. The name has been modestly popular in England ever since the Conquest.

**Millicent** /ˈmɪlɪsənt/ (*f.*) Norman: of Germanic origin, composed of the elements *amal* labour + *swinth* strength, and first introduced to Britain in the form *Melisende*.

**Millie** /ˈmɪli/ (*f.*) Short form of MILLICENT (and occasionally of MILDRED). It is now used as an independent name, and although not common is considerably more common than either of the full forms, which are now generally out of favour.

**Milo** /ˈmaɪləʊ/ (*m.*) Latinized form of MILES, regularly used in documents of the Middle Ages.

**Milton** /ˈmɪltən/ (*m.*) From the English surname, derived from any of the numerous places so called, the majority of which get their name from Old English *middel* + *tūn* 'settlement in the middle'; the rest were originally named as *mylentūn* 'settlement with a mill'. The surname is most famous as that of the poet John Milton (1608–74), and the given name is sometimes bestowed in his honour.

**Mimi** /ˈmiːmiː/ (*f.*) Pet form of MARIA, originally an Italian nursery name. The heroine of Puccini's opera *La Bohème* (1896) announces 'They call me Mimi', and the name has occasionally been chosen in reference to this.

**Minette** /mɪˈnɛt/ (*f.*) Of uncertain origin, possibly a contracted form of MIGNONETTE.

**Minnie** /ˈmɪniː/ (*f.*) Pet form of WILHELMINA, at its peak of popularity in the latter half of the 19th cent. It has now largely fallen out of use, perhaps because of association with cartoon characters such as Minnie Mouse (in Walt Disney's animations) and Minnie the Minx (in the children's comic *Beano*).

**Mirabelle** /ˈmɪrəbel; *French* mɪraˈbɛl/ (*f.*) From French, coined from the Latin word *mīrābilis* wondrous, lovely (cf. MIRANDA). The name was quite common in medieval times, and occasionally the variant **Mirabel** was used for boys as well as girls, but by the 17th and 18th cents. both forms were rare. The Latinate form **Mirabella** also occurs.

**Miranda** /mɪˈrændə/ (*f.*) Invented by Shakespeare for the heroine of *The Tempest*. It represents the feminine form of the Latin gerundive *mīrandus* 'admirable, lovely', from *mīrāri* to admire or wonder at; cf. AMANDA.

**Mireille** /*French* mɪˈrɛj/ (*f.*) French: apparently first used, in the Provençal form *Mireio*, as the title of a verse romance by the poet Frédéric Mistral (1830–1914). The name is probably a derivative of Provençal *mirar* to admire (cf. MIRANDA), but the poet himself declared it to be a form of MIRIAM, in order to overcome the objections of a priest to so baptizing his god-daughter with a non-liturgical name.

**Miriam** /ˈmɪrɪəm/ (*f.*) From a later form of the common Hebrew name *Maryam* (compare MARIA). Of uncertain ultimate origin, the name is first recorded in the Old Testament (Exod. 15:20) as being borne by the elder sister of Moses. Since the names of both Moses and his brother Aaron are probably of Egyptian origin, it is possible that this feminine name is too. It was enthusiastically taken up as a given name by the Israelites, and is still borne mainly, but by no means exclusively, by Jews.

**Mitch** /mɪtʃ/ (*m.*) Short form of MITCHELL.

**Mitchell** /'mɪtʃəl/ (*m.*) From the English surname, derived from a common medieval form of MICHAEL, representing an Anglicized pronunciation of Norman French *Michel* (see MICHELLE).

**Mitzi** /'mɪtsiː/ (*f.*) Swiss pet form of MARIA.

**Moira** /'mɔɪrə/ (*f.*) Anglicized version of the Irish name **Máire** /'mɑːrjə/, the Gaelic form of MARY. The name is also found in English in the spelling **Moyra**.

**Molly** /'mɒliː/ (*f.*) Pet form of MARY, representing an altered version of the earlier *Mally*. The name is rarely used now, and is chiefly associated with Ireland, although the name is not Gaelic.

**Mona** /'məʊnə/ (*f.*) Of Irish origin: from the Gaelic name **Muadhnait** /'muənidʒ/, a feminine diminutive of *muadh* noble. The name is no longer restricted to people with Irish connections, and has sometimes been taken as a short form of MONICA, or alternatively as connected with Greek *monos* one. *Mona* is also found as a girl's name in Arabic.

**Monica** /'mɒnɪkə/ (*f.*) Of uncertain ultimate origin. This was the name of the mother of St Augustine, as transmitted to us by her famous son. She was a citizen of Carthage, so her name may well be of Phoenician origin, but in the early Middle Ages it was taken to be a derivative of Latin *monēre* to warn, counsel, or advise, since it was as a result of her guidance that her son was converted to Christianity.

**Montague** /'mɒntəgjuː/ (*m.*) From the English surname, originally a Norman baronial name borne by the Lords of Montaigu in La Manche. This place name was composed of the Old French elements *mont* hill (Latin *mons*, genitive *montis*) + *aigu* pointed (Latin *acūtus*). Drogo of Montaigu accompanied William the Conqueror in his invasion of England, and *Montague* soon became a noble British family name, whence it was transferred to use as a given name in the 19th cent.

**Montgomery** /mɒntˈgɒməri/ (*m.*) From the English and Irish surname, which is a Norman baronial name in origin, from places in Calvados so called from Old French *mont* hill + the Germanic personal name *Gomeric* 'man power'. It has never been common as a given name, although its popularity was given additional currency by the actor Montgomery Clift (1920–66), and during and after World War II by the British field marshal Bernard Montgomery (1887–1976).

**Montmorency** /ˌmɒntməˈrɛnsi/ (*m.*) A use of the English surname that enjoyed a brief vogue in the 19th cent., but is now regarded as affected and so hardly ever used. The surname is from a Norman baronial name derived from a place in Seine-et-Oise so called from Old French *mont* hill + the Gallo-Roman personal name *Maurentius*.

**Monty** /ˈmɒnti/ (*m.*) Short form of MONTAGUE or of the much rarer MONTGOMERY and MONTMORENCY, all of which have gone through the cycle of transformation from French place-name to Norman baronial name to noble British surname to modern given name. The full forms of all these names are now rare. *Monty* is now often used as an independent name, especially among Jews.

**Morag** /ˈmɔːræg, *Gaelic* ˈmɔːrak/ (*f.*) Of Scottish origin: probably derived from the nickname *Mor* 'Great', with the addition of the diminutive suffix -*ag* (originally meaning 'young'). However, it is also possible that the first element is derived from *muir* sea, a common element in Gaelic personal names. The name is still confined almost completely to Scotland and people of Scottish ancestry.

**Mordecai** /'mɔːdəkaɪ/ (*m.*) Old Testament: the name of Esther's cousin and foster-father, who secured her introduction to King Ahasuerus (Esther 2–9). The name is of Persian origin and seems to have meant 'Devotee of the god Marduk'. The name had some currency among Puritans in the 17th cent. and Nonconformists in the 18th and 19th cents., but has always been and still is mainly a Jewish name, and not a particularly common one.

**Morgan** /'mɔːrgən/ (*m.*, *f.*) Welsh: common both as a given name and as a surname, but of uncertain ultimate derivation. It appears to reflect an old Celtic name composed of the elements *môr* sea + *can* bright. It is normally a boys' name, but occasionally used for girls, in which case it is generally adopted with conscious reference to King Arthur's jealous stepsister Morgan le Fay.

**Morna** /'mɔːnə/ (*f.*) Variant of MYRNA, influenced by MONA.

**Morris** /'mɒrɪs/ (*m.*) From the English surname, which is derived from the medieval Norman given name *Meurisse*, a variant of MAURICE. The spelling *Morris* was quite common as a given name in the Middle Ages, but fell out of use and was readopted from the surname in modern times. Like MORTIMER and MORTON, it is now quite common as a Jewish name, having been widely adopted as an Anglicized equivalent of MOSES.

**Mort** /mɔːt/ (*m.*) Short form of MORTIMER and MORTON, more or less confined to America.

**Mortimer** /'mɔːtɪmə/ (m.) From the English surname, which is derived from a Norman baronial name, originally borne by the lords of Mortemer in Normandy. The place name meant 'Dead Sea' in Old French, and probably referred to a stagnant marsh. It was not used as a given name until the 19th cent. It is now sometimes used as a Jewish name (see MORRIS).

**Morton** /'mɔːtən/ (m.) From the English surname, derived from any of the numerous places named from Old English *mōrtūn* 'settlement by or on a moor'. It is now also used as a Jewish name (see MORRIS).

**Morwenna** /'mɔːrwenə/ (f.) From an old Celtic personal name, derived from an element cognate with Welsh *morwyn* maiden. It was borne by a somewhat obscure Cornish saint of the 5th cent.; churches in her honour have named several places in the West Country. The name was revived in Wales in the mid 20th cent. as a result of nationalistic sentiment.

**Moses** /'məuzɪz/ (m.) Old Testament: name of the patriarch (*Moshe* in Hebrew) who led the Israelites out of Egypt (Exod. 4). His name is probably of Egyptian origin, most probably from the same root as that found in the second element of names such as *Tutmosis* and *Rameses*, where it means 'born of (a certain god)'. Various Hebrew etymologies have been proposed, beginning with the biblical 'Saved (from the water)' (Exod. 2:10), but none is convincing. It is now mainly Jewish, as it has always been, but up until the 20th cent. it also enjoyed some popularity among Christians, especially Puritans and Nonconformists.

**Moss** /mɒs/ (m.) From the usual medieval English form of MOSES or, more commonly, from the English surname derived from it. In recent years it has also come to be used as a short form of MOSTYN.

**Mostyn** /'mɒstɪn/ (*m.*) Welsh: derived from the name
of a place in Clwyd, on the Dee estuary. The place
name is probably composed of the Welsh elements
*maes* open field, plain + *tyn* fortress, settlement.

**Mungo** /'mʌŋgəʊ/ (*m.*) A characteristically Glas-
wegian name. It is recorded as the byname of St Kentigern, the 6th-cent. apostle of south-west Scotland
and north-west England, and glossed in Latin by his
biographer as *carissimus amicus* 'dearest friend',
although the derivation is in fact far from clear. It
does not correspond to any Gaelic elements with this
meaning.

**Munro** /'mən'rəʊ/ (*m.*) From the Scottish surname,
which was originally a local name for someone who
lived by the mouth of the river Roe in Ireland. The
first syllable represents a lenited form of Gaelic *bun*
mouth or root.

**Murdo** /'mɜːdɔː/ (*m.*) Scottish: Anglicized spelling of
the older Gaelic personal name *Muireachadh*, a derivative of *muir* sea. The modern Gaelic form is **Mur-
chadh** /'muːrɪxɪg/. Among English speakers the form
**Murdoch** /'mɜːdɒk/ survived and became quite common, especially as a surname; the modern given
name in part represents a transferred use of this surname.

**Muriel** /'mjuːrɪəl/ (*f.*) Of Celtic origin, composed of
elements meaning 'sea' + 'bright'. Forms are found
not only in Gaelic but also in Welsh and Breton, and
in the Middle Ages the name was relatively common
even in the heart of England, having been introduced
from various sources; the surname *Merrill* is derived
from it. See also MERIEL.

**Murray** /'mʌrɪ/ (*m.*) From the Scottish surname,
originally a local name from the region and former

county of Moray, but in some cases also an Anglicized form of the personal name *Muireach* (see MURDO). Its use as a given name is still mostly restricted to Scotland or to people of Scottish descent.

**Myf** /mɪf/ (*f.*) Short form of MYFANWY.

**Myfanwy** /mə'vænwɪ/ (*f.*) Welsh: from a phrase meaning 'my lovely one'. Its popularity dates only from relatively recent times, when specifically Welsh names have been sought as tokens of Welsh national identity.

**Myles** /maɪlz/ (*m.*) Variant of MILES; cf. MARTYN.

**Myra** /'maɪrə/ (*f.*) Invented in the 17th cent. by the poet Fulke Greville (1554–1628). It is impossible to guess what models he had consciously or unconsciously in mind, but it has been variously conjectured that the name is an anagram of MARY; that it is a simplified spelling of Latin *myrrha* myrrh, unguent; and that it is connected with Latin *mīrārī* to admire or wonder at.

**Myrna** /'mɜːnə/ (*f.*) Anglicized form of Irish **Muirne** 'Beloved'.

**Myron** /'maɪrən/ (*m.*) From an ancient Greek name, derived from Greek *myron* myrrh. The name was borne by a famous sculptor of the 5th cent. BC; but it was taken up with particular enthusiasm by the early Christians because of the gift of myrrh to the infant Christ, and the association of myrrh (as an embalming spice) with death and eternal life. The name was borne by various early saints, notably a 3rd-cent. martyr of Cyzicus and a 4th-cent. bishop of Crete. Their veneration, however, is greater in the Eastern Church than the Western, and the name has not been common in the English-speaking world.

**Myrtle** /ˈmɜːtəl/ (*f.*) From the name of the plant (Old French *myrtille*, Late Latin *myrtilla*, a diminutive of Classical Latin *myrta*); one of the group of plant names that became popular as girls' names in the late 19th cent.

# N

**Nadia** /'nɑːdjə/ (*f.*) Russian: pet form of the name *Nadezhda* 'Hope'. The name has enjoyed a considerable vogue in the English-speaking world in the 20th cent., and even the full form has occasionally been used.

**Nadine** /næ'diːn; *French* nə'diːn/ (*f.*) French elaboration of NADIA. Many names of Russian origin reached Britain via France in the early 20th cent. as a result of the popularity of the Ballet Russe established in Paris by Diaghilev in 1909.

**Nan** /næn/ (*f.*) Originally a nickname from a child's early attempts at speech, it became attached to ANN as a pet form (cf. NED). It is now generally used as a short form of NANCY.

**Nancy** /'nænsɪ/ (*f.*) Originally probably a pet form of CONSTANCE, but in the 18th cent. it came to be associated with ANN. Nowadays it is an independent name, and was especially popular in America between about 1920 and 1960.

**Nanette** /nə'nɛt/ (*f.*) Elaboration of NAN, with the addition of the French feminine diminutive suffix *-ette*.

**Naomi** /'neɪəmɪ/ (*f.*) Old Testament: name (meaning 'Pleasantness' in Hebrew) of the wise mother-in-law of Ruth. The name has long been regarded as typically Jewish, but recently has begun to come into more general use.

**Nat** /næt/ (*m.*) Short form of NATHAN and NATHANIEL. Both of these names and the short form derived from them are now generally borne by Jews, but in America *Nat* also has some currency as an independent given name among non-Jews.

**Natalie** /'nætəlɪ/ (*f.*) French form of the Russian

name *Natalya*, from Late Latin *Natalia* (a derivative of Latin *natālis* (*diēs*) birthday, especially Christ's birthday, i.e. Christmas; cf. NOEL). St Natalia was an inhabitant of Nicomedia who is said to have given succour to the martyrs, including her husband Adrian, who suffered there in persecutions under Diocletian in 303. She is regarded as a Christian saint, although she was not herself martyred. The name is also spelled **Nathalie**.

**Natasha** /nəˈtæʃə/ (*f.*) Russian pet form of *Natalya* (see NATALIE). This name, like NOELLE, is sometimes given to girls born on Christmas Day, but it is of much more widespread occurrence.

**Nathan** /ˈneɪθən/ (*m.*) Old Testament: from a Hebrew word meaning 'Gift' (cf. NATHANIEL). This was the name of a prophet who had the courage to reproach King David for arranging the death in battle of Uriah the Hittite in order to get possession of the latter's wife Bathsheba (Sam. 12:1–15). It was also the name of one of David's own sons.

**Nathaniel** /nəˈθænjəl/ (*m.*) Old Testament: name (meaning 'Gift of God' in Hebrew) of one of the less prominent apostles (John 1:45, 21:2), who is probably identical with BARTHOLOMEW. The Bible actually uses the form **Nathanael**, but this spelling has always been rare in English. The form *Natanaele* is occasionally used as a given name in Italy, but the name is little used in other European languages.

**Ned** /ned/ (*m.*) Short form of EDWARD, possibly originating in the misdivision of phrases such as *mine Ed* (cf. NAN). It was common in the Middle Ages and up to the 18th cent., but in the 19th was almost entirely superseded in the role of short form by TED. *Ned* is now, however, undergoing something of a revival.

**Neil** /ˈniːəl/ (*m.*) Of Irish origin (Gaelic NIALL): apparently a derivative of *niadh* champion. It was adopted by the Scandinavians in the form *Njal* and soon became very popular among them. They first transmitted the name to England at an early period, and its popularity was strengthened when it was later reintroduced by the Normans. Until the 20th cent. this name was characteristic of southern Scotland and northern England, as well as Ireland. The Irish given name gave rise to a fairly common surname, which in turn may in some cases have influenced the choice of given name. The spelling **Neal** is also found.

**Nell** /nɛl/ (*f.*) From the medieval short form of the related names ELEANOR, ELLEN, and HELEN; for the explanation of the initial consonant cf. NED. It was the name by which Charles II's mistress Eleanor Gwyn (1650–87) was universally known to her contemporaries, and at about that time it also became established as an independent name.

**Nellie** /'nɛlɪ/ (*f.*) Diminutive of NELL, with the hypocoristic suffix *-ie*. The spelling **Nelly** also occurs, but the name as a whole is rather out of favour at present.

**Nelson** /'nɛlsən/ (*m.*) From the English surname, originally acquired in the Middle Ages by men who were the sons of either a NEIL or a NELL. Use as a given name probably began as a tribute to the British admiral Lord Nelson (1758–1805); cf. HORATIO. It is, however, now much more common in America than in Britain.

**Nerys** /'nɛrɪs/ (*f.*) Welsh: from a feminine form of *ner* lord. This was not used as a given name in the Middle Ages, and dates only from the recent revival of interest in Welsh culture, which has been accompanied by a desire to give Welsh children names reflecting their national identity.

**Nesta** /'nɛstə/ (*f.*) Of Welsh origin: Latinized version of *Nest*, a Welsh pet form of AGNES. Nesta was the name of the grandmother of the 12th-cent. chronicler Giraldus Cambrensis ('Gerald the Welshman').

**Nettie** /'nɛtɪ:/ (*f.*) Diminutive name derived from an apheatic version of various girls' names ending in the syllable *-nette*, for example ANNETTE and JEANETTE, with the hypocoristic suffix *-ie*. It achieved a brief peak of popularity in the late 19th and early 20th cent.

**Neville** /'nɛvɪl/ (*m.*) From the English surname, derived from a Norman baronial name from any of several places in Normandy called Néville or Neuville 'new settlement'. First used as a given name in the early 17th cent., and with increasing regularity from the second half of the 19th, it is now so firmly established as a given name that it has lost touch with its origin as a surname.

**Niall** /*Gaelic* 'njɪəl/ (*m.*) Modern revival of the Gaelic form of NEIL, gaining steadily in popularity, especially in Ireland.

**Nicholas** /'nɪkələs/ (*m.*) From the post-classical Greek name *Nikolaos*, composed of the elements *nikē* victory + *laos* people. The spelling with *-ch-* first occurred as early as the 12th cent., and became firmly established at the time of the Reformation, although the spelling **Nicolas** is still occasionally found. St Nicholas was a 4th-cent. bishop of Myra in Lycia, about whom virtually nothing factual is known, although a vast body of legend grew up around him, and he became the patron saint of Russia, as well as of children, sailors, merchants, and pawnbrokers. His feast day is 6 December, and among the many roles which legend has assigned to him is that of bringer of Christmas presents, in the guise of 'Santa Claus' (an alteration of the German form of his name, *Sankt Niklaus*, or the Dutch form, *Sinte Claus*).

**Nick** /nɪk/ (*m.*) Usual short form of NICHOLAS.

**Nicky** /'nɪki:/ (*m., f.*) As a boy's name, a diminutive form of NICK. It is occasionally found as a girl's name (see NIKKI).

**Nicol** /'nɪkəl/ (*m.*) From a common medieval form of NICHOLAS, current until a relatively late period in Scotland, and now being revived in more general use. It is also spelled **Nichol** and **Nic(h)oll**, in part being a transferred use of surnames derived from the medieval given name.

**Nicola** /'nɪkələ/ (*f.*) Feminine form of NICHOLAS. This is the regular form of the boy's name in Italian, and the spelling *Nikola* is likewise found in several East European languages as a boy's name, but in English the ending -*a* seems to be inextricably associated with femininity.

**Nicole** /nɪ'kəʊl; *French* nɪ'kɔl/ (*f.*) French feminine form of NICHOLAS, now increasingly used as a more exotic version of NICOLA.

**Nicolette** /nɪkə'lɛt/ (*f.*) French diminutive of NICOLE.

**Nigel** /'naɪdʒəl/ (*m.*) Anglicized form of the medieval name *Nigellus*, a Latinized version (ostensibly representing a diminutive of Latin *niger* black) of the vernacular *Ni(h)el*, i.e. NEIL. Although it is frequently found in medieval records, this form was probably not used in everyday life before its revival by antiquarians in the 19th cent.

**Nikki** /'nɪki:/ (*f.*) Pet form of NICOLA or feminine variant of NICKY, but now quite commonly used as an independent name in its own right.

**Nina** /'ni:nə/ (*f.*) Originally a Russian pet form of ANNA, but later taken as a short form of various longer girl's names ending in -*nina*, such as *Antonina* and *Janina*.

**Ninette** /nɪ'nɛt/ (*f.*) French diminutive of NINA; like NADINE, this was one of the names brought to the English-speaking world from Russian via French in the early 20th cent.

**Ninian** /'nɪnɪən/ (*m.*) Scottish: the name of a 5th-cent. British saint who was responsible for evangelizing the northern Britons and the Picts. His name first appears in the Latinized form *Ninianus* in the 8th cent.; this appears to be the same as the *Nynnyaw* recorded in the *Mabinogion*. The given name was used in his honour until at least the 16th cent. in Scotland and has occasionally been revived in recent years.

**Noah** /'nəʊə/ (*m.*) Old Testament: name of the character whose family alone was saved from the flood ordained by God to destroy mankind because of its wickedness. The origin of the name is far from certain; in the Bible it is implied that it means 'Rest' (Gen. 5:29, 'And he called his name Noah, saying, This same shall comfort us concerning our work and the toil of our hands, because of the ground which the Lord hath cursed').

**Noel** /'nəʊəl/ (*m.*) From Old French *noel*, *nael* Christmas, from Latin *natālis diēs [Domini]* birthday (of the Lord); its meaning is still relatively transparent, partly because the term occurs as a synonym for 'Christmas' in the refrain of Christmas carols. The name is often given to children born at Christmas time.

**Noelle** /nəʊ'ɛl; *French* nɔ'ɛl/ (*f.*) French feminine form of NOEL.

**Nona** /'nəʊnə/ (*f.*) From the feminine form of the Latin ordinal *nonus* ninth, sometimes used as a given name in Victorian times for the ninth-born child in a family if it was a girl, or even to the ninth-born girl. These days it is more generally used, without reference to the etymological sense.

**Noni** /'nəʊniː/ (f.) Pet form of IONE or of NORA. The spelling **Nonie** is also found.

**Nora** /'nɔːrə/ (f.) Short form of names such as HONORA or LEONORA. Although these are not Gaelic in origin, *Nora* was especially popular in Ireland at one time. The name is sometimes spelled **Norah**, giving it a biblical appearance.

**Norbert** /'nɔːbət/ (m.) Norman: of Germanic origin, composed of the elements *nord* north + *beorht* famous. Its most famous bearer was an 11th-cent. saint who founded an order of monks known as Norbertians (also called Premonstratensians from their first home at Premontré near Laon). *Norbert* was one of several names of Germanic origin that were revived in Britain in the late 19th cent., but it is now rather more common in America than Britain.

**Noreen** /'nɔːriːn/ (f.) Diminutive of NORA. The suffix is of Irish origin (Gaelic -*in*), and the name is occasionally spelled **Norene** or **Norine**.

**Norma** /'nɔːmə/ (f.) Apparently invented by Felice Romani in his libretto for Bellini's opera of this name (first performed in 1832). It is identical in form with Latin *norma* rule, standard, but there is no evidence that this word was the actual source of the name. It has also been taken as a feminine equivalent of NORMAN.

**Norman** /'nɔːmən/ (m.) Of Germanic origin, composed of the elements *nord* north + *man* man, i.e. 'Norseman'. This name was in use in England before the Conquest, and was reinforced by its use as a given name among the Norman invaders themselves.

**Norris** /ˈnɒrɪs/ (*m.*) From the English surname, derived from Old Norman French *norreis* (in which the stem represents the Germanic element *nord*), originally a local designation for someone who had migrated from the north.

**Nuala** /ˈnuːələ/ (*f.*) Aphetic short form of the Irish name *Fionnuala* (see FENELLA and FINOLA). It is now in general use as an independent name.

**Nye** /naɪ/ (*m.*) English short form of the Welsh name ANEURIN, representing the middle syllable of that name as commonly pronounced. The name is associated with the Welsh Labour statesman Aneurin Bevan (1897–1960).

**Nyree** /ˈnaɪriː/ (*f.*) English spelling of the Maori name usually transcribed as **Ngaire**. It is relatively common in New Zealand and has been taken up to some extent in Britain due to the fame of the New Zealand-born actress Nyree Dawn Porter (b. 1940).

# O

**Obadiah** /ˌəʊbəˈdaɪə/ (*m.*) Old Testament: name (meaning 'servant of God' in Hebrew, cf. Arabic *Abdullah* 'servant of Allah') of a prophet who gave his name to one of the shorter books of the Old Testament, and of two other minor biblical characters: a porter in the Temple (Neh. 12:25), and the man who introduced King Ahab to the prophet Elijah (I Kings 18).

**Oberon** /ˈəʊbərɒn/ (*m.*) Variant spelling of AUBERON.

**Octavia** /ɒkˈteɪvɪə/ (*f.*) Of Latin origin, representing a feminine form of OCTAVIUS. It was borne by various female members of the Roman imperial family.

**Octavian** /ɒkˈteɪvɪən/ (*m.*) Usual English form of the Latin name *Octāviānus*, a derivative of OCTAVIUS. The first Roman emperor, now generally known by the imperial title Augustus, was born Caius Octavius, but when he was adopted by Julius Caesar became Caius Julius Caesar Octavianus. Another Octavianus was a 5th-cent. Carthaginian saint who was put to death with several thousand companions by the Asiatic Vandal king Hunneric.

**Octavius** /ɒkˈteɪvɪəs/ (*m.*) From the Roman family name, derived from Latin *octāvus* eighth. The name was fairly frequently given to the eighth child (or eighth son) in large Victorian families. It is much less common these days, when families rarely extend to eight children, but is occasionally selected for reasons of family tradition or for some other reason without regard to its original meaning.

**Odette** /əʊˈdet; *French* oˈdɛt/ (*f.*) French: feminine diminutive form of the common medieval man's name *Oda*, which is of Germanic origin (cf. OTTO).

**Odile** /əʊˈdiːl; *French* oˈdiːl/ (*f.*) French: from the

medieval Germanic name *Odila* (a derivative of the
element *od* riches, prosperity, fortune; cf. OTTO). This
was the name of an 8th-cent. saint who founded a
Benedictine convent at what is now Odilienburg in
North Germany. See also OTTILIE.

**Olaf** /'əʊlæf/ (*m.*) Of Scandinavian origin, from a name
composed of the elements *ans* god + *leifr* relic. It was
introduced to Britain before the Norman Conquest,
but modern use as a given name in the English-speaking world originated in America, where it was taken
by recent Scandinavian immigrants.

**Olga** /'ɒlgə/ (*f.*) Russian variant of HELGA, taken to
Russia by the Scandinavian settlers who founded the
first Russian state of Kiev in the 9th cent. It was introduced to the English-speaking world in the late 19th
cent.

**Olive** /'ɒlɪv/ (*f.*) One of the earliest and most successful of the names from plants coined during the 19th
cent., no doubt partly because an olive branch has
been a symbol of peace since biblical times. The Latinate form *Oliva* was a given name in medieval times,
but dropped out of use after its pronunciation
became indistinguishable from that of the boy's name
OLIVER. See also OLIVIA.

**Oliver** /'ɒlɪvə/ (*m.*) Norman French, of Germanic origin. It was first used as the name (French *Olivier*) of
one of Charlemagne's paladins or retainers, the close
companion in arms of Roland in the *Chanson de
Roland*, an Old French narrative poem of the 11th or
12th cent. Ostensibly it derives from Late Latin *oli-
vārius* olive tree (cf. OLIVE), but Charlemagne's other
paladins all bear solidly Germanic names, so it is
more probably an altered form of some Germanic
name, perhaps OLAF.

**Olivia** /ə'lɪvɪə/ (*f.*) Latinate name, first used by Shakespeare as the name of the rich heiress who is wooed by the duke in *Twelfth Night*. It is possibly derived from Latin *oliva* olive, perhaps influenced by the medieval given name *Oliva*, although this had dropped out of use by the 16th cent.

**Ollie** /'ɒlɪ/ (*m.*, *f.*) As a boy's name, a pet form of OLIVER; as a girl's name, a pet form of the various woman's names beginning with the first syllable *Ol-*, such as OLIVE and OLWEN. It is not now much used.

**Olwen** /'ɒlwɛn/ (*f.*) Welsh: composed of the elements *ôl* footprint, track + *gwen* white. A character of this name in Welsh legend had the magical property of causing flowers to spring up behind her wherever she went.

**Omar** /'əʊmɑː/ (*m.*) Old Testament: name (meaning 'Talkative' or 'Eloquent' in Hebrew) of a character fleetingly mentioned in a genealogy (Gen. 36:11). It has been occasionally used from Puritan times down to the present day in America. More often, however, it is of Arabic origin, as in the case of the film actor and international bridge player Omar Sharif (b. 1926 in Egypt).

**Oonagh** /'uːnə/ (*f.*) An ancient Irish name of uncertain origin. The form **Oona** is also quite common.

**Opal** /'əʊpəl/ (*f.*) One of the rarer girl's names taken from gemstones. The word *opal* is ultimately derived (via Latin and Greek) from Sanskrit *upala* precious stone.

**Opaline** /'əʊpəliːn/ (*f.*) Diminutive of OPAL, with the productive suffix of female names *-ine*. A comparatively recent coinage.

**Ophelia** /ə'fiːlɪə/ (*f.*) Of Shakespearian origin: name of a character in *Hamlet*, the beautiful daughter of Polonius; she loves Hamlet, and eventually goes mad and drowns herself. In spite of the ill omen of this literary association, the name has enjoyed moderate popularity since the 19th cent. Apparently it was first used by the Italian pastoralist Jacopo Sannazzaro (1458–1530), who presumably intended it as a feminine form of the Greek name *Óphelos* 'Help'. Shakespeare seems to have borrowed the name from Sannazzaro, without giving any thought to whether it was an appropriate name for a play set in medieval Denmark.

**Orla** /Irish 'ɔːrlə/ (*f.*) Irish (older Gaelic form **Orfhlaith**); a feminine derivative of Gaelic *ór* gold, probably with reference to golden hair.

**Orlando** /ɔː'lændəʊ/ (*m.*) Italian form of ROLAND, occasionally used as a given name in the English-speaking world. It is the name of the hero in Shakespeare's comedy *As You Like It*.

**Ormond** /'ɔːmənd/ (*m.*) Irish: originally an ethnic name for someone who came from East Munster; cf. DESMOND.

**Orson** /'ɔːsən/ (*m.*) From an Old Norman French nickname meaning 'Bearcub' (a diminutive of *ors* bear, Latin *ursus*), used occasionally in medieval times. In the 20th cent. it has come to public notice as a result of the fame of the American actor Orson Welles (1915–85), who dropped his more prosaic first name, George, in favour of his middle name before embarking on his acting career.

**Orville** /'ɔːvɪl/ (*m.*) Though in appearance a surname of Norman baronial origin, this name seems to have been invented (with the intention of evoking such associations) by the novelist Fanny Burney for the hero, Lord Orville, of her novel *Evelina* (1778).

**Osbert** /'ɒzbəːt/ (*m.*) From a Late Old English personal name, composed of the elements *os* god (of Scandinavian origin; cf. OLAF) + *beohrt* bright, famous. It is not now common in the English-speaking world, but has been borne for example by the British cartoonist Osbert Lancaster and the writer Osbert Sitwell.

**Osborn** /ˈɒzbɔːn/ (*m.*) From a Late Old English personal name, composed of the elements *os* god + *bearn* bear, warrior (both of Scandinavian origin). As a modern given name it generally represents a transferred use of the surname that was derived from this name during the Middle Ages. The spellings **Osborne**, **Osbourn**, and **Osbourne** are also found.

**Oscar** /ˈɒskə/ (*m.*) An 18th-cent. revival of a Late Old English name, of Scandinavian origin, composed of the elements *os* god + *gār* spear. It seems to have been resuscitated by the antiquarian poet James Macpherson (1736–96); cf. MALVINA. It is now once again a characteristically Scandinavian name; it was reintroduced there because Napoleon, being an admirer of the works of Macpherson, imposed the name on his godson Oscar Bernadotte, who became King Oscar I of Sweden in 1844.

**Osmond** /ˈɒzmənd/ (*m.*) From a Late Old English personal name, composed of the elements *os* god (of Scandinavian origin; cf. OLAF) + *mund* protection. The name was also in use among the Normans and was borne by an 11th-cent. saint who was appointed to the see of Salisbury by William the Conqueror. As a modern given name it may in part represent a transferred use of the surname derived from this name during the Middle Ages. The spelling **Osmund** is also in use.

**Oswald** /ˈɒzwəld/ (*m.*) A 19th-cent. revival of a Late Old English name, of Scandinavian origin, composed of the elements *os* god + *weald* rule. St Oswald was a 10th-cent. Bishop of Worcester and Archbishop of

York, of Danish parentage. The name more or less died out after the Middle Ages, but underwent a modest revival in the 19th cent. as part of the vogue for pre-Conquest English names.

**Oswin** /ˈɒzwɪn/ (*m.*) From a late Old English personal name, composed of the elements *os* god (of Scandinavian origin; cf. OLAF) + *wine* friend. St Oswin was a 7th-cent. king venerated as a martyr, although the reasons for his death at the hand of his brother Oswy seem to have been political and personal rather than religious.

**Otis** /ˈəʊtɪs/ (*m.*) From the English surname, derived from the genitive case of the medieval given name *Ote* or *Ode* (of Norman and ultimately Germanic origin; cf. OTTO). It originally denoted a man who was the 'son of Ote'. It came to be used as a given name in America in honour of the Revolutionary hero James Otis (1725–83), and is still much more common in America than elsewhere in the English-speaking world.

**Ottilie** /ˈɒtɪli/ (*f.*) From French: of Germanic origin, from the woman's given name *Odila* (see ODILE), a feminine derivative of OTTO.

**Otto** /ˈɒtəʊ/ (*m.*) German: from a Germanic element *od, ot* prosperity, fortune, riches (cf. the corresponding Old English *ēad* in names such as EDWARD and EDWIN). *Otto* was relatively recently introduced from Germany, where it has been popular in various noble and ruling families for centuries.

**Ottoline** /ˈɒtəlaɪn, ˈɒtəliːn/ (*f.*) From French: originally a diminutive of OTTILIE. It now has independent status in the English-speaking world, partly due to the influence of the literary hostess Lady Ottoline Morrell (1873–1938).

**Owen** /ˈəʊɪn/ (*m.*) From Welsh: apparently of the

same origin as the Gaelic EWAN, i.e. 'borne of the yew'. The name is often chosen by Welsh patriots in honour of Owen Glendower (Welsh *Owain Glyndwr*), who led a revolt against Henry IV's rule in Wales in the early years of the 15th cent. The more authentic Welsh spelling **Owain** is now also used. In Ireland this name is sometimes used as an Anglicization of EOGHAN.

**Oz** /ɒz/ (*m.*) Informal short form of OSWALD, OSBERT, OSBORN, or OSMOND.

# P

**Paddy** /'pædi:/ (*m.*) Diminutive of PATRICK or of its Irish equivalent *Padraig*. It has been in use since medieval times, and has come to function also as a generic nickname for an Irishman.

**Pamela** /'pæmələ/ (*f.*) An invention of the Elizabethan pastoral poet Sir Philip Sidney (1554–86), in whose verse it is stressed on the second syllable. There is no clue to the sources that influenced Sidney in this coinage. The name was taken up as the name of the heroine of Samuel Richardson's novel *Pamela* (1740). In Henry Fielding's *Joseph Andrews* (1742), which started out as a parody of *Pamela*, Fielding comments that the name is 'very strange'.

**Pansy** /'pænzi:/ (*f.*) A 19th-cent. flower name, from the garden flower that got its name from Old French *pensee* thought. This was never especially popular, and is seldom chosen at all now that the word *pansy* is also used in the slang sense 'effeminate'.

**Pascal** /'pæs'kɑːl/ (*m.*) From French: from Late Latin *Paschālis* 'relating to Easter' (Latin *Pascha*, from Hebrew *pesach* Passover). In France the name was often given to sons born at this time of the year. Its popularity may have been influenced by the fame of the French philosopher Blaise Pascal (1623–62), whose *Pensées* ('Thoughts') were published posthumously in 1670. The name is now occasionally used in the English-speaking world, mainly by Roman Catholics. The spelling **Paschal** is also used.

**Pascale** /'pæs'kɑːl/ (*f.*) French feminine form of PASCAL, which has been occasionally used in the English-speaking world since about 1960. The Spanish form **Pascuala** is also found.

**Pat** /pæt/ (*m.*, *f.*) Short form of PATRICK or PATRICIA.

**Patience** /ˈpeɪʃəns/ (f.) From the English vocabulary
word, denoting one of the Seven Christian Virtues.
This name was a favourite with the Puritans, and survived better than many similar names, but now seems
somewhat old-fashioned. The word is derived from
Latin *pati* to suffer, and was associated by the early
Christians with those who endured persecution and
misfortune without complaint or loss of faith.

**Patricia** /pəˈtrɪʃə/ (f.) Feminine equivalent of
PATRICK, Latinate in form.

**Patrick** /ˈpætrɪk/ (m.) Anglicized version of Irish
**Pádraig** /ˈpɑːdrɪgʲ/, the name of the apostle and
patron saint of Ireland (c. 389–461). In his own Latin
autobiography, as well as in later tradition, his name
appears as *Patricius* 'Patrician' (i.e. belonging to the
Roman senatorial or noble class), but this may
actually represent a Latinization of some lost Celtic
(British) name.

**Patsy** /ˈpætsi/ (f., m.) Pet form, mainly Irish, of PATRI-
CIA or PATRICK. It is rather more common as a girl's
name, and is fairly well established in independent
use. As a boy's name it is almost completely
restricted to Irish communities. Its popularity does
not seem to have been seriously affected by its use in
derogatory senses in the general vocabulary, in
America meaning a dupe and in Australia a homosexual.

**Patti** /ˈpæti/ (f.) Short form of PATRICIA. The spellings
**Pattie** and **Patty** also occur.

**Paul** /pɔːl/ (m.) From a Latin family name, originally a
nickname meaning 'Small', from Latin *paulus*, used
in the post-classical period as a given name. Pre-emi-
nently this is the name of the saint who is generally
regarded, with St Peter, as co-founder of the Christian Church. He was a Roman citizen and a Jew, born

in Tarsus, originally named SAUL, and at first found employment as a minor official persecuting Christians. He was converted to Christianity by a vision of Christ while on the road to Damascus, and thereafter undertook extensive missionary journeys, converting people, especially gentiles, to Christianity all over the eastern Mediterranean. His preaching aroused considerable official hostility, and eventually he was beheaded at Rome in about AD 65. He is the author of the fourteen epistles to churches and individuals which form part of the New Testament.

**Paula** /ˈpɔːlə/ (*f.*) Feminine form of PAUL, from the Latin name *Paula*, feminine of *Paulus*. This was the name of various minor early saints and martyrs.

**Paulette** /pɔːˈlɛt/ (*f.*) French feminine diminutive of PAUL, a more recent importation to the English-speaking world than PAULINE.

**Paulina** /pɔːˈliːnə/ (*f.*) Feminine form of the Late Latin name *Paulīnus*, a derivative of *Paulus* (see PAUL). It was borne by several minor early martyrs.

**Pauline** /ˈpɔːliːn/ (*f.*) French version of PAULINA, now very commonly used in the English-speaking world. It is occasionally found in the spellings **Paulene**, **Pauleen**, and **Paulyne**.

**Pearl** /pɜːl/ (*f.*) In modern use, one of the group of names coined in the 19th cent. from precious and semi-precious stones. It has a longer history as a Jewish name, representing an Anglicized form of Yiddish *Perle*, an affectionate nickname or vernacular equivalent of MARGARET.

**Peg** /pɛg/ (*f.*) Short form of PEGGY.

**Peggy** /ˈpɛgɪ/ (*f.*) Variant of MEGGIE or MAGGIE, pet forms of MARGARET. It is also spelled **Peggie**. The reason for the alternation of *M-* and *P-*, which occurs also in *Molly*/*Polly*, is not known; it has been ascribed to Celtic influence, but this seems unlikely.

**Penelope** /pə'nɛləpi:/ (*f.*) From Greek mythology: name of the wife of Odysseus who sat patiently awaiting his return for twenty years, fending off by persuasion and guile a pressing horde of suitors for her hand in marriage as a supposed wiðow. Her name would seem to derive from Greek *pēnelops* duck, and play is made with this word in the *Odyssey*, but this may be a legend obscuring a more complex origin, now no longer known.

**Penny** /'pɛni:/ (*f.*) Pet form of PENELOPE, now quite commonly used as an independent name.

**Percival** /'pɜːsɪvəl/ (*m.*) From Old French versions of Arthurian legend, where the name is spelled *Perceval*. According to Chrestien de Troyes (12th cent.) and Wolfram von Eschenbach (*c.* 1170–1220), Perceval (German *Parzifal*) was the perfectly pure and innocent knight who alone could succeed in the quest for the Holy Grail (a cup or bowl with supernatural powers, which in medieval legend was identified with the chalice that had received Christ's blood at the Crucifixion). Later versions of the Grail legend assign this role to Sir Galahad. The name *Perceval* probably represents a drastic remodelling of the Celtic name *Peredur*, as if from Old French *perce(r)* to pierce + *val* valley. This may well have been influenced by PERCY, which was similarly analysed as a compound of *perce(r)* + *haie* hedge.

**Percy** /'pɜːsi:/ (*m.*) Originally a surname, but long established as a given name, and now often taken as a short form of PERCIVAL. In its first use it was a Norman territorial name borne by a baron who held a fief in Normandy called *Perci* (from Late Latin *Persiācum*, composed of the Gallo-Roman personal name *Persius* and the local suffix *-ācum*). As a given name

*pos*, composed of the elements *philein* love + *hippos*
horse, which was popular in the classical period and
after. It was the name of the father of Alexander the
Great. It was also the name of one of Christ's apostles, of a deacon ordained by the apostles after the
death of Christ, and of several other early saints. The
spelling **Phillip** is sometimes used, although not etymologically justified; it is in part a result of the
influence of the English surname *Phillips*, which is
generally spelt with two *l*'s.

**Philippa** /ˈfɪlɪpə/ (*f.*) Latinate feminine form of PHI-
LIP. In the Middle Ages the vernacular name *Philip*
was borne by women as well as men, but female
bearers were distinguished in Latin records by this
form. It was not, however, used as a regular given
name until the 19th cent. The spellings **Philipa** and
**Phillip(p)a** are also used.

**Philippina** /fɪlɪˈpiːnə/ (*f.*) Latinate feminine derivative of PHILIP. In the Middle Ages it was sometimes
interpreted as a compound of Greek *philein* to love +
*poinĕ* pain, punishment, since Christians were supposed to rejoice in purging themselves of their sins by
pain and punishment, such as flagellation and the
wearing of hair-shirts. The spellings **Philipina** and
**Phillip(p)ina** are also used.

**Phillida** /ˈfɪlɪdə/ (*f.*) Variant of PHYLLIS, derived from
the genitive case (Greek *Phyllidos*, Latin *-dis*) with
the addition of the Latin feminine ending *-a*. The
spelling **Phyllida** is also found.

**Philomena** /fɪləˈmiːnə/ (*f.*) From the name of an
obscure saint (probably of the 3rd cent.) with a local
cult in Italy. In 1527 the bones of a young woman
were discovered under a church altar, together with a
Latin inscription declaring them to be the body of St
Filomena. Her name seems to be a feminine form of
Latin *Philomenus*, from Greek *Philomenēs*, com-

posed of the elements *philein* to love + *menos*
strength. The name became popular in the 19th cent.,
as a result of the supposed discovery in 1802 of the
relics of another St Philomena in the catacombs at
Rome. All the excitement, however, resulted from
the misinterpretation of the Latin inscription *Filu-
mena pax tecum* 'peace be with you, beloved' (from
Greek *philoumena* beloved).

**Phineas** /'fɪnɪəs/ (*m.*) Old Testament: Anglicized
form of the name borne in the Bible by two minor
characters: a grandson of Aaron, who preserved the
purity of the race of Israel and deflected God's wrath
by killing an Israelite who had taken a Midianite
woman to wife (Num. 25:6–15), and a son of the
priest Eli, killed in combat with the Philistines over
the Ark of the Covenant (I Sam. 1:3). The name is
spelled *Phinehas* in the Authorized Version, and has
been taken to mean 'Serpent's Mouth' (i.e. 'Oracle')
in Hebrew. It was popular among the Puritans in the
17th cent., and has been occasionally used since,
especially in America.

**Phoebe** /'fi:bi:/ (*f.*) From classical mythology: Latinized form of the name of a Greek deity, *Phoibē*
(from *phoibos* bright), partially identified with Artemis, goddess of the moon and of hunting, sister of the
sun god Apollo, who was also known as *Phoibos*
(Latin *Phoebus*).

**Phyl** /fɪl/ (*f.*) Short form of PHYLLIS or of any of the
various women's names beginning with the syllable
*Phil-*.

**Phyllis** /'fɪlɪs/ (*f.*) From Greek mythology: name of a
character who killed herself for love and was trans-
formed into an almond tree; the Greek word *phyllis*
means 'foliage', so clearly her name doomed her
from the start.

**Pia** /'piːə/ (*f.*) From the feminine form of Latin *pius* pious, respectful, honourable. The name is common in Italy, and is also regularly used in Eastern Europe and Scandinavia, but is a recent introduction to the English-speaking world.

**Piers** /pɪəz/ (*m.*) A regular Middle English form of PETER (from the Old French nominative case, as against the oblique *Pier*). In the form *Pierce* it survived into the 18th cent., although in part this may be a transferred use of the surname derived from the medieval given name. *Piers* was revived in the mid 20th cent., perhaps partly under the influence of William Langland's great rambling medieval poem *Piers Plowman* (1367–86), in which the character of Piers symbolizes the virtues of hard work, honesty, and fairness.

**Pip** /pɪp/ (*m.*) Pet form of PHILIP, best known as the name of the main character in Charles Dickens's *Great Expectations* (1861), whose full name was Philip Pirrip.

**Pippa** /'pɪpə/ (*f.*) Contracted pet form of PHILIPPA, now quite commonly used as an independent name. It was popularized in the 19th cent. by Browning's narrative poem *Pippa Passes* (1841), in which the heroine is a child worker in an Italian silk mill, whose innocent admiration of 'great' people is ironically juxtaposed with their sordid lives. The name is presumably supposed to be Italian, but is not in fact used in Italy.

**Poll** /pɒl/ (*f.*) Short form of POLLY.

**Polly** /'pɒli/ (*f.*) Variant of MOLLY, now sometimes used as a given name in its own right. The reason for the interchange of *P* and *M* is not clear; cf. PEGGY.

**Poppy** /'pɒpiː/ (*f.*) From the name of the flower, Old English *popæg* (ultimately from Latin *papāver*). It

has been used as a given name since the latter years
of the 19th cent., and reached a peak of popularity in
the 1920s.

**Portia** /ˈpɔːʃə/ (f.) Of Shakespearian origin: it occurs
twice in Shakespeare, once as the name of the wife of
Brutus in *Julius Caesar*, which was historically fairly
accurate. Brutus' wife was called *Porcia*, feminine
form of the Roman family name *Porcius*, which is
apparently a derivative of Latin *porcus* pig. However, the main influence on the choice of this given
name is undoubtedly the heiress in *The Merchant of
Venice* who, disguised as a man, shows herself to be a
brilliant advocate.

**Primrose** /ˈprɪmrəʊz/ (f.) One of the several girls'
names taken from words for flowers in the late 19th
cent. The word is from Latin *prima rosa* first rose,
although it does not in fact have any connection with
the rose family and does not bloom particularly early.

**Prince** /prɪns/ (m.) A nickname from the royal title.
The Old French title *prince* (Latin *princeps*, from *pri-
mus* first + *capere* to take, i.e. one who took the first
place) was introduced to Britain by the Normans;
before the Conquest young members of the royal
house had been known as *æðelingas* (from Old English *æðel* noble). As a given name, *Prince* is common
among Blacks in America; it was often bestowed on
slaves with cruel irony, but has been perpetuated by
their descendants with pride.

**Priscilla** /prɪˈsɪlə/ (f.) New Testament: from a post-
classical Latin given name, a feminine diminutive of
the Roman family name *Priscus* (originally a nickname meaning 'Ancient'). *Priscilla* was the name of a
woman with whom St Paul stayed at Corinth (Acts
18:3); she is also referred to as *Prisca* (II Tim. 4:19).
The name was extremely popular among the Puritans
in the 17th cent. and again in the 19th cent.

**Prosper** /ˈprɒspə/ (*m.*) From the Latin name *Prosper-us*, derived from the adjective *prosper* fortunate, prosperous. This was the name of various early saints, including a 5th-cent. theologian and contemporaneous bishops of Orleans and Reggio. It was a favourite among the Puritans, partly because of its association with the English verb to *prosper*. It is still used in the English-speaking world, but only very occasionally. It has always been more common in France, and is particularly associated with the French writer Prosper Mérimée (1803–70).

**Prudence** /ˈpruːdəns/ (*f.*) Originally a medieval form of the Latin name *Prūdentia*, a feminine form of *Prūdentius*, from *prūdens* provident. The Blessed Prudentia was a 15th-cent. abbess who founded a new convent at Como in Italy. Later it was used as a quality-name among the Puritans in the 17th cent, taken from the vocabulary word.

**Prue** /pruː/ (*f.*) Short form of PRUDENCE, also spelled **Pru**.

**Prunella** /pruːˈnɛlə/ (*f.*) A Latinate name that seems to belong to the class of flower names coined in the 19th cent., from a diminutive of Late Latin *pruna* plum (originally the plural form of Classical Latin *prunum*).

# Q

**Queenie** /'kwiːniː/ (*f.*) From the affectionate nick-name *Queen* (going back to Old English *cwēne* woman, respelled as if derived from Latin), with the addition of the diminutive suffix *-ie* (originally characteristic of Northern England and Scotland). In the Victorian era it was sometimes used as an allusive pet form for VICTORIA.

**Quentin** /'kwɛntɪn/ (*m.*) From the Old French form of the Latin name *Quintīnus*, a derivative of the given name *Quintus* 'Fifth' (itself sometimes used as a given name in England, mainly in the 19th cent. for the fifth child or the fifth boy to be born into a family; cf. OCTAVIUS). The name was borne by a 3rd-cent. saint who worked as a missionary in Gaul.

**Quincy** /'kwɪnsiː/ (*m.*) From the English surname, originally a Norman baronial name borne by the family that held lands at Cuinchy in the Pas-de-Calais, Normandy, so called from the Gallo-Roman name *Quintus* (see QUENTIN) and the local suffix *-ācum*. Use as a given name is more common in America than the rest of the English-speaking world, and seems to derive from the fame of President John Quincy Adams (1767–1848). The name is sometimes also spelled **Quincey**.

**Quintin** /'kwɪntɪn/ (*m.*) Less common variant of QUEN-TIN, with the Latin vowel restored in the first syllable.

# R

**Rabbie** /'ræbɪ:/ (*m.*) Scottish pet form of ROBERT, a diminutive version of the short form *Rab, Rob*. It is chiefly associated with the poet Robert Burns (1759–96).

**Rachel** /'reɪtʃəl/ (*f.*) Old Testament: name (meaning 'Ewe' in Hebrew) of the wife of Jacob and mother (after long barrenness) of Joseph. In the Middle Ages and later this was a characteristically Jewish name, and still retains something of a Jewish flavour, although it is now much more widely used.

**Rae** /reɪ/ (*f.*) Apparently originating as a short form of RACHEL, but now often taken as a feminine form of RAY or RAYMOND. Occasionally it may represent a transferred use of the Scottish surname *Rae*, originally a nickname from the roebuck. It is often used in combinations such as *Rae Ellen* and *Mary Rae*.

**Raelene** /'reɪliːn/ (*f.*) Australian fanciful coinage of recent origin, from RAE + the feminine suffix *-lene*.

**Raina** /raɪ'iːnə/ (*f.*) From Eastern Europe, where it is a form of REGINA. It seems to have been first introduced to the English-speaking world by George Bernard Shaw, as the name of a character in *Arms and the Man* (1894).

**Raine** /reɪn/ (*f.*) Of relatively modern origin and uncertain derivation: possibly a respelling of French *reine* queen (cf. REGINA and RAINA), or from the surname *Raine* or *Rayne*. The surname is derived from various medieval given names beginning with the Germanic element *ra(g)in* might.

**Ralph** /rælf, reɪf/ (*m.*) Norman: a contracted form of the Germanic name *Radulf*, composed of the elements *rad* counsel + *wulf* wolf. The spelling with -*ph* is the result of classically influenced 'improvement' in the 18th cent. The spelling **Ralf** is also used, but is rarer. The pronunciation with silent *l* (rhyming with *waif*), which was universal in the 19th cent., is now unusual.

**Ramon** /rə'məun; *Spanish* ra'mɔn/ (*m.*) Spanish version of RAYMOND, in frequent use in the U.S. among people of Hispanic descent, but not taken up outside such communities to anything like the same extent as the feminine form RAMONA.

**Ramona** /rə'məunə; *Spanish* ra'mɔnə/ (*f.*) Spanish feminine form of RAMON, which has been gaining popularity in recent years with non-Hispanic parents in America and, to a lesser extent, in Britain.

**Randall** /'rændəl/ (*m.*) From a regular medieval form of RANDOLF, now sporadically reintroduced from the surname that was derived from the given name. The spelling **Randal** also occurs, together with the less frequent **Randel(l)** and **Randle**.

**Randolf** /'rændɒlf/ (*m.*) Norman: of Germanic origin, composed of the elements *rand* rim, edge (of a shield) + *wulf* wolf. The spelling **Randolph** is about equally common.

**Randy** /'rændi:/ (*m.*, *f.*) As a boy's name this originated as a pet form of RANDALL and RANDOLF. As a girl's name it may have originated either as a transferred use of the boy's name or else as an aphetic pet form of MIRANDA. It is now fairly commonly used as an independent name by both sexes, in spite of the unfortunate connotations of the slang term *randy* lustful. As a girl's name it is also spelled **Randi**.

**Raoul** /'rəuəl; *French* ra'ul/ (*m.*) French version of RALPH, occasionally used in the English-speaking world. The form **Raul** (sometimes pronounced as a single syllable) is either a simplified spelling or a use of the Spanish or Italian form.

**Raphael** /'ræfeɪəl/ (m.) From early Christian tradition: name (composed of Hebrew elements meaning 'to heal' and 'God') of one of the archangels (cf. GABRIEL and MICHAEL). He is not named in the canonical text of the Bible, but plays a part in the apocryphal tale of Tobias. The name has always been much more common on the Continent than in Britain, and use in the English-speaking world today generally reflects European influence.

**Raquel** /'rækɛl; *Spanish* ra'kɛl/ (f.) Spanish form of RACHEL, brought to public attention by the fame and good looks of the film actress Raquel Welch (born Raquel Tejada in 1942).

**Rastus** /'ræstəs/ (m.) New Testament: short form of the Latin name *Erastus* (Greek *Erastos*, from *erān* to love). This was the name of the treasurer of Corinth converted by St Paul (Rom. 16:23). In the early 20th cent. *Rastus* came to be regarded as a typically Black name, for reasons which are unclear.

**Ray** /reɪ/ (m.) Short form of RAYMOND, now often used as an independent name. In a few instances it may represent a transferred use of the surname *Ray*, which was normally first acquired as a nickname, from Old French *rei, roi* king (cf. ROY and LEROY).

**Raymond** /'reɪmənd/ (m.) Norman: of Germanic origin, composed of the elements *ra(g)in* might + *mund* protection. It was revived in the middle of the 19th cent., together with several other given names of Anglo-Saxon and Norman Germanic origin.

**Rebecca** /rɪ'bɛkə/ (f.) Old Testament: from the Latin form of *Rebekah* (meaning possibly 'Heifer', or alternatively 'Noose', in Hebrew), borne by the wife of Isaac and mother of Esau and Jacob. The name has always been common among Jews; it began to be used also by Christians when Old Testament names became popular at the time of the Reformation, was very popular among the Puritans in the 17th cent., and is now widely used by people of many different creeds.

**Reg** /rɛdʒ/ (*m.*) Short form of REGINALD, often preferred by bearers of that name for use in almost all situations, but rarely actually bestowed as an independent name.

**Regan** /'riːgən/ (*f.*) Of Shakespearian origin: name of one of the three daughters in *King Lear*, who is in fact a most unattractive character. It is not known where Shakespeare got the name; he presumably believed it to be of Celtic origin. Modern use has been reinforced by the Irish surname *Re(a)gan* (Gaelic *Ó Riagáin*).

**Reggie** /'rɛdʒi/ (*m.*) Pet form of REGINALD, common in the 19th and early 20th cent., but now less so.

**Regina** /rɪ'dʒaɪnə/ (*f.*) From a Latin nickname meaning 'Queen'. It seems to have been occasionally used among early Christians; a St Regina, probably of the 3rd cent., was venerated as a virgin martyr at Autun from an early date. In modern use it is normally borne by Roman Catholics in allusion to the Marian title *Regina Coeli* 'Queen of Heaven'.

**Reginald** /'rɛdʒɪnəld/ (*m.*) Norman: from *Reginaldus*, a Latinized form of REYNOLD, influenced by Latin *regina* queen. It is now regarded as extremely formal, and bearers generally shorten it to REG.

**Renée** /'rɛniː; *French* rə'ne/ (*f.*) French feminine form of the boy's name *René*, which is much less common in the English-speaking world. It means 'Reborn (i.e. in Christ)', from Latin *Renātus*.

**Reuben** /'ruːbən/ (*m.*) Old Testament: Hebrew name of uncertain origin, borne by one of the twelve sons of Jacob, who passed it on to one of the twelve tribes of Israel. It has been taken to mean 'Behold, a son' (Gen. 29:32 'and Leah conceived, and bare a son, and she called his name Reuben: for she said, Surely the Lord hath looked upon my affliction: now therefore my husband will love me'). The spelling **Reuven** is rare, but more accurately reflects the Hebrew pronunciation of the name.

**Rex** /rɛks/ (*m.*) From Latin *rex* king; not used as a given name in Latin of the classical period or in the Middle Ages. Its adoption as a given name seems to have been a 19th-cent. innovation.

**Reynard** /'rɛnɑːd/ (*m.*) Norman: of Germanic origin, composed of the elements *ra(g)in* might + *hard* hardy, brave, strong. In French *renard* (derived from this name) has become the generic name for a fox, as a result of the popularity of medieval beast tales featuring *Re(y)nard le goupil* 'Reynard the Fox'.

**Reynold** /'rɛnəld/ (*m.*) Norman: of Germanic origin, composed of the elements *ra(g)in* might + *wald* rule. See also RONALD and REGINALD.

**Rhiannon** /hri'ænon/ (*f.*) Welsh: name (meaning 'Nymph, Goddess') borne in Celtic mythology by a minor deity associated with the moon, but not used as a given name before the 20th cent. The spelling **Rhianon** is also found.

**Rhoda** /'rəʊdə/ (*f.*) From the post-classical Greek name *Rhoda*, derived either directly from *rhodon* rose, or else as an ethnic name meaning 'woman from Rhodes', an island which possibly originally got its name from the same word *rhodon*. In the New Testament, Rhoda was a servant in the house of Mary the mother of John, where Peter went after his release from prison by an angel (Acts 12:13).

**Rhona** /'rəʊnə/ (*f.*) Of uncertain derivation: apparently originating in Scotland sometime around 1870.

The spelling **Rona** is also found, and it is possible that the name was devised as a feminine form of RONAN. The spelling was then probably altered by association with RHODA.

**Rhonwen** /'hronwɛn/ (f.) Welsh: composed of the elements *rhon* pike, lance + *gwen* white, fair. It is now fairly common in Wales.

**Rhydderch** /'hrəðɛrx/ (m.) Welsh: originally a byname meaning 'Reddish-brown'. This was a relatively common name in the Middle Ages, when it gave rise to the surname *Prothero(e)* (Welsh *ap Rhydderch* 'Son of Rhydderch'), and has recently been revived by parents proudly conscious of their Welsh roots.

**Rhys** /hrɪs/ (m.) Welsh: meaning 'Ardour'. It is occasionally also used in the Anglicized spelling **Rees** /riːs/, and has also been influenced by the surname so spelled.

**Ria** /'riːə/ (f.) Aphetic short form of MARIA, of German origin.

**Rich** /rɪtʃ/ (m.) Short form of RICHARD. There was a medieval name *Rich(e)*, but it is not directly connected with the modern form: it represents a short form of several medieval names, including not only *Richard* but also other rarer Germanic names with the same first element, as for example *Rich(i)er* 'Power Army' and *Richaud* 'Power Rule'. It also came to be used independently.

**Richard** /'rɪtʃəd/ (m.) One of the most enduringly successful of the Germanic names introduced into Britain by the Normans. It is composed of the elements *ric* power + *hard* hardy, brave, strong; it has enjoyed continuous popularity from the Conquest to the present day, reinforced by its having been borne by three kings of England.

**Richie** /'rɪtʃiː/ (*m.*) Diminutive of RICH; the suffix *-ie*
was originally characteristic of Scotland and northern
England, and this name is still very largely Scottish. It
is also commonly spelled **Ritchie**.

**Rick** /rɪk/ (*m.*) Short form of RICHARD, and currently
gaining ground on DICK, though the latter is still more
common.

**Rikki** /'rɪkiː/ (*f.*) Respelled version of the relatively
rare boy's name *Ricky* or *Rickie* (a diminutive of
RICK), on the lines of *Nikki* and *Vikki*.

**Riley** /'raɪliː/ (*m.*) From the English surname, originally a local name from various places (for example
in Devon and Lancs.) named with the Old English
elements *ryge* rye + *lēah* wood, clearing. In some
uses it may represent a respelling of the Irish surname
*Reilly*, which is from an old Irish personal name,
*Rogheallach*, of unknown origin.

**Rita** /'riːtə/ (*f.*) Short form of *Margarita*, the Spanish
form of MARGARET, or of *Margherita*, the Italian form.
This short form is far more common in England and
the U.S. than either of the full versions.

**Rob** /rɒb/ (*m.*) Short form of ROBERT.

**Robert** /'rɒbət/ (*m.*) One of the many Germanic
names introduced into Britain by the Normans. This
one is somewhat tautologously composed of the two
elements *hrod* fame + *berht* bright, famous. It had a
native Old English predecessor of similar form
(*Hreodbeorht*), which was completely overwhelmed
by the Norman name. See also RUPERT.

**Roberta** /rə'bɜːtə/ (*f.*) Latinate feminine form of
ROBERT, not used in the English-speaking world
before the 1870s; it is probably from Italian.

**Robin** /'rɒbɪn/ (*m.*, *f.*) Originally a diminutive of
ROBERT, from the short form ROB and the diminutive
suffix *-in* (of Old French origin), but now nearly

always used as an independent name. It is now also given to girls, and is also spelled **Robyn**.

**Rocky** /ˈrɒki:/ (*m.*) Of recent American origin, originally a nickname for a tough individual. The name came to public notice through the American heavyweight boxing champion Rocky Marciano (1923–69). He was of Italian extraction, and Anglicized his original name (*Rocco*, of Germanic origin, from *hrok* rest) into a form that seems particularly appropriate for a fighter.

**Rod** /rɒd/ (*m.*) Short form of RODNEY or RODERICK.

**Roderick** /ˈrɒdrɪk/ (*m.*) Of Germanic origin: composed of the elements *hrod* fame + *ric* power, this name was introduced into England in slightly different forms by earlier Scandinavian settlers and by the Normans, but did not survive long into the Middle Ages. In modern use it is taken as an Anglicized form of the cognate Spanish RODRIGO, of Scottish RORY, and of Welsh RHYDDERCH.

**Rodney** /ˈrɒdni:/ (*m.*) Originally from an English surname, but in independent use as a given name since at least the 18th cent., when it was bestowed in honour of Admiral Lord Rodney (1719–92), who comprehensively defeated the French navy in 1759–60. The surname probably derives ultimately from a place name, but the location and etymology of this are uncertain. Stoke Rodney in Somerset is named from the surname, having been held by Richard de Rodene in the early 14th cent. An unidentified place called *Redaneleye* appears in a Glastonbury document of 1282.

**Rodrigo** /rɒˈdriːgəʊ; *Spanish* rɔˈðrigo/ (*m.*) Spanish: of Germanic origin, composed of elements meaning 'fame' and 'power'; cf. RODERICK. This was the name of the last king of the Visigoths, who was defeated by

Arab invaders in 711, and of a saint martyred under the Arabs at Cordoba in 857. It is now occasionally used in the English-speaking world, mainly in families of Hispanic descent.

**Roger** /'rɒdʒə/ (*m.*) Of Germanic origin: composed of the elements *hrod* fame + *geri* spear. A continental form was introduced to Britain by the Normans, swamping the native Old English cognate *Hroðgar*. The short form *Rodge* is occasionally used in a more or less jocular way, but the medieval *Hodge* and *Dodge* are extinct.

**Roisin** /rɒˈʃiːn/ (*f.*) Of Irish origin: from Gaelic **Róisín** /'rɔːʃiːnʲ/, diminutive of **Ros** /rɔːʃ/, the Gaelic form of ROSE. The Anglicized spelling **Rosheen** is also found.

**Roland** /'rəʊlənd/ (*m.*) Norman, of Germanic origin: composed of the elements *hrod* fame + *land* land, territory. It was very popular in the Middle Ages as the name of a legendary Frankish hero, a vassal of Charlemagne, whose exploits are related in the *Chanson de Roland*.

**Rolf** /rɒlf/ (*m.*) Of Germanic origin; popular among the Normans, who brought it to Britain, but also representing a more recent importation of the same name from Germany. It represents a contracted form of a continental Germanic name composed of the elements *hrod* fame + *wulf* wolf. See also RUDOLPH.

**Rollo** /'rɒləʊ/ (*m.*) Latinized form of *Roul*, the Old French version of ROLF (cf. *Raoul* for *Ralph*). This form appears regularly in Latin documents of the Middle Ages, but does not seem to have been used in everyday vernacular contexts. Its use in a few families in modern times is a consciously archaistic revival.

**Romy** /'rəʊmi/ (*f.*) Pet form of ROSEMARY, made famous by the Austrian film actress Romy Schneider

(b. 1938). Her original given name was *Rosemarie*. The spelling **Romey** is also found.

**Ron** /rɒn/ (*m.*) Short form of RONALD.

**Ronald** /'rɒnəld/ (*m.*) From the Scandinavian form (Old Norse *Rognvaldr*) of Norman REYNOLD. *Ronald* was the form regularly used in the Middle Ages in northern England and Scotland, where Scandinavian influence was strong.

**Ronan** /'rəʊnən/ (*m.*) From Irish (Gaelic **Rónán** /'ro:nɑn/): of uncertain origin, apparently a diminutive form of *ron* seal. It was borne by various early Celtic saints, but there has been much confusion in the transmission of their names. The most famous is a 5th-cent. Irish saint who was consecrated bishop by St Patrick and subsequently worked as a missionary in Cornwall and Brittany.

**Ronnie** /'rɒni:/ (*m.*, *f.*) Pet form of RON, or, as a girl's name, of VERONICA.

**Rory** /'rɔ:ri:/ (*m.*) Anglicized form of the old Gaelic name *Ruaidhri*, now found in Scottish Gaelic as **Ruairi** and in Irish as **Ruarí**, both pronounced approximately /'ruərzɪ:/. It is composed of Celtic elements meaning 'red' and 'rule, power', and is common in both Scotland and Ireland. RODERICK is sometimes taken as an Anglicization of it.

**Ros** /rɒz/ (*f.*) Short form of ROSAMUND and ROSALIND.

**Rosa** /'rəʊzə/ (*f.*) Spanish, Italian, and Latin form of ROSE.

**Rosalie** /'rɒzəli:, 'rəʊzəli:; *French* rozə'li/ (*f.*) French form of the Latin name *Rosalia* (from *rosa* rose), introduced to the English-speaking world in the latter part of the 19th cent. St Rosalia was a 12th-cent. Sicilian virgin, and is the patron of Palermo.

**Rosalind** /'rɒzəlɪnd/ (*f.*) Originally a Germanic girl's name, composed of the elements *hrod* fame + *lind* lime (wood), shield, which was introduced to Britain by the Normans. Its popularity owes much to its use by Shakespeare as the name of the heroine in *As You Like It*.

**Rosalyn** /ˈrɒzəlɪn/ (*f.*) Altered form of ROSALIND. **Rosalin** was a common medieval form, since the letter *d* tended to attach itself to and detach itself from final *n* with great readiness. The name has been further altered to coincide in form with the productive suffix of girl's names, *-lyn(ne)*. The spelling **Rosalynne** is also found.

**Rosamund** /ˈrɒzəmənd/ (*f.*) From a Germanic girl's name composed of the elements *hrod* fame + *mund* protection, introduced to Britain by the Normans. In the Middle Ages it was reanalysed as Latin *rosa munda* 'pure rose' or *rosa mundi* 'rose of the world', titles given to the Virgin Mary. The spelling **Rosamond** has been common since the Middle Ages, when scribes sometimes used *o* for *u*, to distinguish it from *n* and *m*, all of which consisted of very similar down strokes of the pen.

**Rose** /rəʊz/ (*f.*) From the name of the flower (Latin *rosa*). However, the name was in use throughout the Middle Ages, long before any of the other girls' names derived from flowers, which are generally of 19th-cent. origin. In part it may refer to the flower as a symbol of the Virgin Mary, but it seems likely that it also has a Germanic origin, probably as a short form of various girls' names with the first element *hrod* 'fame'. As well as being a name in its own right, it is currently used as a short form of ROSEMARY and, less often (because of their different pronunciation), of other names beginning *Ros-*, such as ROSALIND and ROSAMUND.

**Rosemary** /ˈrəʊzmərɪ/ (*f.*) A 19th-cent. coinage,

from the name of the herb (which is from Latin *ros marīnus* sea dew). It is often also assumed to be a combination of the names ROSE and MARY.

**Rosie** /'rəʊzi:/ (*f.*) Diminutive form of ROSE, ROSA, or ROSEMARY. It was first used in the 1860s and is now well established as an independent name, particularly in America.

**Ross** /rɒs/ (*m.*) From a British surname relatively recently taken into use as a given name. The surname has different origins in different parts of Britain, but the use of it as a given name is fairly strongly localized to Scotland; the most common sources of the surname there are the numerous places named with the Gaelic element *ros* headland.

**Rowan** /'rəʊən/ (*m.*, *f.*) As a boy's name this is from a surname of Irish origin, which is derived from an old Irish personal name *Ruadhán* 'Little Red One' (a diminutive of *ruadh* red; cf. ROY). This was borne by a 6th-cent. saint who founded the monastery of Lothra, and it is an alternative name of the 5th-cent. saint also known as RONAN. As a girl's name it is taken from the name (of Scandinavian origin) of the tree, an attractive sight with its clusters of bright red berries.

**Rowena** /rəʊ'i:nə/ (*f.*) Apparently a Latinized form of a Saxon name (of uncertain original form and derivation, perhaps composed of the Germanic elements *hrod* fame + *wynn* joy). It first occurs in the Latin chronicles of Geoffrey of Monmouth (12th cent.), as the name of a daughter of the Saxon invader Hengist, and was taken up by Sir Walter Scott as the name of a Saxon woman, Lady Rowena of Hargottstanstede, who marries the eponymous hero of his novel *Ivanhoe* (1819).

**Rowland** /'rəʊlənd/ (*m.*) Variant of ROLAND, or a

transferred use of the surname derived from that
name in the Middle Ages.

**Roxanne** /rɒk'sæn; *French* rok'san/ (*f.*) French form
of Latin *Roxan(n)a*, Greek *Roxanē*, recorded as the
name of the wife of Alexander the Great. She was the
daughter of Oxyartes the Bactrian, and her name is
presumably of Persian origin; it is said to mean
'Dawn'. In the 1980s the name is in vogue.

**Roy** /rɔɪ/ (*m.*) Originally a Scottish name, representing
an Anglicized spelling of the Gaelic nickname *Ruadh*
'Red' (cf. RONAN). It has since spread to other parts
of the English-speaking world, where it is often reanalysed as Old French *roy* king (cf. LEROY).

**Royston** /'rɔɪstən/ (*m.*) From the English surname,
derived from the name of the place in Hertfordshire,
named in the Middle Ages as the 'settlement of
Royce' (which name is an obsolete variant of ROSE,
from its Germanic form). It is now used as a given
name especially among British West Indians,
although the reasons for its popularity among them
are not clear. It may in some cases be being taken as a
version of 'Roy's son'.

**Ruby** /'ru:bi:/ (*f.*) From the vocabulary word for the
gem stone (Latin *rubīnus*, from *rubeus* red). The
name was chiefly common between the middle of the
19th cent. and the middle of the 20th, and is now
rare.

**Rudolph** /'ru:dɒlf/ (*m.*) From a classicized version,
*Rudolphus*, of the German name ROLF, introduced to
the English-speaking world from Germany in the
19th cent. It also represents an Anglicized version of
the Italian and Spanish name *Rodolfo*, *Rodolpho*,
made popular by the American silent-film actor
Rudolph Valentino (1895–1926), born in Italy as
Rodolpho di Valentina d'Antonguolla. The spelling

**Rudolf** is about equally common, but the name in either spelling is out of fashion at present.

**Rufus** /ˈruːfəs/ (*m.*) From a Latin nickname meaning 'Red(-haired)', sometimes used in medieval documents as a translation of various surnames with the same sense. It began to be used as a given name in the 19th cent.

**Rupert** /ˈruːpət/ (*m.*) Low German form of ROBERT, first brought to England by Prince Rupert of the Rhine (1618–92), who came to help his uncle, Charles I, in the Civil War.

**Russ** /rʌs/ (*m.*) Short form of RUSSELL, now also used as an independent name.

**Russell** /ˈrʌsəl/ (*m.*) From a surname, itself originally from the Old French nickname *Rousel* 'Little Red One' (a diminutive of *rous* red, from Latin *russus*).

**Ruth** /ruːθ/ (*f.*) Old Testament: name (of uncertain derivation, perhaps meaning 'Friendship' in Hebrew) of a Moabite woman who left her own people to remain with her mother-in-law Naomi, and became the wife of Boaz and an ancestress of David. Her story is told in the book of the Bible that bears her name. It was popular among the Puritans, partly because of its association with the term *ruth* meaning 'compassion'. It is now as common among Gentiles as among Jews.

**Ryan** /ˈraɪən/ (*m.*) From an Irish surname, whose correct Gaelic form is much disputed, along with its derivation and meaning. There has been considerable confusion with REGAN, but it seems clear that they were originally distinct names.

# S

**Sabine** /sə'bi:n, sə'bi:nə; *French* sa'bi:n; *German* za'bi:nə/ (*f.*) From a French and German name, which is derived from the Latin name *Sabīna* 'Sabine woman'. The Sabines were an ancient Italic race whose territory was early taken over by the Romans. According to tradition the Romans made a raid on the Sabines and carried off a number of their women, but when the Sabines came for revenge the women succeeded in making peace between the two groups. The given name was borne by three minor early Christian saints, in particular a Roman maiden martyred in about 127.

**Sabrina** /sə'bri:nə/ (*f.*) Romano-British: name of a character in Celtic legend, who supposedly gave her name to the River Severn. In fact this is one of the most ancient of all British river-names, and its true origins are obscure. Legend has it that Sabrina was the illegitimate daughter of a Welsh king called Locrine, drowned in the river on the orders of the king's wife Gwendolen. The river name is found in the form *Sabrina* in the Latin writings of Tacitus, Gildas, and Bede; it is of uncertain derivation. The name of the legendary character is almost certainly derived from that of the river, rather than vice versa.

**Sacha** /'sæʃə; *French* sa'ʃa/ (*m.*) French version of SASHA. Many names of Russian origin were introduced to the English-speaking world via French, at the time (1909–20) when Diaghilev's Ballet Russe made a great impact in Paris.

**Sacheverell** /sə'ʃevərəl/ (*m.*) From an English surname, probably of Norman origin, from an unidentified place in Normandy called Saute-Chevreuil, which means 'Roebuck leap'. It was made familiar as a given name by the writer Sacheverell Sitwell

(1897–1985), who was named in honour of William
Sacheverell (1638–91), an early Whig statesman,
about whose ancestry little is known.

**Sadie** /ˈseɪdɪ/ (*f.*) Pet form of SARAH, sometimes used
as an independent name, particularly in America.
The exact formation is not clear; it is paralleled by
the much rarer *Maidie* from MARY.

**Sal** /sæl/ (*f.*, *m.*) English short form of SALLY. In America it is sometimes used as a boy's name, a short form
of Spanish *Salvador* or Italian *Salvatore* 'Saviour',
given in honour of Jesus Christ.

**Sally** /ˈsælɪ/ (*f.*) English: in origin a pet form of
SARAH, but in the 20th cent. normally treated as a
name in its own right. It derives from the short form
SAL (*r* and *l* being readily interchangeable), with the
addition of the diminutive suffix *-y*. It is frequently
used as the first element in combinations such as
*Sally-Anne* and *Sally-Jane*.

**Salome** /ˈsæləmeɪ, səˈləʊmɪ/ (*f.*) New Testament:
Greek form of an Aramaic name derived from the
Hebrew word *shalom* peace. It was common at the
time of Christ, and was borne by one of the women
who were at his tomb at the time of the Resurrection
(Mark 16: 1–8). This would normally have led to its
common use as a Christian name, and it is indeed
found in early medieval times. However, according
to the historian Josephus, it was also the name of the
daughter of Queen Herodias and stepdaughter of
King Herod. Salome danced for her stepfather, and
so pleased him that he offered to give her anything
she wanted. Prompted by her mother, she asked for
(and got) the head of John the Baptist, who was in
one of Herod's prisons. This story so gripped medieval imagination that the name Salome became more
or less taboo until the 20th cent.

**Sam** /sæm/ (*m.*, *f.*) Short form of the boy's name
SAMUEL (or, occasionally, of SAMSON), or (especially
in recent years) of the girl's name SAMANTHA.

**Samantha** /sə'mænθə/ (*f.*) Of problematic and much
debated origin. It seems to have originated in the
southern U.S. in the 18th cent., possibly as a combination of SAM (from SAMUEL) + a feminine suffix
*-antha* (perhaps suggested by ANTHEA).

**Sammy** /'sæmi:/ (*m.*, *f.*) Diminutive of SAM. As a girl's
name, it is more often spelled **Sammie**.

**Samson** /'sæmsən/ (*m.*) Old Testament: name
(Hebrew *Shimshon*, probably from *shemesh* sun) of a
Jewish champion and strong man, who was betrayed
by his mistress, Delilah, and enslaved and blinded by
the Philistines; nevertheless he brought the pillars of
the temple of the Philistines crashing down, in a final
suicidal act of strength (Judges 13–16). In the Middle
Ages the popularity of the given name was increased
in Celtic areas by the fame of a 6th-cent. Celtic saint
who bore it, probably as a classicized form of some
Celtic name. A variant spelling with intrusive *p* is
found, **Sampson**; when found as a given name, this
is usually a transferred use of the surname.

**Samuel** /'sæmjʊəl/ (*m.*) Old Testament: name of one
of the greatest of the biblical prophets, after whom
two books of the Old Testament are named. His
name (Hebrew *Shemuel*) means '(God) hearkened'
(presumably to the prayers of a mother for a son).

**Sandra** /'sɑːndrə, 'sændrə/ (*f.*) Aphetic short form of
*Alessandra*, the Italian version of ALEXANDRA. In Italian the masculine form *Sandro* is even more frequently used, but this has not been adopted in the
English-speaking world in the same way as the feminine form.

**Sandy** /'sændi:/ (*m.*, *f.*) Short form, originally Scot-

tish, of the boy's name ALEXANDER. It is now also
used for girls called ALEXANDRA or SANDRA, and as an
independent girl's name. It is also sometimes given as
a nickname to people of either sex who have a crop of
'sandy' (light reddish brown) hair. For girls the spelling **Sandie** is also in use.

**Sara** /'seɪrə/ (f.) Variant of SARAH. This is the form
used in the Greek of the New Testament (Heb.
11:11).

**Sarah** /'seɪrə/ (f.) Old Testament: name of the wife of
Abraham, who was originally called *Sarai* (probably
meaning 'Contentious'), but had her name changed
by God to the more auspicious *Sarah* 'Princess' in
token of a greater blessing (Gen. 17:15; 'and God
said unto Abraham, As for Sarai thy wife, thou shalt
not call her name Sarai, but Sarah shall her name
be').

**Sasha** /'sæʃə/ (m.; occasionally also f.) Russian pet
form of ALEXANDER, recently adopted in the English-
speaking world as an independent name. It was introduced via France; the French spelling **Sacha** is also
used, and occasionally even the German **Sascha**. Its
adoption as a girl's name seems to be due to the fact
that it ends in -*a*, a characteristically feminine name
ending.

**Saul** /sɔːl/ (m.) Old Testament: name (from a Hebrew
word meaning 'asked for' or 'prayed for') of one of
the first kings of Israel, and also, before his conversion, of St Paul. It was popular among the Puritans,
but is now once again mainly a Jewish name.

**Sawney** /'sɔːnɪ/ (m.) Scottish variant of SANDY,
resulting from a pronunciation reflected also in the
surname *Saunders*. The name declined in popularity
in the 19th and 20th cents., perhaps as a result of

association with the legendary Highland mass-murderer and cannibal Sawney Bean.

**Scarlett** /ˈskɑːlət/ (*f.*) Name popularized by the central character in the novel *Gone with the Wind* (1936) by Margaret Mitchell, later made into a famous film. Her name was Katie Scarlett O'Hara (the middle name representing her grandmother's maiden surname), but in keeping with the fashion in the southern U.S. for unusual names, she was always known as Scarlett. The surname originally denoted someone who made or traded in scarlet cloth.

**Scott** /skɒt/ (*m.*) Although used as a personal name both before the Norman Conquest and in the Middle Ages, modern use seems to derive from the surname which originated as a nickname for a migrant from Scotland, the land of the Scots (the Gaelic-speaking Celtic people who originally came from Ireland). The given name is often chosen by parents of Scottish descent, but is also used more widely.

**Séamas** /ˈʃeːməs/ (*m.*) Irish form of JAMES. The Scottish form is SEUMAS. The spelling **Seamus** is also found, especially outside Ireland.

**Sean** /ʃɔːn, *Irish* ʃɑːn/ (*m.*) Irish form of JOHN (sometimes spelled **Shaun**, representing the usual pronunciation of the Irish name). It has always been common in Ireland, but is now chosen also by parents who have no Irish connections.

**Seb** /sɛb/ (*m.*) Short form of SEBASTIAN.

**Sebastian** /səˈbæstɪən/ (*m.*) Borne by a 3rd-cent. Christian saint, a Roman soldier martyred by the arrows of his fellow officers, whose sufferings were a favourite subject for medieval artists. His name means 'man from Sebasta', a town in Asia Minor so called from Greek *Sebastos*, a translation of the Latin imperial title *Augustus*.

**Selima** /sə'li:mə/ (*f.*) Of uncertain origin: name used by Oliver Goldsmith for his cat, 'drowned in a tub of goldfish'. The metre shows it to be stressed on the first syllable, but there is no clue to its derivation. It is possibly derived from the Arabic name *Selim* 'Peace'.

**Selina** /sə'li:nə/ (*f.*) Of uncertain origin; first occurs in the 17th cent. It may be an altered form of *Selena* (Greek *Selēnē*), the name of a goddess of the moon, or of *Celina* (Latin *Caelīna*), a derivative of CELIA. The name suddenly became more popular in Britain in the 1980s, partly perhaps because of the familiarity of the TV newsreader Selina Scott.

**Selma** /'selmə/ (*f.*) Of uncertain origin, probably a contracted form of SELINA.

**Selwyn** /'selwɪn/ (*m.*) From an English surname, which is of disputed origin. There was a given name *Selewyn* in use in the Middle Ages, which probably represents a survival of an unrecorded Old English name composed of the elements *sēle* prosperity + *wine* friend. Alternatively, the surname may be Norman, derived from *Seluein*, an Old French form of Latin *Silvānus* (from *silva* wood; cf. SILAS).

**Seònaid** /'ʃɔ:natʃ/ (*f.*) Scottish Gaelic form of JANET; cf. Irish Gaelic SINEAD.

**Septimus** /'septɪməs/ (*m.*) Late Latin name representing Latin *septimus* seventh. It was fairly commonly used in large Victorian families for the seventh child or seventh son, but is now rare.

**Seraphina** /serə'fi:nə/ (*f.*) Latinate derivative of Hebrew *Seraphim* 'Burning Ones', the name of an order of angels (Isa. 6:2). It was borne by a rather shadowy saint who was martyred at the beginning of the 15th cent. in Italy, Spain, or Armenia.

**Serena** /sə'ri:nə/ (*f.*) From a Latin name, representing the feminine form of the adjective *serēnus* calm, serene. It was borne by an early Christian saint, about whom little is known. In her *Life* she is described as a wife of the emperor Domitian (AD 51–96), but there is no mention of her in any of the historical sources that deal with this period.

**Serge** /*French* sɛrʒ/ (*m.*) French form of the Russian name *Sergei*, from the old Roman family name *Sergius*, which is of uncertain, probably Etruscan, origin. (It was borne for example by the conspirator denounced by Cicero, Lucius Sergius Catalina.) St Sergius of Radonezh (*c.* 1314–92) is one of the most famous of all Russian saints, hence the great popularity of the name in that country. There is no connection with the type of material called *serge* (Old French *sarge*, from Latin *sericum* silk).

**Seth** /seθ/ (*m.*) Old Testament: name (from a Hebrew word meaning 'Substitute') of the third son of Adam, who was born after the murder of Abel (Gen. 4:25; 'and Adam knew his wife again; and she bare a son and called his name Seth: For God, said she, hath appointed me another seed instead of Abel, whom Cain slew'). It was popular among the Puritans (particularly for children born after the death of an elder brother), and has been occasionally used since, but received a setback from the absurdity of the darkly passionate rural character Seth Starkadder in Stella Gibbons's comic novel *Cold Comfort Farm* (1932).

**Seumas** /'ʃeɪməs/ (*m.*) Scottish Gaelic form of JAMES, from which is derived HAMISH. See also SÉAMUS.

**Seymour** /'siːmɔː/ (*m.*) From the English surname, originally a Norman baronial title from Saint-Maur in Normandy. This place was so called from the dedication of its church to an unidentified St Maurus, whose Latin name means 'Moor', i.e. North African.

**Shane** /ʃeɪn/ (*m.*) An early Anglicized form of SEAN (also used as a surname), which represents the Gaelic pronunciation somewhat less accurately than SHAUN and SHAWN.

**Sharon** /'ʃærən/ (*f.*) A 20th-cent. coinage, from a biblical place-name, meaning 'plain' in Hebrew. The derivation is from the phrase 'I am the rose of Sharon, and the lily of the valleys' (S. of S. 2:1). Subsequently the name 'rose of Sharon' was used for a shrub of the genus *Hypericum*, with yellow flowers, and for a species of hibiscus with purple flowers. In John Steinbeck's novel *The Grapes of Wrath* (1936), Rosasharn (Rose of Sharon) is the name of the daughter. Nowadays the spelling **Sharron** is also found.

**Shaun** /ʃɔːn/ (*m.*) Anglicized spelling of SEAN, somewhat less common than SHAWN in America, but more so in Britain.

**Shaw** /ʃɔː/ (*m.*) From the English surname, a topographic name from Old Norse *skogr* or Old English *sceaga* wood.

**Shawn** /ʃɔːn/ (*m.*) Anglicized spelling of SEAN, found mainly in America.

**Sheena** /'ʃiːnə/ (*f.*) Anglicized spelling of SÌNE, the Scots Gaelic form of JANE.

**Sheila** /'ʃiːlə/ (*f.*) Anglicized spelling of the Irish given name SÍLE, now so common that it is hardly felt to be Irish any longer. In Australia since the 19th cent. it has been a generic term for any woman.

**Shelagh** /'ʃiːlə/ (*f.*) Another Anglicized form of SÍLE (see also SHEILA). The final consonants in the written form seem to have been added to restore a Gaelic feel to the name, since they occur at the end of many Gaelic words and are silent, but they are not used in the Irish form of the name. The spelling **Sheelagh** is also found.

**Shelley** /ˈʃɛli/ (f.; occasionally m.) From the English surname, borne most notably by the English Romantic poet Percy Bysshe Shelley (1792–1822). The surname is from one of the various places (in Essex, Suffolk, and Yorkshire) named in Old English as the 'sloping meadow'. The name is now nearly always given to girls only, perhaps as a result of association with SHIRLEY (the actress Shelley Winters was born in 1922 as Shirley Schrift), and the normally feminine suffix -ie, -y.

**Sheridan** /ˈʃɛrɪdən/ (m.) From the surname, made famous by the Irish playwright Richard Brinsley Sheridan (1751–1816). The surname is from Gaelic Ó Sirideáin 'Descendant of Sirideán', an Old Irish personal name of uncertain origin, possibly connected with sirim to seek.

**Sherry** /ˈʃɛri/ (f.) Probably a respelling of French Chérie 'Beloved', but now more closely associated with the fortified wine, earlier sherry wine, so named from the port of Jerez in southern Spain.

**Shirley** /ˈʃɜːli/ (f.; formerly m.) From the English surname, itself from any of the various places (in the West Midlands, Derbyshire, Hampshire, and Surrey), named in Old English from the elements scir county, shire + lēah clearing. It was given by Charlotte Brontë to the heroine of her novel Shirley (1849), whose parents had selected the name in prospect of a male child and used it regardless. It is probable that Shirley had earlier been used for boys (Charlotte Brontë refers to it as a 'masculine cognomen'), but this literary influence fixed it firmly as a girl's name. It was strongly reinforced during the 1930s and 40s by the popularity of the child film star Shirley Temple (b. 1928).

**Sian** /ʃæːn/ (*f.*) Welsh form of JANE, made familiar by the actress Sian Phillips.

**Sibb** /sɪb/ (*f.*) Short form of SYBIL, popular in the Middle Ages, but now rare.

**Sibilla** /sɪˈbɪlə/ (*f.*) Latinate variant of SYBIL, also found occasionally as **Sibella**.

**Sibyl** /ˈsɪbəl/ (*f.*) Variant of SYBIL. Even in classical times there was confusion between the vowels in this word.

**Sid** /sɪd/ (*m.*) Short form of SIDNEY.

**Sidney** /ˈsɪdnɪ/ (*m.*; occasionally *f.*) From the English surname, which is usually said to be a Norman baronial name from Saint-Denis in France. However, at least in the case of the family of the poet and soldier Sir Philip Sidney (1554–86) it appears to have a more humble origin, being derived from lands in Surrey named as the 'wide meadow' (Old English *sīden* wide (dative case) + *ēg* island in a river, riverside meadow). The popularity of the boy's name increased considerably in the 19th cent., probably under the influence of Sidney Carton, hero of Dickens's novel *A Tale of Two Cities* (1859). As a girl's name it is perhaps in part a contracted form of SIDONY, but is quite rare.

**Sidony** /ˈsɪdənɪ/ (*f.*) From a Latin byname, *Sidōnius* (*m.*) or *Sidōnia* (*f.*) 'person from Sidon' (in Phoenicia). This quite early came to be associated with Greek *sindon* winding-sheet. Two saints called Sidonius are venerated in the Catholic Church: Sidonius Apollinaris, a 4th-cent. bishop of Clermont, and a 7th-cent. Irish monk who was the first abbot of the monastery of Saint-Saens (named with a much mutilated form of his name). *Sidonius* does not seem to have been used as a given name in the later Middle Ages, but the feminine form *Sidonia* (English

*Sidony*) was comparatively popular and has continued in occasional use ever since. The spelling **Sidonie** is also found, probably under the influence of French.

**Sigmund** /'sɪgmənd/ (*m.*) Of Germanic origin, composed of the elements *sige* victory + *mund* protection. It was introduced to Britain both before and after the Conquest, from Scandinavia and Normandy, but there was much confusion with SIMON (final -*d* being added and dropped in the Middle Ages with great abandon) and it eventually fell out of use. As a modern given name it is a recent re-introduction from Germany.

**Sigrid** /'sɪgrɪd/ (*f.*) Recent importation to the English-speaking world from Scandinavia, composed of the Norse elements *sigr* victory + *riðr* fair, beautiful.

**Sigurd** /'sɪgɜːd/ (*m.*) Of Scandinavian origin, composed of the elements *sigr* victory + *orð* word. According to Germanic legend, a character of this name slew the dragon Fafnir, who was guarding an accursed treasure; according to Wagner's treatment in the *Ring* cycle, this role is taken by Siegfried.

**Silas** /'saɪləs/ (*m.*) New Testament: Greek name, a short form of *Silouanus* (Latin *Silvānus*, from *silva* wood). This name was borne by a companion of St Paul, who is also mentioned in the Bible in the full form of his name. The Eastern Church recognizes two separate saints, Silas and Silvanus, but honours both on the same day (20 July).

**Sile** /'ʃɪːljə/ (*f.*) Irish: of uncertain origin, probably a Gaelic version of CELIA. It is now most commonly found in the Anglicized spelling SHEILA.

**Silvana** /sɪl'vɑːnə/ (*f.*) From the feminine form of the Latin word *silvānus* 'of the woods'. This is a comparatively rare girl's name; the masculine form has not been used at all as a given name in the English-speaking world. Compare SILAS.

**Silvester** /sɪlˈvɛstə/ (*m.*) From the Latin name, meaning 'of the woods'. It was borne by various early saints, most notably by the first pope to govern a Church free from persecution (314–335). His feast is on 31 December, and in various parts of Europe New Year is celebrated under his name. The given name has been continuously, if modestly, used from the Middle Ages to the present day.

**Silvestra** /sɪlˈvɛstrə/ (*f.*) Latinate feminine form of SILVESTER.

**Silvia** /ˈsɪlvɪə/ (*f.*) From Latin: Rhea *Silvia* was, according to mythological tradition, the mother of the twins Romulus and Remus, who founded Rome. Her name probably represents a reworking, by association with Latin *silva* wood, of some pre-Roman form. It was borne by a 6th-cent. saint, mother of Gregory the Great, and has always been relatively popular in Italy. Shakespeare used it as a typically Italian name in his *Two Gentlemen of Verona*.

**Sima** /ˈsiːmə/ (*f.*) Russian pet form of SERAPHINA.

**Simeon** /ˈsɪmɪən/ (*m.*) Biblical: from Hebrew, meaning 'Hearkening'. It is borne by several Old and New Testament characters, rendered in the Authorized Version variously as *Shimeon*, *Simeon*, and SIMON. In the New Testament, it is the spelling used for the man who blessed the infant Christ (Luke 2:25).

**Simon** /ˈsaɪmən/ (*m.*) Usual English form of SIMEON. This form of the name is borne in the New Testament by various characters: two apostles, a brother of Jesus, a Pharisee, a leper, a tanner, a sorcerer (who offered money for the gifts of the Holy Ghost, giving

rise to the term *simony*), and the man who carried
Jesus' cross to the Crucifixion.

**Simone** /sɪˈməʊn; *French* sɪˈmɔn/ (*f.*) French feminine
form of SIMON.

**Sinclair** /ˈsɪŋkleə/ (*m.*) From the Scottish surname,
which originated as a Norman baronial name borne
by the families who held various seats called Saint-
Clair, notably Saint-Clair-sur-Elle in La Manche and
Saint-Clair-l'Évêque in Calvados.

**Sindy** /ˈsɪndi/ (*f.*) Pet form of CYNTHIA that came into
use in about 1950 and is most common in America
(cf. CINDY).

**Sìne** /ˈʃiːnə/ (*f.*) Scottish Gaelic form of JANE, which
has given rise to the increasingly popular Anglicized
name SHEENA.

**Sinéad** /ˈʃɪnjeːd/ (*f.*) Irish: the Gaelic form of JANET.

**Siobhan** /ʃɪˈvɔːn; *Irish* ˈʃuwɑːn/ (*f.*) Irish: a Gaelic
form of JOAN. It has recently come to be more widely
popular, together with various Anglicized spellings,
representing the usual pronunciation, such as **She-
vaun** and **Chevonne**.

**Sissie** /ˈsɪsi/ (*f.*) Pet form of CICELY that came into use
about 1890 and fell out of use again after about 1920,
no doubt because of the homonymous slang word
*sissy* 'effeminate' (which is probably from the kinship
term *sister*). In recent years it has undergone something of a revival, and the spellings **Sissy** and **Sissey**
are also used.

**Solly** /ˈsɒli/ (*m.*) Jewish: pet form of SOLOMON.

**Solomon** /ˈsɒləmən/ (*m.*) Old Testament: name
(Hebrew *Shlomo*, derived from *shalom* peace) of a
king of Israel, son of David and Bathsheba, who was
legendary for his wisdom (2 Sam. 12–24; 1 Kings
1–11; 2 Chron. 1–9). The books of Proverbs and

Ecclesiastes were ascribed to him, and the Song of Solomon, otherwise known as the Song of Songs, bears his name. It has been sporadically used since the Middle Ages, often by parents who wished wisdom for their child, but is still largely a Jewish name.

**Sonia** /'sɒnjə, 'səunjə/ (f.) Russian pet form of SOPHIA (Russian *Sofya*), popular in Britain since the 1920s.

**Soo** /su:/ (f.) Fanciful variant of SUE.

**Sophia** /sə'faɪə/ (f.) From the Greek name meaning 'Wisdom'. The Eastern legend of St Sophia seems to be the result of misinterpretation of the phrase *Hagia Sophia* 'Holy Wisdom' as if it meant 'Saint Sophia'. The name became popular in England in the 17th and 18th cents. The heroine of Fielding's novel *Tom Jones* (1749) is called Sophia Weston. In recent years, its popularity may have been increased by the fame of the Italian film actress Sophia Loren (b. 1934).

**Sophie** /'səufi:/ (f.) Variant, of French origin, of SOPHIA. In the English-speaking world it is often taken as a pet form of *Sophia*, and is sometimes spelled **Sophy**. It has been popular since the 18th cent.

**Sorcha** /'sɔ:xə; *Irish* 'ʃɔrəxə/ (f.) Irish: Gaelic name derived from an old Celtic element meaning 'brightness'. It has long been taken as a Gaelic form of SARAH, but this is based on no more than a slight phonetic similarity.

**Spencer** /'spɛnsə/ (m.) From the English surname, originally an occupational name for a 'dispenser' of supplies in a manor house. This is the name of a great English noble family, traditionally supposed to be descended from someone who performed this function in the royal household. Its popularity was increased in the mid 20th cent. by the fame of the American film actor Spencer Tracy (1900–67).

**Stacy** /'steɪsɪ/ (*f.*) Apparently a pet form of ANASTA-SIA, respelled perhaps as a result of association with EUSTACE. It is not clear why this name, together with its variants **Stacey** and **Stacie**, should have become so common in the 1970s and 1980s.

**Stan** /stæn/ (*m.*) Short form of STANLEY.

**Stanley** /'stænlɪ/ (*m.*) From an English surname, derived from any of numerous places (in Derbys., Durham, Gloucs., Staffs., Wilts., and Yorks.), named in Old English from *stān* stone + *lēah* clearing. The name has been widely used as a given name since the 1880s, although it had been in occasional use earlier. Its popularity seems to have stemmed mainly from the fame of the explorer Sir Henry Morton Stanley (1841–1904), who was born John Rowlands but later took the surname of his adoptive father.

**Stella** /'stelə/ (*f.*) From Latin *stella* star. This was not used as given name before the 16th cent., when Sir Philip Sidney seems to have been the first to use it (as a name deliberately far removed from the prosaic range of everyday names) in his sonnets supposedly addressed by Astrophel to his lady Stella.

**Stephan** /'stefən/ (*m.*) Variant of STEPHEN, preserving the vowels of the Greek name. It is in most cases a relatively recent importation from Eastern Europe (cf. Polish **Stefan**, which spelling is also in use in the English-speaking world).

**Stephanie** /'stefənɪ/ (*f.*) French form of Latin *Stephania*, a variant of *Stephana*, which was in use among early Christians as a feminine form of *Stephanus* (see STEPHEN).

**Stephen** /'stiːvən/ (*m.*) Usual English spelling of the name of the first Christian martyr, whose feast is accordingly celebrated next after Christ's own (26 December). His name is derived from the Greek word *stephanos* garland or crown.

**Steve** /stiːv/ (*m.*) Short form of STEVEN.

**Steven** /ˈstiːvən/ (*m.*) Variant of STEPHEN, established in England since medieval times.

**Stewart** /ˈstjuːət/ (*m.*) Variant of STUART, less common as a given name, although more common as a surname.

**Storm** /stɔːm/ (*f.*) Apparently a 20th-cent. coinage, although it may be slightly earlier. The name is presumably derived from the climatic phenomenon, although it is hard to see why it should be chosen. It derives perhaps from the Romantic commitment to emotional drama, and may sometimes have been given in the hope that a child would have a dramatic personality. In other cases, it may have been used for a child born during a storm.

**Stuart** /ˈstjuːət/ (*m.*) From the French version (introduced in the 16th cent. by Mary Stuart, Queen of Scots, who was brought up in France) of the surname *Stewart*. This was originally an occupational name for someone who served as a *steward* in a manor or royal court house. The Scottish royal family of this name are traditionally supposed to be descended from a family who were hereditary stewards in Brittany before the Conquest. The given name was originally Scottish, but is now widespread throughout the English-speaking world.

**Sue** /suː/ (*f.*) Short form of SUSAN and, less commonly, of SUSANNA and SUZANNE.

**Sukie** /ˈsuːkiː/ (*f.*) Pet form of SUSAN, very common in the 18th cent., but now rare.

**Susan** /'suːzən/ (*f.*) Anglicized form of SUSANNA, and always the most common of this group of names.

**Susanna** /suːˈzænə/ (*f.*) New Testament form (Luke 8:3) of the Hebrew name *Shoshana* (from *shoshan* lily). The name is also spelled **Susannah**, a transliteration used in the Old Testament. The tale of Susannah, wife of Joachim, and the elders who falsely accused her of adultery, found in the Apocrypha in the book that bears her name, was popular in the Middle Ages and later.

**Susie** /'suːziː/ (*f.*) Pet form of SUSAN and SUSANNA, occasionally used as an independent name. It is also spelled **Suzie** and **Suzy**.

**Suzanne** /suːˈzæn/ (*f.*) French version of SUSANNA.

**Suzette** /suːˈzɛt/ (*f.*) French pet form of SUZANNE.

**Sybil** /'sɪbəl/ (*f.*) From classical mythology: name (Greek *Sibylla* or *Sybilla*, with confusion over the vowels from an early period) of a class of ancient prophetesses inspired by Apollo. According to medieval theology they were pagans denied the knowledge of Christ but blessed by God with some insight into things to come and accordingly admitted to Heaven. It was thus regarded as a respectable name to be borne by Christians. The classical form **Sybilla** and the French form **Sybille** are also occasionally used in the English-speaking world.

**Sydney** /'sɪdnɪ/ (*m.*) Variant of SIDNEY, in part representing an alternative form of the surname (which may reflect a medieval practice of writing *y* for *i* for greater clarity).

**Sylvia** /'sɪlvɪə/ (*f.*) Variant, respelled for elegance, of SILVIA. It is now rather more common than the plain form.

**Sylvie** /'sɪlviː/ (*f.*) French form of SILVIA.

# T

**Tabitha** /'tæbɪθə/ (f.) New Testament: Aramaic name, meaning 'Doe' or 'Roe', borne by a woman restored to life by St Peter (Acts 9:36–41); in the biblical account this form of the name is given, together with its Greek equivalent DORCAS. It is now rarely given to girls, being more commonly bestowed on pets, especially cats.

**Tadhg** /taig/ (m.) Irish: from Gaelic **tadhg** poet; sometimes Anglicized as TIM.

**Taliesin** /tæl'jɛsɪn/ (m.) Welsh: composed of the elements *tâl* brow + *iesin* shining. This was the name of a legendary 6th-cent. Welsh poet, which has been revived in recent times.

**Talitha** /'tælɪθə/ (f.) New Testament: from an Aramaic word meaning 'little girl'. Jesus raised a child from the dead with the words TALITHA CUMI 'which is, being interpreted, Damsel, I say unto thee arise' (Mark 5:41).

**Tallulah** /tə'lu:lə/ (f.) A rare name, chosen occasionally as a result of the fame of the American actress Tallulah Bankhead (1903–68). In spite of its exotic appearance, her given name was not adopted for the sake of her career but inherited from her grandmother. It is taken from the place name Tallulah Falls, Georgia, which is of American Indian origin.

**Tamara** /tə'mɑ:rə/ (f.) Russian: probably derived from Hebrew *Tamar* 'Palm tree', with the addition of the feminine suffix *-a*. The name Tamar is borne in the Bible by two female characters: the daughter-in-law of Judah, who is involved in a somewhat seamy story of sexual intrigue (Gen. 38), and a daughter of King David (II Sam. 13), the full sister of Absolom, who is raped by her half-brother Amnon, for which Absolom kills him. It is rather surprising, therefore,

that it should have given rise to such a popular given
name. However, Absolom himself later has a
daughter named Tamar, who is referred to as 'a
woman of a fair countenance' (II Sam. 14:27), and
the name may derive its popularity from this reference. It is also possible that the name is a feminine
form of *Tammarus*, which was the name of an
obscure 5th-cent. male saint who, together with St
Priscus, was cast adrift from Africa and washed
ashore in Italy. *Tammarus* is probably a Latinized
form of a Germanic name composed of the elements
*tank* thought + *mar* fame.

**Tammy** /'tæmi:/ (*f.*) Pet form of TAMARA and TAMSIN.

**Tamsin** /'tæmzin/ (*f.*) Contracted form of THOMASINA,
relatively common throughout Britain in the Middle
Ages, but confined to Cornwall immediately before
its recent revival.

**Tansy** /'tænzi:/ (*f.*) A flower name, derived from
Greek *athanasia* immortal. It has enjoyed some
popularity as a given name in the 20th cent.

**Tanya** /'tænjə, 'tɑːnjə/ (*f.*) Russian pet form of
TATIANA.

**Tara** /'tɑːrə/ (*f.*) Irish: from the name (meaning 'hill')
of a place in Co. Meath, seat of the High Kings of Ireland. It has been used as a girl's name in America
since 1940, probably as a result of the immense success of the film *Gone with the Wind*, in which the
estate of this name has great emotional significance.
In Britain it was not much used before the 1960s, and
its popularity since then seems to be a result of its use
for the character Tara King in the television series
*The Avengers*. *Tara* is also an Indian name, from the
Sanskrit vocabulary word for star (cognate with Latin
*stella* and English *star*), originally borne by the wife
of Brhaspati (preceptor of the gods) in Hindu texts,

or by the wife of Buddha or a goddess in Buddhist ones.

**Tatiana** /tætɪˈɑːnə/ (*f.*) Russian: of early Christian origin. This was the name of various early saints honoured particularly in the Eastern Church. In origin it is a feminine form of Latin *Tatiānus*, apparently a derivative of *Tatius*, a Roman family name of obscure origin. Titus Tatius was a king of the Sabines who later ruled jointly with Romulus.

**Ted** /ted/ (*m.*) Short form of EDWARD, also used for THEODORE.

**Teddy** /ˈtedɪ/ (*m.*) Pet form of TED. Teddy bears were so named from the American president Theodore Roosevelt (1858–1919).

**Tel** /tel/ (*m.*) Modish short form of TERRY or TERENCE.

**Terence** /ˈterəns/ (*m.*) From the Latin name *Terentius*, which is of uncertain origin. It was borne by the Roman playwright Marcus Terentius Afer (who was a former slave, and took his name from his master, Publius Terentius Lucanus), and later by various minor early Christian saints. As a modern given name it is a 'learned' back-formation from the supposed pet form TERRY.

**Teresa** /təˈriːzə/ (*f.*) Italian and Spanish variant of THERESA, often chosen in this spelling with particular reference to the Spanish saint Teresa of Ávila (Teresa Cepeda de Ahumada, 1515–82).

**Terri** /ˈterɪ/ (*f.*) A mainly American name, a pet form of TERESA, or feminine spelling of TERRY.

**Terry** /ˈterɪ/ (*m.*) In the Middle Ages this was a Germanic name composed of elements meaning 'tribe' and 'power', introduced to England by the Normans in the form *T(h)ierri*. (A fuller form is represented by the name of the emperor *Theodoric*, where the spelling has been influenced by association with THEO-DORE; see also DEREK and DERRICK). In modern English use it seems at first to have been a transferred use of the surname *Terry*, which is derived from the medieval given name, and later to have been taken as a pet form of TERENCE.

**Tessa** /ˈtɛsə/ (*f.*) This name and its shortened form **Tess** are generally considered to be pet forms of TER-ESA, although now often used independently. However, the formation is not clear, and *Tessa* may be of distinct origin. Literary contexts of the late 19th cent. show that the name was thought of as Italian, although it is in fact unknown in Italy.

**Thaddeus** /ˈθædɪəs/ (*m.*) New Testament: byname of one of the lesser-known of Christ's apostles, who bore the given name *Lebbaeus* (Matt. 10:3). It is of uncertain origin, but seems to represent a Greek spelling of an Aramaic version of a short form of the Greek names *Theodoros* 'Gift of God' (see THEO-DORE) and *Theodotos* 'Given by God'.

**Thea** /ˈθiːə/ (*f.*) Aphetic short form of DOROTHEA.

**Thecla** /ˈθɛklə/ (*f.*) Contracted form of the Greek name *Theokleia*, composed of the elements *theos* god + *kleia* glory. The name was borne by a 1st-cent. saint (the first female martyr), who was particularly popular in the Middle Ages because of the lurid details of her suffering recorded in the apocryphal *Acts of Paul and Thecla*.

**Thelma** /ˈθɛlmə/ (*f.*) First used by the novelist Marie Corelli for the heroine of her novel *Thelma* (1887). She was supposed to be Norwegian, but it is not an old Scandinavian name. Greek *thelēma* (neuter) means 'wish, (act of) will', and the name could perhaps be interpreted as a contracted form of this.

**Theo** /'θiːəʊ/ (*m.*) Short form of THEODORE and, less commonly, of THEOBALD.

**Theobald** /'θiːəbəʊld/ (*m.*) Latinized form, first found in medieval documents, of a Norman name of Germanic origin, composed of the elements *theud* tribe + *bald* bold, brave; the first element has been altered under the influence of Greek *theos* god.

**Theodora** /θiːə'dɔːrə/ (*f.*) Feminine form of THEODORE, borne most notably by a 9th-cent. empress of Byzantium, the wife of Theophilus the Iconoclast.

**Theodore** /'θiːədɔː/ (*m.*) From the French form of the Greek name *Theodōros*, composed of the elements *theos* god + *dōron* gift. The name was popular among early Christians and was borne by several early saints.

**Theodosia** /θiːə'dəʊzɪə/ (*f.*) Greek: derived from the elements *theos* god + *dōsis* giving. It was borne by various early saints venerated mostly in the Eastern Church, and is only very occasionally used in the English-speaking world today.

**Theophilus** /θiː'ɒfɪləs/ (*m.*) New Testament: name of the addressee of Luke's gospel and the Acts of the Apostles; also borne by various early saints. It is composed of the Greek elements *theos* god + *philos* friend, and was popular among early Christians because of its well-omened meaning 'Lover of God' or 'Beloved by God'.

**Theresa** /tə'riːzə/ (*f.*) Of problematic origin: it seems to have been first used in Spain and Portugal, and according to tradition was the name of the wife of St Paulinus of Nola, who spent most of his life in Spain; she was said to come from (and to have derived her name from) the Greek island of Thera. However, this theory is neither factually nor etymologically reliable. The German form *Theresia* (much used in the combination *Maria Theresia* in families claiming connection with the royal Habsburg line) is also occasionally used in the English-speaking world. See also TERESA.

**Thomas** /ˈtɒməs/ (*m.*) New Testament: Greek form of an Aramaic byname meaning 'Twin'. It is the name of an apostle, referred to as 'Thomas, called Didymus' (John 11:16, 20:24), where *Didymos* is the Greek word for 'twin'. The given name has always been popular throughout Christendom, perhaps because St Thomas's doubts and reassurance have made him seem a very human character.

**Thomasina** /tɒməˈsiːnə/ (*f.*) Latinate feminine derivative of THOMAS; see also TAMSIN.

**Tiffany** /ˈtɪfəni/ (*f.*) Usual medieval English form of Greek *Theophania* 'Epiphany', from *theos* god + *phainein* to appear. This was once a relatively common name, given particularly to girls born on the Feast of the Epiphany (6 January), and it gave rise to an English surname. As a given name, it fell into disuse until revived in the 20th cent. under the influence of the famous New York jewellers Tiffany's and the film, starring Audrey Hepburn, *Breakfast at Tiffany's* (1961).

**Tilly** /ˈtɪli/ (*f.*) Pet form of MATILDA, much used from the Middle Ages to the late 19th cent., latterly also as an independent given name. It is rare in either use nowadays.

**Tim** /tɪm/ (*m.*) Short form of TIMOTHY, also used in Ireland as an Anglicization of the Gaelic name TADHG.

**Timmy** /ˈtɪmi/ (*m.*) Diminutive of TIM.

**Timothy** /ˈtɪməθi/ (*m.*) English form, used in the Authorized Version of the Bible (alongside the Latin form *Timotheus*), of Greek *Timotheos*, composed of the elements *tīmē* honour + *theos* god. This was the name of a companion of St Paul; according to ancient

tradition he was stoned to death for denouncing the
worship of Diana, but there is no historical evidence
for this. Surprisingly, the name was not used in England at all before the Reformation.

**Tina** /'ti:nə/ (f.) Short form of CHRISTINA and, less commonly, of other girl's names ending in *-tina*.

**Titus** /'taɪtəs/ (m.) From an ancient Roman given
name, of unknown origin. It was borne by a companion of St Paul who became the first Bishop of
Crete; also by the Roman emperor who destroyed
Jerusalem in AD 70. It is not common in English.

**Toby** /'təʊbi/ (m.) English form of Hebrew *Tobiah*
'God is good'. This name is borne by several characters in the Old Testament (appearing in the Authorized Version also as *Tobijah*), but in the Middle Ages
it was principally associated with the tale of Tobias (a
Greek form) and the angel. According to the book of
Tobit in the Apocrypha, Tobias, the son of Tobit, a
rich and righteous Jew of Nineveh, was lucky enough
to acquire the services of the angel Raphael as a travelling companion on a journey to Ecbatana. He
returned wealthy, married, and with a cure for his
father's blindness.

**Todd** /tɒd/ (m.) From an English surname, which was
originally a nickname from a medieval English dialect
term meaning 'fox'.

**Tom** /tɒm/ (m.) Short form of THOMAS, in use since the
Middle Ages, and recorded as an independent name
since the 18th cent.

**Tommy** /'tɒmi:/ (m.) Pet form of THOMAS or its shortened form TOM.

**Toni** /'təʊni:/ (f.) Mainly American: it seems to have originated as a pet form of ANTONIA or directly as a feminine spelling of TONY. The variants **Tonia** /'təʊnjə/ and
**Tonie** are found, but are much less common.

**Tony** /'təʊnɪ/ (*m.*) Short form of ANTHONY, now widely used as an independent name in the English-speaking world.

**Torquil** /'tɔːkwɪl/ (*m.*) Norman: of Scandinavian origin, from the Old Norse personal name *Thorkell*, a contracted form of *Thorketill*, meaning 'Thor's cauldron'.

**Tracy** /'treɪsɪ/ (*f.*, formerly *m.*) Originally from an English surname, derived from a Norman baronial name, from places in France called Tracy 'place of Thracius'. Formerly, *Tracy* was occasionally given as a first name to boys, as were the surnames of other English noble families. Later, it was given also to girls and taken as a pet form of THERESA. In recent years it has become a massively popular girl's name (with variants **Tracey** and **Tracie**), influenced especially by Tracy Lord, the character played by Grace Kelly in the film *High Society* (1956).

**Travis** /'trævɪs/ (*m.*) From the English surname, derived from the Norman French occupational name (from *traverser* to cross) for someone who collected a toll from users of a bridge or of a particular stretch of road. It is now regularly used as a given name, especially in America and Australia.

**Trevor** /'trevə/ (*m.*) An originally Welsh given name derived from a surname, which in turn is from a place name. There are a large number of places in Wales called Trefor, from the elements *tref* settlement + *fôr*, mutated form of *môr* large. In recent years, *Trevor* has also become popular as a given name among people who have no connection with Wales. The Welsh spelling **Trefor** is also used as a given name.

**Tricia** /'trɪʃə/ (*f.*) Short form of PATRICIA.

**Trina** /'triːnə/ (*f.*) Short form of KATRINA.

**Trisha** /ˈtrɪʃə/ (*f.*) Phonetic respelling of TRICIA, comparatively recent in origin. It is currently fairly popular, and sometimes bestowed as a given name in its own right.

**Tristan** /ˈtrɪstən/ (*m.*) Variant of TRISTRAM. Both forms of the name occur in medieval and later versions of the legend.

**Tristram** /ˈtrɪstrəm/ (*m.*) From Celtic legend, the name borne by a hero of medieval romance. There are many different versions of the immensely popular tragic story of Tristram and his love for Isolde. Generally, they agree that Tristram was an envoy sent by King Mark of Cornwall to bring back his bride, the Irish princess Isolde. Unfortunately, Tristram and Isolde fall in love with each other, having accidentally drunk the love potion intended for King Mark's wedding night. Tristram eventually leaves Cornwall to fight for King Howel of Brittany. Wounded in battle, he sends for Isolde. She arrives too late, and dies of grief beside his bier. The name *Tristram* is of unknown derivation; it has been altered from an irrecoverable original as a result of transmission through Old French sources that insisted on associating it with Latin *tristis* sad, a reference to his tragic fate.

**Trixie** /ˈtrɪksiː/ (*f.*) Pet name derived from BEATRIX, occasionally used as an independent given name.

**Troy** /trɔɪ/ (*m.*, *f.*) Probably originally derived from the Norman surname, which is a local name from Troyes in France. Now, however, the given name is principally associated with the ancient city in Asia Minor whose fate has been a central topic in epic poetry from Homer onwards. It was sacked by the Greeks after a siege of ten years; according to classical legend, a few survivors got away to found Rome (and, according to medieval legend, another group founded Britain).

**Trudy** /'tru:di:/ (*f.*) From the Swiss German name *Trudi*, representing a pet form of GERTRUDE, ERMIN-TRUDE, and various more characteristically German names such as *Waltrude*. It has been adopted in the English-speaking world, with a variant spelling **Trudie**, and is now a popular given name even though the full forms are out of favour.

**Tybalt** /'tɪbəlt/ (*m.*) Usual medieval form of THEO-BALD, rarely used nowadays. It occurs in Shakespeare's *Romeo and Juliet* as the name of a brash young man who is killed in a brawl.

**Tyler** /'taɪlə/ (*m.*) From the English surname, originally an occupational name borne by a *tiler* of roofs, now sometimes used as a given name.

**Tyrone** /'taɪrəʊn, taɪ'rəʊn/ (*m.*) From the name of a county in Northern Ireland and a town in Pennsylvania. Its use as a given name seems to be entirely due to the influence of the two film actors (father and son) called Tyrone Power.

# U

**Ulric** /ˈʊlrɪk/ (*m.*) In the Middle Ages, this represented an Old English name composed of the elements *wulf* wolf + *rīc* power. In its occasional modern use it is probably an Anglicized spelling of German *Ulrich*, composed of Germanic elements meaning 'prosperity' + 'power'.

**Ulrike** /*German* ʊlˈriːkə/ (*f.*) German feminine form of *Ulrich* (see ULRIC), recently introduced from Germany to the English-speaking world. The Swedish form **Ulrika** is also occasionally used.

**Ulysses** /ˈjuːlɪsiːz/ (*m.*) Latin form of the Greek name *Odysseus*, the famous wanderer of Homer's *Odyssey* and of subsequent legend. The name is of uncertain derivation, nor is it clear why the Latin form should be so altered (mediation through Etruscan has been one suggestion). As a given name it has occasionally been used in the 19th and 20th cents., especially in America (like other names of classical origin such as HOMER and VIRGIL). It was the name of the 18th president of the United States, Ulysses S. Grant (1822–85).

**Una** /ˈjuːnə/ (*f.*) Variant of the Irish name OONAGH, respelled to coincide in form with Latin *una* alone, single, only.

**Urban** /ˈɜːbən/ (*m.*) From Latin *urbānus* 'of the city'. This name was borne by numerous early saints, and was adopted by several popes (who may have felt the name to be particularly appropriate since they ruled from the city of Rome).

**Uriah** /juːˈraɪə/ (*m.*) Old Testament: name (from Hebrew, meaning 'God is Light') borne by a Hittite warrior treacherously disposed of by King David after he had made Uriah's wife Bathsheba pregnant (II Sam. 11). The Greek form *Urias* occurs in the

New Testament (Matt. 1:6). The name was in use in the 19th cent., especially among Nonconformists, but is now most closely associated with the character of the obsequious Uriah Heep in Dickens's *David Copperfield* (1850) and has consequently undergone a sharp decline in popularity.

**Ursula** /'ɜːsjʊlə/ (*f.*) From Latin *Ursula*, a diminutive of *ursa* (she-)bear. This was the name of a 4th-cent. Christian saint martyred at Cologne with a number of companions varying, in different versions of the legend, from eleven to eleven thousand. The given name has long been popular in Germany and is now used increasingly also in the English-speaking world.

# V

**Val** /væl/ (*f.*; occasionally *m.*) Short form of VALERIE or, occasionally, of VALENTINE.

**Valda** /'vældə/ (*f.*) Fanciful extension of VAL; a 20th-cent. coinage.

**Valene** /vəl'iːn/ (*f.*) Fanciful extension of VAL, with the feminine suffix *-ene*; a 20th-cent. coinage, apparently of Australian origin.

**Valentine** /'væləntaɪn/ (*m.*, occasionally *f.*) English form of the Latin name *Valentīnus*, a derivative of *valens* 'healthy, strong'. This was the name of a Roman martyr of the 3rd cent. whose feast is celebrated on 14 February, the date of a pagan fertility festival marking the first stirrings of spring, which survived in an attenuated form under the patronage of the saint.

**Valerie** /'væləriː/ (*f.*) From the French form of the Latin name *Valĕria*, the feminine form of the old Roman family name *Valĕrius*, which was apparently

derived from *valēre* to be healthy, strong. The name
was popular in France in the Middle Ages as a result
of the fame of a 3rd-cent. saint (probably spurious)
converted by Martial of Limoges.

**Vanessa** /və'nesə/ (*f.*) Invented by Jonathan Swift
(1667–1745) for his intimate friend Esther Vanhom-
righ. It seems to have been derived from the first syllable of her (Dutch) surname, with the addition of the
suffix *-essa* (perhaps influenced by the first syllable of
her given name).

**Vaughan** /vɔːn/ (*m.*) From the Welsh surname, which
derives from Welsh *bychan* small. This was originally
a nickname; the initial *v* results from the mutation of
Welsh *b* to *f* (pronounced *v*) in combination after a
personal name.

**Vera** /'vɪərə/ (*f.*) From the Russian name, meaning
'Faith', introduced to England from the beginning of
the 20th cent. It coincides in form with the feminine
form of the Latin adjective *vērus* true, and this has no
doubt enhanced its popularity as a given name.

**Verity** /'verɪtɪ/ (*f.*) From the archaic abstract noun
*verity* truth (via Old French from Latin *vēritās*). It
was a popular Puritan name, and is still occasionally
used.

**Vernon** /'vɜːnən/ (*m.*) From the English surname,
which was originally a Norman local name from various places in Normandy, so called from Gaulish
elements meaning 'place of alders'.

**Veronica** /və'rɒnɪkə/ (*f.*) Latin form, somewhat gar-
bled, of BERENICE, influenced from an early date by
association with the Church Latin phrase *vera icon*
'true image', of which this form is an anagram. The
legend of the saint who wiped Christ's face on the
way to Calvary and found an image of his face

imprinted on the towel seems to have been invented
to account for this derivation.

**Vesta** /'vestə/ (*f.*) From Roman religion: name of the
Roman goddess of the hearth, cognate with that of a
Greek goddess with similar functions, *Hestia*, but of
uncertain derivation.

**Vi** /vaɪ/ (*f.*) Short form of VIOLET, now rather old-
fashioned.

**Vicky** /'vɪkiː/ (*f.*) Pet form of VICTORIA, found also in
the spellings **Vickie**, **Vicki**, and **Vikki**.

**Victor** /'vɪktə/ (*m.*) From a Latin name, meaning
'Conqueror'. This was popular among early Christians as a reference to Christ's victory over death and
sin, and was borne by several saints.

**Victoria** /vɪk'tɔːrɪə/ (*f.*) From the feminine form of
the Latin name *Victōrius*, a derivative of VICTOR, also
perhaps a direct use of Latin *victōria* victory. It was
little known in England until the accession in 1837 of
Queen Victoria (1819–1901), who got it from her
German mother Mary Louise Victoria of Saxe-
Coburg. It did not begin to be a popular name among
commoners in Britain until the 1940s, reaching a
peak in the 1970s.

**Vikki** /'vɪkiː/ (*f.*) Pet form of VICTORIA.

**Vince** /vɪns/ (*m.*) Short form of VINCENT, in use at least
since the 17th cent., and probably earlier, since it has
given rise to a surname.

**Vincent** /'vɪnsənt/ (*m.*) Norman: from the Old French
form of the Latin name *Vincens* 'Conquering', from
*vincere* to conquer. This name was borne by various
early saints particularly associated with France, most
notably the 5th-cent. Vincent of Lérins.

**Viola** /vaɪ'əʊlə, 'vaɪələ/ (*f.*) From Latin *viōla* violet.

The name is relatively common in Italy and was used by Shakespeare in *Twelfth Night* (where most of the characters have Italianate names). However, in England it seems largely to have been given in modern times as a result of its association with the somewhat larger flower so called in English (a single-coloured pansy).

**Violet** /'vaɪələt/ (*f.*) From the name of the flower (Old French *violette*, Late Latin *violetta*, a diminutive of *viola*). This was one of the earliest flower names to become popular in Britain, being well-established before the middle of the 19th cent., but it is now out of favour.

**Violetta** /viː'lɛtə/ (*f.*) Italian form of VIOLET.

**Violette** /vaɪə'lɛt, *French* viːoˈlɛt/ (*f.*) French form of VIOLET.

**Virgil** /'vɜːdʒəl/ (*m.*) Usual English form of the name of the most celebrated of Roman poets, Publius Vergilius Maro (70–19 BC). The correct Latin spelling is *Vergilius*, but it was early altered to *Virgilius* by association with *virgo* maiden or *virga* stick. Today the name is almost always given with direct reference to the poet, but medieval instances may have been intended to honour instead a 6th-cent. Bishop of Arles or an 8th-cent. Irish monk who evangelized Carinthia and became Archbishop of Salzburg, both of whom also bore the name. In the case of the later saint it was a classicized form of the Gaelic name *Feargal*, composed of the elements *fear* man + *gal* valour.

**Virginia** /vəˈdʒɪnɪə/ (*f.*) From the feminine form of Latin *Virginius* (more correctly *Verginius*; cf. VIRGIL), a Roman family name. It was borne by a Roman maiden killed, according to legend, by her own father to spare her the attentions of an importunate suitor. It does not seem to have been used as a given name in the Middle Ages. It was bestowed on the first American child of English parentage, borne at Roanoke, Virginia, in August 1587, and has since become very popular. Both child and province were named in honour of Elizabeth I, the 'Virgin Queen'.

**Vita** /'viːtə/ (f.) A 19th-cent. coinage: from Latin *vita* life, or else a feminine form of the Late Latin name *Vitus* (probably itself from *vita*) or Italian *Vito*. It has been borne most notably by the English writer Vita Sackville-West (1892–1962), in whose case it was a pet form of her Christian name, VICTORIA.

**Viv** /vɪv/ (f., m.) Short form of VIVIEN, VIVIENNE, or VIVIAN.

**Vivian** /'vɪvɪən/ (m.) Norman: from an Old French form of the Latin name *Viviānus* (probably a derivative of *vivus* alive). The name was borne by a 5th-cent. bishop of Saintes in western France, who protected his people during the invasion of the Visigoths.

**Vivien** /'vɪvɪən/ (f., formerly m.) Originally the more common Old French form of VIVIAN, but used by Tennyson in his poem *Merlin and Vivien* (1859) as a girl's name in place of the usual feminine form VIVIENNE. In this case the name seems to represent an altered form of some Celtic name.

**Vivienne** /'vɪvɪən; *French* vɪ'vjɛn/ (f.) French feminine form of VIVIEN.

**Vyvyan** /'vɪvɪən/ (m.) Fanciful spelling of VIVIAN.


# W

**Wade** /weɪd/ (m.) From the English surname, derived from a medieval given name or from the medieval vocabulary word *wade* ford. The former represents an Old English personal name derived from *wadan* to go, borne, according to legend, by a great sea-giant.

**Wallace** /'wɒləs/ (*m.*) From the English surname, from Old French *waleis* foreign, Celtic, which was originally given by the Normans to members of various Celtic races in areas where they were in the minority—Welshmen in the Welsh marches, Bretons in East Anglia, and surviving Britons in the Strathclyde region. The given name seems to have been first used in Scotland, given in honour of the Scottish patriot William Wallace (?1272–1305), who was probably descended from Strathclyde Britons.

**Wally** /wɒlɪ/ (*m.*) Pet form of WALTER, now out of fashion, having acquired connotations of stupidity or incompetence.

**Walter** /'wɒltə/ (*m.*) Of Norman and Old English origin: from a medieval given name composed of the Germanic elements *wald* rule + *heri* army. There was a native Old English form of the name, *Wealdhere*, but it was strongly reinforced (or replaced) at the time of the Conquest by the Continental forms popular among the Normans.

**Wanda** /'wɒndə/ (*f.*) Of uncertain origin: attempts have been made to derive it from various Germanic and Slavonic roots, and it was certainly in use in Poland in the 19th cent. However, it does not seem to have been used in the Middle Ages, and it was probably introduced to the English-speaking world by Ouida (Louise de la Ramée), who used it for the heroine of her novel *Wanda* (1883).

**Ward** /wɔːd/ (*m.*) From the English surname, from Old English *weard* guard or watchman.

**Warren** /'wɒrən/ (*m.*) From the English surname, from a Norman name, which is derived partly from a place in Normandy called La Varenne 'The Game-park' and partly from a Germanic personal name, from an element meaning 'to guard' (cf. WERNER). In America it has sometimes been given in honour of Joseph Warren, the first hero of the American Revolution, who was killed at Bunker Hill (1775).

**Washington** /'wɒʃɪŋtən/ (*m.*) From the surname of the first president of the U.S. George Washington (1732–99), whose family came originally from North-amptonshire in England, but had been established in Virginia since 1656. Their name is derived from the village of Washington in Co. Durham. It is very rarely used as a given name in Britain, but relatively frequent in America, especially among Blacks.

**Wat** /wɒt/ (*m.*) The usual medieval short form of WALTER, based on the normal vernacular pronunciation *Water*; occasionally found in modern use as a short form of WATKIN, which was originally derived from it in the first place.

**Watkin** /'wɒtkɪn/ (*m.*) From the English surname, derived in the Middle Ages from WAT + the hypocoristic suffix -*kin*.

**Wayne** /weɪn/ (*m.*) From the English surname, orig-inally an occupational name for a carter or cart-wright, from Old English *wægen* cart, waggon. It was adopted as a given name in the 20th cent. mainly as a result of the popularity of the American actor John Wayne (1907–82). He was born Marion Michael Morrison; his screen name was chosen in honour of the American Revolutionary general Anthony Wayne (1745–96).

**Wendy** /'wendi:/ (*f.*) Invented by J. M. Barrie for the 'little mother' in his play *Peter Pan* (1904). He took it from the nickname *Fwendy-Wendy* (i.e. 'Friend') used for him by a child acquaintance, Margaret Henley.

**Werner** /'wɜːnə; *German* 'vɛrnər/ (*m.*) German: recently introduced to the English-speaking world, most common in America. It is composed of the old Germanic elements *warin* guard + *heri* army.

**Wes** /wɛz/ (*m.*) Short form of WESLEY.

**Wesley** /'wɛzli:/ (*m.*) From the surname of the founder of the Methodist Church, John Wesley (1703–91), and his brother Charles (1707–88), who was also influential in the movement. Their family must have come originally from one or other of the various places in England called Westley, the 'western meadow'. The given name was at first confined to members of the Methodist Church, but is now more widely used among English-speaking people of other creeds, without reference to its religious connotations.

**Wilbur** /'wɪlbə/ (*m.*) From the comparatively rare surname, now a fairly common given name, especially in America. The surname probably derives from a medieval girl's name composed of the Old English elements *will* will, wish + *burh* fortress.

**Wilfrid** /'wɪlfrɪd/ (*m.*) From an Old English personal name composed of the Germanic elements *will* will, wish + *frid* peace. The Old English form was in use before the Conquest, and was borne by two saints. There is some doubt about the name of the more famous, who played a leading role at the Council of Whitby (664); it may have been *Walfrid* 'Strangerpeace'. Wilfrid the Younger was an 8th-cent. bishop of York. The name was not used in the Middle Ages, but revived in the 19th cent. The variant spelling **Wilfred** is almost equally common.

**Wilhelmina** /wɪlheɪ'miːnə, *German* vɪlhɛl'miːnə/ (f.) German feminine form of WILLIAM, from the German boy's name *Wilhelm* + the Latinate feminine suffix

*-ina*. This name was introduced to the English-speaking world from Germany in the 19th cent.

**Will** /wɪl/ (*m.*) Short form of WILLIAM, well established in medieval times, but now less common and rather more formal than BILL.

**William** /'wɪljəm/ (*m.*) The most successful of all the Germanic names introduced to England by the Normans; it is composed of the elements *will* will, wish + *helm* helmet, protection. The fact that it was borne by the Conqueror himself does not seem to have inhibited its favour with the 'conquered' population: in the first century after the Conquest it was the commonest boy's name of all, not only among Normans. In the later Middle Ages it was overtaken by JOHN, but continued to run second to that name until the 20th cent., when the picture became more fragmented.

**Wilma** /'wɪlmə/ (*f.*) Contracted form of WILHELMINA, or a girl's name formed directly from WILLIAM by altering the ending.

**Windsor** /'wɪndzə/ (*m.*) From the English surname, derived from a place in Berkshire (or from *Broadwindsor* in Dorset), originally named in Old English as *Windels-ōra* i.e., 'landing-place with a windlass'. Its use as a given name dates from the mid 19th cent., and was reinforced by the fact that this was adopted in 1917 as the surname of the British royal family (from their residence at Windsor in Berkshire). It was felt necessary to replace the name *Wettin*, introduced by Queen Victoria's husband Albert, as German names were not in favour at the time.

**Winifred** /'wɪnɪfrəd/ (*f.*) From the Welsh personal name *Gwenfrewi*, composed of the elements *gwen* white, fair, holy + *frewi* reconciliation. This was borne by a 7th-cent. Welsh saint around whom a body of legends grew up. The name has been altered

by association with the Old English name elements
*wynn* joy + *frið* peace.

**Winston** /'wɪnstən/ (*m.*) From the English surname:
although there was an Old English personal name,
*Wynnstan*, composed of the elements *wynn* joy +
*stān* stone, which would have had this form if it had
survived, the modern given name originated in the
Churchill family. The first Winston Churchill (b.
1620) was christened with the surname of his
mother's family, who had come originally from the
hamlet of Winston in Gloucs. The name has continued in this family ever since, and has recently been
more widely used in honour of the statesman Winston Spencer Churchill (1874–1965).

**Winthrop** /'wɪnθrəp/ (*m.*) From the surname of a
leading American pioneering family, and still largely
confined to America. John Winthrop (1588–1649)
was one of the first governors of the Massachusetts
Bay Colony, and his son (1606–76) and grandson
(1638–1707), who bore the same name, were also col-
onial governors. Their family probably came originally from one of the places in England called
Winthorpe (named in Old English as the 'village of
Wynna').

**Wolfgang** /'wʊlfgæŋ; *German* 'vɔlfgaŋ/ (*m.*) German:
composed of the elements *wolf* wolf + *gang* going,
and occasionally bestowed in the English-speaking
world in honour of the composer Wolfgang Amadeus
Mozart (1756–91).

**Woodrow** /'wʊdrəʊ/ (*m.*) From the English surname,
originally given to someone who lived in a row of
houses by a wood, occasionally borne as a given
name in honour of the American President Woodrow
Wilson (1856–1924).

**Wyndham** /'wɪndəm/ (*m.*) From the English surname, derived from a contracted form of the place

Wymondham in Norfolk, originally named in Old
English as the 'homestead of Wigmund'.

**Wynne** /wɪn/ (*m.*, *f.*) As a boy's name, a derivative of
the English surname, which is itself derived from the
Old and Middle English given name *Wine* 'Friend'.
As a girl's name it is probably an 'elegant' re-spelling
of a short form of WINIFRED.

**Wystan** /'wɪstən/ (*m.*) From an Old English name
composed of the elements *wīg* battle + *stān* stone. It
is comparatively rare, being best known as the given
name of the poet Wystan Hugh Auden (1907–73).

# X

**Xavier** /'zævɪə, *Spanish* xa'βɪɛr/ (*m.*) From the sur-
name of the Spanish soldier-saint Francis Xavier
(1506–52), founder of the Society of Jesus (Jesuits).
He was born on the ancestral family estate at Xavier
(now Javier) in Navarre. In the early Middle Ages
Navarre was an independent Basque kingdom;
*Xavier* seems to represent a Hispanicized form of the
Basque place name *Etcheberria* 'the new house' (*x*
was pronounced in the Middle Ages as *sh*, now as *h*).
The given name is used almost exclusively among
Catholics.

**Xaviera** /zævɪ'ɛrə/ (*f.*) Feminine form of XAVIER.

**Xenia** /'zi:njə/ (*f.*) A comparatively rare given name,
coined from the Greek vocabulary word *xenia* hospi-
tality, from *xenos* stranger, foreigner.

# Y

**Yolanda** /jəʊ'lændə/ (*f.*) Latinate form of YOLANDE,
perhaps reflecting the common Italian *Iolanda*.

**Yolande** /jəʊˈlænd; *French* joˈlād/ (*f.*) Of uncertain origin: it is found in Old French in this form, and seems to be ultimately of Germanic origin, but if so it has been deformed beyond recognition by attempted associations with various Greek and Latin elements. It is also sometimes identified with the name of St *Jolenta* (d. 1298), daughter of the King of Hungary, whose name is sometimes rendered as HELEN.

**Yorick** /ˈjɒrɪk/ (*m.*) The name of the (defunct) court jester in Shakespeare's *Hamlet*; it seems to be a re-spelling of *Jorck*, a Danish form of GEORGE.

**Ysanne** /iːˈzæn/ (*f.*) Of uncertain origin: apparently a modern Frenchified invention, composed of *Ys-* (as in *Yseult*) + *Anne*.

**Yseult** /iːˈzəʊlt/ (*f.*) Medieval French form of ISOLDE, still occasionally used as a given name, also spelled **Iseult**..

**Yves** /*French* iːv/ (*m.*) French: of Germanic origin, a short form of various compound names containing the element 'yew' (cf. IVOR); the final *-s* is the mark of the Old French nominative case. The name was introduced to Britain from France at the time of the Norman Conquest and again in the 20th cent.

**Yvette** /ɪˈvɛt; *French* iːˈvɛt/ (*f.*) French feminine diminutive form of YVES.

**Yvonne** /ɪˈvɒn; *French* ɪˈvon/ (*f.*) French feminine diminutive form of YVES (or simply a feminine form based on the Old French oblique case).

# Z

**Zachary** /ˈzækəri/ (*m.*) English form (not used in the Bible) of Hebrew *Zacharaiah* 'God has remembered' (Greek form *Zacharaias*). The name was borne in the Old Testament by the last king of Israel of the race of